The Good Doctor

PHILIP DODDRIDGE
of
NORTHAMPTON

———————

A tercentenary tribute

Alan C. Clifford

CHARENTON
REFORMED PUBLISHING

© Alan C. Clifford 2002

First published in Great Britain 2002
by Charenton Reformed Publishing
8 Le Strange Close, Norwich NR2 3PN

Typeset in Sabon

British Library Cataloguing in Publication Data.
A catalogue record for this book is available from the
British Library

Printed by Barkers Print & Design
Attleborough, Norfolk

To
precious
MARIAN,
Our beloved
John, Katie, Hywel and David
(who all share Northampton origins),
daughter-in-law Fiona, granddaughter Hannah
and son-in-law David
and our dear brothers and sisters
of
Norwich and Norfolk,
the Netherlands and Northampton,
especially Les and Joyce Sandall
and
the memory of
Charles Lawrence
(who delighted in Doddridge's 'warm heart')

May we all worship, trust, love and serve
the Lord Jesus Christ
as Philip Doddridge did.

Contents

List of Illustrations

Acknowledgements

Reproduced by kind permission of:
  a Dr Williams's Library, London (from a photograph)
  b National Library of Wales, Aberystwyth
  c Central Library Northampton
  d Revd Malcolm Deacon, Northampton

Preface

Dr Philip Doddridge's dates (1702-51) provide us with two contiguous anniversaries: the 250th anniversary of his death occurred this year (October 26) and the tercentenary of his birth takes place next year (June 26). But why should we hold a celebration at all? With regard to worship, the first reason is obvious. Indeed, the hymnbooks of many denominations suggest that Doddridge's name will not be forgotten. 'Hark the glad sound' and 'O happy day' still find a place in the worship of God's people. The new book *Praise!* includes several albeit rather mangled examples. Yet Doddridge's hymns were just a fraction of his vast literary output – and an even smaller part of his many and widely creative activities. They were written to reinforce and apply the sermon, and given out, line by line, after it had been preached. This fact reminds us that Doddridge was primarily a minister of the Gospel of Jesus Christ, a calling that he considered 'the most desirable employment in the world.'

To earlier generations, Doddridge's various activities as pastor, evangelist, academy tutor, author, philanthropist and patriot won him many admirers. The editors of the centenary edition of his complete *Works* (1802-5) claimed that Doddridge 'ranks with the brightest ornaments of the British nation, and of the Christian Church'. Praise was also international. After reading the Dutch translation of some of Doddridge's sermons, a pastor of the Reformed Church at Amsterdam, Wilhelmus Peiffers declared to the printer: 'Herewith I gratefully return you the work of Dr Doddridge, concerning the New Birth, Salvation by Grace, &c which I have read more than once with such uncommon pleasure, that I long to see all that excellent author has published. I did not know him by name; but from this incomparable masterpiece, in which the oratory of the ancients seems to be revived, he appears to be a very great man.'

The following tercentenary tribute is an attempt to demonstrate the validity of these assessments. More than that, in endorsing them enthusiastically, I wish to share with others the personal enrichment I have received through a study of Philip Doddridge. Indeed, I thank God for all the providential possibilities which opened up in my early years. The story really began during the late 1950s when, as a young Christian, I discovered those two wonderful hymns, Charles Wesley's 'O for a thousand tongues' and Doddridge's 'Hark, the glad sound!' My attachment to these and other hymn writers grew as church history and Christian biography became major preoccupations. These interests were largely encouraged by the late Dr D. Martyn Lloyd-Jones of Westminster Chapel, London, whose ministry I attended from 1963-66. Among other things, these years proved ideal tuition for the ministry!

Having left a scientific career at the RAF Institute of Aviation Medicine, Farnborough to study history, philosophy and psychology at the University College of North Wales, Bangor, I developed an interest in the interface between philosophy and theology. Even before my philosophy finals in the summer of 1969, I had received a pastoral call from Primrose Hill Congregational Church, Northampton, chiefly on the recommendation of Dr R. Tudur Jones, principal of Coleg Bala-Bangor. (I had hoped to pursue a BD but 'Dr Tudur' considered this unnecessary in view of my age and background.) Since Northampton had been the scene of Doddridge's labours as both pastor and academy tutor, my interest increased on discovering the range of his interests, activities and achievements. My wife and I moved to Northampton in July, and my ordination took place in August. During the following three years, spare time was taken up with Doddridge research. This did not stop with our move to Gateshead in 1972, and in December of that year, I had the privilege of giving a paper on Doddridge at the Westminster Conference in London. After deciding to omit any discussion of the paper, the chairman, Dr Lloyd-Jones immediately urged me to expand the lecture into a paperback, promising at the same time to put me in touch with a publisher. However, despite completing my manuscript by July 1973, nothing came of this venture. Instead, these efforts became channelled into part-time, external Masters degree research in the Department of Religious

Studies at the University of Newcastle upon Tyne. Guided by Professor B.M.G. Reardon, I was eventually awarded the degree (MLitt, 1978) for my thesis 'Orthodoxy and the Enlightenment'. In the meantime, we had moved to a rural pastorate at Great Ellingham in Norfolk, a twenty-year settlement which, among other things, provided opportunity for continuing research. The Doddridge work stimulated a four-year period of further part-time doctoral study which, under the excellent guidance of Dr Tudur Jones, led to the award of my PhD from the University of Wales in 1984. Oxford University Press eventually published my thesis *Atonement and Justification* in 1990.

While periodic lectures on Doddridge have kept my interest alive, other concerns have held my attention in recent years. Then, on June 26, 2001 – Doddridge's birthday - I suddenly realised that the two Doddridge anniversaries were nigh. Since previous plans to publish my MLitt thesis (commended by OUP but declined on commercial grounds) had come to nothing, I turned my attention to the less-ambitious idea of publishing a reworked version of the MS originally produced for Dr Lloyd-Jones nearly thirty years ago. The present work is the result. Lack of time and opportunity have prevented me from producing a larger book more worthy of the subject. Who knows, retirement – if, and whenever it comes – might help to remedy what is inevitably an inadequate offering. However, if *The Good Doctor* helps to inspire others to study Doddridge and his distinctive contribution, the author will be well satisfied.

While Doddridge is not entirely unknown to students of church history and theology, he is probably forgotten more than he deserves. That said, an Internet search reveals much useful information. However, when one recalls that Bedford, Bristol, Kidderminster and Southampton have statues of John Bunyan, the Wesley brothers, Richard Baxter and Isaac Watts respectively, it is sad to reflect that Northampton preferred to honour the Victorian atheist MP Charles Bradlaugh instead of the saintly and patriotic Doddridge! As the largely forgotten 'fifth man' of the eighteenth-century English Evangelical quintet (including Watts, Whitefield and the Wesleys), Doddridge's place is not recognised as it should be. A musical analogy is perhaps helpful. The Viennese composer-group of Haydn, Mozart, Beethoven and Schubert is arguably completed by the too-little-known virtuoso pianist-composer Johann Nepomuk Hummel (1778-1837). As surely as his romantic classicism is a refreshing, charming and surprisingly interesting change to the standard classical repertoire, so Doddridge's significant achievements are worthy of a place beside the contributions of Isaac Watts, George Whitefield and the Wesley brothers. Perhaps even this assessment is too modest. As we shall see, Professor Alan Everitt has suggested that a pioneering role in the evangelical revival actually belongs to Doddridge. One may add that in several respects, the overall Christian legacy of Doddridge was sounder than those of John Wesley and George Whitefield, not least on the matrimonial level.

Another factor justifies a renewed interest in Doddridge. Despite the legacy of his fervent Trinitarian evangelicalism, the clouds of controversy have never lifted from this gifted and gracious man of God. Indeed, few Christian leaders have been more misrepresented than Philip Doddridge with errors ranging from the comical to the almost criminal! Described as the 'champion "howler" of the century', one writer in 1926 (see letter to the editor, *Christian World*, April 8) related Dr Doddridge's 'execution', confusing him with a disreputable Dr Dodd who was hanged about twenty years after Doddridge died! In less bizarre ways, his reputation has repeatedly suffered. One example is unjustified neglect. Indeed, he deserved better from J. C. Ryle who confined himself to Anglicans in his *Christian Leaders of the Last Century* (1885). Furthermore, Doddridge has frequently been exploited by ecumenical liberals who conveniently disregard his unambiguous protestant convictions. While Doddridge's life-long priority was clearly the spread of the Gospel and the salvation of souls, the tercentenary essays of 1951, *Philip Doddridge (1702-51): His contribution to English Religion*, presented a different picture on the dust jacket. The impression given is that Doddridge was chiefly 'tireless in the cause of Christian Unity.'

Although Doddridge the Christian intellectual and biblical theologian actually grappled with philosophical issues at the interface between Reformation and Enlightenment thought, Colin Brown lamented in *Philosophy and the Christian Faith* (1969) that 'no one in the Evangelical Revival sought to work out the philosophical implications of their faith.' Ignorance became insult in *The New International Dictionary of the Christian Church* (1978) which states that several alleged heresies of Doddridge 'are probably due to lack of necessary mental equipment to articulate his thoughts clearly'! Can this possibly apply to a scholar proficient in Hebrew, Greek, Latin and French, whose international theological and pastoral reputation guaranteed a constant stream of enquiries for nearly a quarter of a century?

While he rejects the allegations of heresy (notably Arianism, or Unitarianism), Professor Donald Macleod has recently complained that Doddridge's radical appeal to *sola scriptura* against subscribing to man-made confessions is, although 'honest', utterly 'simplistic'. Failing himself to assess Doddridge's theology correctly, Macleod describes Doddridge's theological posture as 'inept' (see 'God or god? Arianism, Ancient and Modern' in *The Evangelical Quarterly*, 68.2, 1996). Even more at odds with the facts, Dr George Ella absurdly asserts that Doddridge's Calvinism is 'higher' than Dr John Gill's (see *The Banner of Sovereign Grace*, 6.7, 1998). These and other criticisms of Doddridge make his career a focus of considerable interest, not least because the issues he had to confront in his day are still with us. Thus, unavoidably, the following tribute includes an 'apologetic' dimension for which the author refuses to apologise in the least!

A few remarks are required about literature. Since I produced my first MS, three major Doddridge publications have appeared. First, Dr Geoffrey Nuttall's long-awaited *Calendar of the Correspondence of Philip Doddridge DD* (1702-1751) was published in 1979, followed in 1980 by Malcolm Deacon's excellent and informative biography, *Philip Doddridge of Northampton 1702-51*. Third, Drs J. van den Berg and Nuttall co-authored *Philip Doddridge (1702-1751) and the Netherlands*, published in 1987. These three works made significant new information available for Doddridge scholars, and I am greatly indebted to them. For a wealth of personal and local information, the first two works are indispensable. Pursuing a rather different and more personal plan, I assume rather than duplicate the largely descriptive approach of the authors; my tribute will combine piety with objectivity, and admiration with analysis. The third work is of great importance for our appreciation of Doddridge the theologian and I am grateful for the highly significant Continental dimension it brings to a long-neglected and vaguely grasped subject.

Several acknowledgements are due. First, I am grateful for the initial encouragement received from Dr Lloyd-Jones in this project nearly thirty years ago. Now in fellowship with Doddridge 'above', I believe he would generally approve of the contents of this book. In response to my very first Doddridge essay (1971), Dr Lloyd-Jones wrote: 'I think you have established your case beyond any question'. Following his suggestion to submit the work to the *Evangelical Quarterly*, a modified article was eventually published in that journal in 1984. Second, the many authoritative Doddridge writings and friendship of Dr Geoffrey Nuttall continue to be a major source of information and inspiration. I thank him and wish him well as he approaches his ninetieth birthday (November 8), an event which is being celebrated by yet another Doddridge publication. Since several items of Doddridge correspondence have come to light since 1979, Dr Williams's Library is shortly to publish an addendum to Dr Nuttall's *Calendar*. In view of the close proximity of our two publication dates, Dr Nuttall recently wrote: 'It seems we are running neck and neck, and I am reminded of Doddridge and Guyse with their respective *Paraphrases* [see *Calendar*, Introduction, p. xix and Letters 472, 474]'.

Next, I wish to thank my MLitt tutor Professor Bernard Reardon whose guidance and encouragement were everything a young scholar needed. Speaking with him today on the telephone gave me the opportunity to thank him again personally for his help. Next, my PhD tutor Dr Tudur Jones (also 'above') always shared my enthusiasm for Doddridge. In 1984 he wrote: 'Thank you... for sending me your very delightful salutation to Doddridge. It is a fine and appropriate tribute. I shall treasure it'. I trust he would say no less regarding my latest offering. In addition to his excellent book, I am grateful for the friendship and help of the Revd Malcolm Deacon, minister of Castle Hill United Reformed Church, Northampton. I shall always remember a happy afternoon in July 2001 as we looked together at Doddridge MSS and visited the old vestry. It was thrilling to see - and stand on - the original portable pulpit regularly used by Doddridge when preaching in the open-air at Creaton, Northants! I am also grateful to Mr Terry Bracher and Mr Colin Eaton of the Central Library, Northampton. Their prompt assistance in several instances is much appreciated, especially the provision of graphic material for the cover design and other illustrations. Thanks are likewise due to the staff of Dr William's Library and the National Library of Wales, Aberystwyth. Mr Colin Barker and the staff of Barker's Print & Design Ltd, Attleborough are heartily thanked for their excellent and patient assistance in this and several other publishing projects.

When I issued my 'Doddridge Day' (June 26) e-mail announcement concerning the proposed book, several friends responded with enthusiasm including the Revd Geoffrey Thomas of Aberystwyth (who preached at my ordination in 1969) and the Revd Iain H. Murray of Edinburgh. While they will not endorse all Doddridge's distinctives, I trust these brethren will find several things to rejoice about. I am also greatly indebted to David Bond for his time and care in reading and assessing the Appendix. Despite its length, I am happy that he agreed on the need to be thorough. On a lighter note, I wish to thank the Revd James L. Wilson of Loughgilly, Northern Ireland. Besides his many intelligent observations, James' Hibernian humour has been a tonic in the midst of intense theological analysis. We often amused ourselves over the telephone as we compared the relative merits of 'four' and 'five' legged Calvinism. Of the two, we concluded that the former moves with the greater biblical elegance!

Warm gratitude is also due to my dear brothers and sisters of Norwich Reformed Church. I thank them for sharing my many enthusiasms and patiently allowing me to concentrate on the Doddridge project for a few months. Special thanks are due to my dear friend and fellow pastor, the Revd Stephen Quinton whose perceptive and valuable comments during many discussions are greatly appreciated. Special thanks are also due to our administrator, Mike Quinton and our treasurer Heber Martin for their particular help and encouragement.

As a local aside, one may be thankful for Doddridge's numerous personal links with Norwich and Norfolk. Writing to his wife from Great Yarmouth in July 1744, he considered Norfolk as 'one of the most elegant counties in England'. Writing to her four days later from Kings Lynn, he thought Castle Rising was 'the finest old ruin we have met in all our travels'. Ten months before his death, Doddridge told Samuel Wood, pastor of the Old Meeting House, Norwich that 'there are no associations of ministers any where, which I attend with greater delight than those of Norfolk and Suffolk'. As we shall see, the Northampton-Norwich connection was of considerable personal importance to Doddridge.

Before mentioning my wife, our youngest son David deserves warm thanks for time saving help; he scanned the original 130-page typescript into the computer and, with the aid of OCR software, produced an editable text. Then, at a late stage in the reworking, a near computer-catastrophe threatened the book's very existence, but David's skills saved the day! Last, to my beloved wife Marian I owe more than words can tell. Her unfailing support and enthusiasm have always been inspirational as well as practical. While Doddridge's Mercy always needed her husband's help with spelling, 'my Mercy' has frequently saved me from embarrassments of this and related kinds. Should eagle-eyed readers spot any mistakes, they are the author's responsibility alone!

Concluding on a personal note, I believe that Philip Doddridge is one of the greatest Christian men of all time. I endorse the verdict of his pupil Andrew Kippis that 'Dr Doddridge was not only a great man, but one of the most excellent and useful Christians, and Christian ministers, that ever existed.' What remains true of Paul is arguably true of Doddridge: he is to be 'imitated as he imitated Christ' (1 Cor. 11: 1). By the grace of God, Doddridge excelled in so many areas. In him, the mystical, intellectual, experiential and practical features of Christian life and character shone with remarkable brilliance and balance. In his hymns, we find devotion without sentimentality; in his academy lectures and books we see intellectual integrity without arrogance; in his experience we detect great fervency blended with humility; in his public activities we observe a deep concern to enrich and benefit those around him. Truly, he loved God and his fellow human beings 'with all his heart, soul, mind and strength' (Mk. 12: 30-1). His spirituality continues to challenge and inspire us. His very first sermon preached at Hinckley, Leicestershire in July 1722 on love for Christ (from 1 Corinthians 16: 22) was a personal manifesto, and no one loved

Jesus more than Doddridge did. I am thankful to God that I have been spared a decade longer than Doddridge's forty-nine years and granted the privilege and pleasure of setting before the reader the evidence for such a verdict.

Three things remain to be said. First, in view of the likelihood that readers will be denied modern editions or reprints of his works, my method is chiefly to allow Doddridge to speak to us fully in his letters, sermons, lectures and hymns. (As the eminent Huguenot pastor Jean Daillé would rightly remind us, we may thereby gain a better impression of Doddridge than any statue could create!*) Second, my aim is to persuade readers that the Doddridge celebration will have been a tercentenary well spent. Lastly, my motive is, I trust, the one which obviously drove Doddridge himself:

SOLI DEO GLORIA!

Alan C. Clifford

Attleborough, Norfolk
(through which Doddridge passed en route for Norwich in June 1741)

26 October 2001
(the 250th anniversary of Doddridge's entry into heaven in 1751)

* [Instead] of these cold and dumb representations of their bodies, [God] has taken care to draw to the very life in His Word the portraits of [His servants'] minds; there portraying by the pen of His Spirit their piety, their faith, their charity, and other virtues, in a way which neither the pencil, the crayon, the colours, the metals, the marble of human artists are able to express; and has erected these divine statues in the books of Scripture' (Sermon XXII in *An Exposition of the Epistle to the Philippians*, tr. J. Sherman, London, 1863, p. 133).

Philip Doddridge
(1702 - 51)

1
The Formation of Character

In the year 1745, during the reign of King George II, a book was published which was destined to pass through many editions by the dawn of the twentieth century. The reader could be in no doubt over the nature and purpose of this volume, as his eye scanned the title page:

The
Rise and Progress
of
RELIGION IN THE SOUL
Illustrated in a
Course of serious and practical Addresses
Suited to persons of every character and circumstance
with a Devout meditation or prayer
Added to each chapter.

Testifying... Repentance towards God, and faith towards our Lord Jesus Christ, Acts 20: 21. Whom we preach; warning every man, and teaching every man in all wisdom; that we may present every man perfect in Christ Jesus, Col. 1: 28.

The author was at the peak of his usefulness as a theologian, pastor, tutor, author, hymn writer, philanthropist and above all, saint, when, with only a few more years to live, Doddridge launched the *Rise and Progress* into an ocean of spiritual indifference. In doing so, he uttered a prayer, which perfectly reveals the kind of man he was:

Let not my Lord be angry, if I presume to ask, that however weak and contemptible this work may seem in the eyes of the children of this world, and however imperfect it really be, as well as the author of it unworthy, it may nevertheless live before

Thee; and through a divine power, be mighty to produce the rise and progress of religion in the minds of multitudes in distant places, and in generations yet to come! Impute it not, O God, as a culpable ambition, if I desire, that whatever becomes of my name, about which I would not lose one thought before Thee, this work, to which I am now applying myself in Thy strength, may be completed and propagated far abroad; that it may reach to those that are yet unborn, and teach them Thy name and Thy praise, when the author has long dwelt in the dust... But if this petition be too great to be granted to one, who pretends no claim, but Thy sovereign grace, to hope for being favoured with the least, give him to be in Thine almighty hand the blessed instrument of converting and saving one soul: and if it be but one, and that the weakest and meanest of those who are capable of receiving this address, it shall be most thankfully accepted as a rich recompense for all the thought and labour it may cost; and though it should be amidst a thousand disappointments with respect to others, yet it shall be the subject of immortal songs of praise to Thee, O blessed God, for and by every soul, whom, through the blood of Jesus, and the grace of Thy Spirit, Thou hast saved, and everlasting honours shall be ascribed to the Father, to the Son, and to the Holy Spirit, by the innumerable company of angels, and by the general assembly and church of the firstborn in heaven. Amen.[1]

Like the *Rise and Progress*, Philip Doddridge remains, in the words of an article in the *Sword and Trowel* of 1881, 'too much forgotten in the present day[2]. More than a hundred years later, there is little to justify any revision of this lamentably accurate assessment.

In the popular religious mind, the figure of John Wesley tends to dominate the eighteenth century. As one who spanned the century, besides being the generally recognised leader of the Methodist movement, this is understandable. There are others who, it may be argued, have suffered an unwarranted eclipse, deserving more attention than is usually given to them. The mid-twentieth century witnessed a resurgence of interest in the greatest of the Methodist preachers, George Whitefield, a development long overdue. If Philip Doddridge has failed to gain access into the inner circle of our eighteenth century heroes, there is a great deal of evidence to qualify him for a place. The facts of his life and work, if known, cannot fail to be a source of spiritual encouragement to the reader of Christian biography.

When one considers how varied and different the personalities used by God in His unfolding purpose of salvation have been, one is reminded of an orchestra. If the Divine symphony of the grace of God in Jesus Christ has brought the glad sound of salvation to countless generations, our appreciation of God's work is enhanced when we think of the instruments He has used. It would be a gross error to think that the success of a symphony or concerto depends only on such spectacular instruments as trumpets, timpani, violins and pianofortes. Other instruments are just as essential for the overall richness of sound. With this analogy in mind, we can survey with greater accuracy that great movement of the Spirit of God during the eighteenth century, which, in many ways, was a repeat performance of the Acts of the Apostles. So, if George Whitefield may be likened to a trumpet, and John Wesley a trombone, Philip Doddridge may be looked upon as a horn. Without exaggerating the extent of his usefulness, it is still true to say that Philip Doddridge made a greater contribution to the revival than many are aware of. While the observant worshipper will have noticed that such popular hymns as 'Hark the glad sound', 'O God of Bethel' and 'O happy day' were written by Doddridge, a student of church history should have discovered that he was the principal tutor of the famous nonconformist academy at Northampton. Too few people know anything more about this man, whose life was so closely tuned to the Saviour he loved and served. In days when the discordant noise of sin is everywhere heard, a truly saintly life demands a hearing.

Philip Doddridge made his debut upon the stage of history a year before John Wesley made his. On June 26, 1702, the wife of a London tradesman gave birth to a son. Daniel and Monica Doddridge had known much domestic sadness; Philip was their twentieth child, joining a sister in being the only infants to reach maturity. Even Philip was set aside as stillborn, when a sigh proved evidence of life. The sole male heir of the happy parents was destined not only to live but also to be a 'blessed instrument' in the gracious purposes of God. Philip grew up in a London which was only then taking the shape we now take for granted. The scars of the great fire of 1666 could still be seen, as Philip witnessed some of the scenes of its reconstruction. He would have seen Sir Christopher Wren's masterpiece, St Paul's Cathedral, in the final stages of its completion. The sights of his youth left an indelible impression upon him. In a sermon preached at the famous Salters' Hall only a year before he died, Doddridge could not hide his affection for the city of his nativity, when he cried, 'Oh London, London! dear city of my birth and education.'[3] Ancestry can be a dull and fruitless study. Such is not the case with the forebears of Philip Doddridge. Philip was very much the product of an age in which the foundations of Britain's greatness were still being laid. Great men are invariably the products of great influences, and Philip Doddridge was a child of Protestant Nonconformity. His paternal grandfather was numbered with the faithful company of puritan ministers who suffered in the Great Ejection of 1662. John Doddridge had been educated for the ministry at Oxford University, later becoming a minister at Shepperton in Middlesex. Dr Edmund Calamy described the Revd John Doddridge as 'an ingenious man and a scholar, an acceptable preacher, and a very peaceable divine'.[4] Describing a picture that was commonplace among the ejected, Philip wrote of his grandfather in a letter to a friend, that 'he had a family of ten children unprovided for; but he quitted his living, which was worth to him about two hundred pounds per annum, rather than he would violate his conscience, in the manner he must have done, by submitting to the subscriptions and declarations required, and the usages imposed, by the Act of Uniformity'.[5] This worthy man, having ministered to a Dissenting congregation for some years near Brentford, died in 1689.

Philip could also claim a distinguished past in his great grandfather, Sir John Doddridge, who was one of the Judges of the King's bench in the reign of King James I. Educated at Oxford, he later studied law, becoming Solicitor General and Member of Parliament for Horsham in Sussex. A portrait of Sir John hangs in the National Gallery. Since he possessed estates in Devon, he was buried in the Lady Chapel of Exeter Cathedral at his own request. When called to explain his reasons for a legal decision before the House of Lords in 1628, Sir John declared: "It is no more fit for a judge to decline to give an account of his doings, than for a Christian of his faith. God knoweth I have endeavoured always to keep a good conscience; for a troubled one who can bear?"[6]

Of decidedly equal interest are the connections of Philip's mother. She was the daughter of the Revd John Bauman of Prague, who left his homeland in 1626 following the persecution of the Lutheran pastors during the Thirty Years war (1618-1648). Having spent some time in Germany, he came to England, eventually becoming the master of the free school at Kingston-upon-Thames. This worthy man died in 1668, leaving one daughter who was to become Philip's mother. As a result of his grandfather's exile, Philip came into possession of a copy of Luther's Bible, dated 1526. Job Orton, a student of Doddridge and his first biographer wrote that 'The Doctor thought it a great honour to be descended from these suffering servants of Christ, who had made such sacrifices to conscience and liberty'.[7]

Godly parents and an alert child are calculated to work for good in the spiritual nurture of the child. The future theological tutor received his earliest Bible knowledge from his mother. She taught young Philip with the aid of the Dutch tiles which lined the fireplace of their home. These tiles were a common feature in puritan homes; they were decorated with pictures of Bible stories, an early form of visual aid. This early instruction had a deep and lasting impression upon Philip. It is not surprising to find him exhorting parents to give due attention to it in his tract *Family Religion*, published only a year before he died:

> Family worship is a most proper way of teaching children religion, as you teach them language, by insensible degrees; a little one day and a little another; for to them, line must be upon line, and precept upon precept. They may learn to conceive aright of divine perfections, when they hear you daily acknowledging, and adoring them...[8]

In 1712, after attending a private school in London, Philip became a pupil at the grammar school at which his grandfather had taught. He also came under the influence of the Revd Daniel Mayo, minister of the Dissenting church at Kingston. Mayo was one of a number of ministers who were responsible for the completion of Matthew Henry's *Commentary*. Philip remained at Kingston-upon-Thames until 1715, for on July 17 of that year, his father died. The

Philip and his mother

Matthew Henry
(1662 - 1714)

first real indications of spiritual life are to be seen at this time. Soon after his father's death, Philip wrote in his diary:

> God is an immortal Father, my soul rejoiceth in Him; He hath hitherto helped me and provided for me; may it be my study to approve myself a more affectionate, grateful and dutiful child.[9]

His parents' piety and instruction had not been in vain; Philip knew where to turn in his hour of deepest sorrow. It would seem that his mother died not long after this, for in later years, in a sermon entitled *The Orphan's Hope*, we find Philip saying:

> I know the heart of an orphan, having myself been deprived of both my parents, at an age, in which it might reasonably be supposed a child should be sensible of such a loss.[10]

Following the death of his parents, Philip moved to St Albans. But for the kindness and wisdom of the Presbyterian minister there, the Revd Samuel Clark, the young lad's future could have been placed at great risk through the incompetence of his guardian. Mr Clark took Philip under his wing, despite being a total stranger to him. While there is little evidence to suggest the time or circumstances of Philip's conversion, there were clear evidences of growth in grace at this time. He was received into church membership at the hands of Mr Clark on New Year's day, 1718. In his diary he wrote:

> I rose early this morning, read that part of Mr [Matthew] Henry's book on the Lord's supper, which treats of a due approach to it. I endeavoured to excite in myself those dispositions and affections, which he mentions as proper for that ordinance. As I endeavoured to prepare my heart, according to the preparation of the sanctuary, though with many defects, God was pleased to meet me, and give me sweet communion with Himself, of which I desire always to retain a grateful sense. I this day, in the strength of Christ, renewed my covenant with God and renounced my covenant with sin. I vowed against every sin, and resolved carefully to perform every duty. The Lord keep this in the imagination of my heart, and grant I may not deal treacherously with Him![11]

This was not the occasion of his writing the famous hymn 'O happy day' but it is more than likely that the memories of that day in 1718 were called to mind when he was composing it.

The year 1718 was to be an important one in the life of Philip Doddridge as he began to think more particularly about his future. He was conscious of a desire to enter the ministry. However, he was to encounter temptation and disappointment before the Lord finally made his way clear. Philip had an uncle, after whom he was named, who had been employed by the Duke of Bedford. The Duchess of Bedford knew of the circumstances and aspirations of Philip the nephew, offering to finance his education for the ministry. However, there was a snag. A condition was that Philip should conform to the Church of England. This tempting proposition was declined. Although Philip had puritan blood in his veins, he made a convinced and deliberate choice to preach the gospel as a 'Protestant Dissenter'. Philip consulted the eminent nonconformist leader, Dr Edmund Calamy, only to be advised contrary to his desire. God was testing His young servant. Philip wrote:

> I waited upon Dr Edmund Calamy to beg his advice and assistance, that I might be brought up a minister, which has always been my great desire. He gave me no encouragement in it, but advised me to turn my thoughts to something else. It was with great concern, that I received such advice; but I desire to follow providence and not force it. The Lord give me grace to glorify Him in what ever station He sets me: Then, here am I, let Him do with me what seemeth good in His sight.[12]

Whatever were the reasons for Dr Calamy's advice, Philip had to be patient until it was proved, fortunately for us, how even an eminent man of God can misjudge the ways and purposes of God. In the meantime, on further advice, Philip began to consider the legal profession. On receiving some definite proposals from a lawyer, Philip wrote a letter of acceptance. Before posting it, he spent an entire morning in prayer to seek the Lord's will. While in the very act of praying, the postman called with a letter from Mr Clark of St. Albans. As he quickly opened the letter, Philip could hardly believe his eyes! Mr Clark was promising to gain Philip admittance to a Dissenting Academy if his resolution for the ministry continued. The clouds dispersed and his heart lifted. In joy Philip recorded:

> This I looked upon almost as an answer from heaven; and while I live shall adore so seasonable an interposition of Divine providence. I have sought God's direction in this matter, and I hope I have had it. My only view in my choice hath been that of more extensive service; and I beg God to make me an instrument of doing much good in the world.[13]

Through this amazing example of the gracious providence of God, Philip did not follow in the footsteps of his illustrious ancestor, Sir John Doddridge, but those of his two grandfathers. His call was to the 'law and testimony' of the King of Heaven. And so, in October, 1719, Philip entered the Academy of the Revd John Jennings at Kibworth Harcourt in Leicestershire. It was here that Philip received both his higher academic and ministerial education.

It is important for us, at this stage, to understand a little of the educational scene at this time. The Nonconformist academies are an important part of the history of education in this country[14]. The seventeenth and eighteenth centuries were times in which religious beliefs were necessary as entrance qualifications, just as 'A-levels' are today. Unless a student was a member of the Church of England, there was no possibility of gaining admittance to the universities of Oxford and Cambridge. The situation was not so difficult at the pre-university level; there were free schools, such as the one Doddridge attended at Kingston-upon-Thames, and private schools. The chief problem for the Nonconformists was how to obtain a higher education, especially in preparation for the ministry. The solution to this problem was the rise of the academies, which occurred in two phases. In the period prior to the revolution of 1688, ministers would gather around them in their homes, a group of young men, whom they would train specifically for the ministry. The course would consist principally of classics, history and theology. These academies were not institutions as such. There were famous examples of this type of academy in the eighteenth century, particularly the one at Tewkesbury under the direction of the Revd Samuel Jones. Here, the noted Christian apologist, Joseph Butler, afterwards Bishop of Durham, received his education prior to entering university. The academy at Taunton is an example of the earlier type of academy, being founded in the 1680s, which later became a more organised institution, with a principal and staff of tutors. A further and very significant development was that the academies provided an education for non-ministerial as well as ministerial students, the curriculum becoming broader in scope. These institutions reached the zenith of their development in Doddridge's academy at Northampton, about which we shall learn more as we proceed. The academies served the educational purposes of the Nonconformists well for several generations; not until the year 1871 did religious restrictions on university entrance come to an end. The academy at Kibworth, where Doddridge attended, was like the earlier type, in that it centred around Jennings himself. The course was for ministerial students only, but the curriculum included philosophy, the classics and other non-theological subjects. It was here that Doddridge discovered the model of his own academy.

Jennings, like Mayo and Clark, was to have a considerable influence on the young Doddridge. He was noted for his wide learning and his deep spirituality. Several of Jennings' works were published. In particular, a work on preaching - *Two Discourses: Preaching Christ* and *Particular and Experimental Preaching* - was so highly regarded, that it was translated into German and published by the famous Dr August Herman Franke, a prominent leader in the German Pietist movement and Professor of Divinity at the University of Halle, in Saxony. Jennings' early death in the year 1723 was a great loss to the churches in the Midlands. Two days before his former tutor died, Doddridge revealed his own estimate of Jennings' character and abilities, in a letter to his sister:

> Good Mr Jennings is fallen ill of the smallpox. It is of the very worst sort, and I am afraid he will be dead before this comes to your hand. May God avert so dreadful a loss to the dissenting interest in general, and especially to this part of England.[15]

This sad event was to have a direct bearing on Doddridge's future since Jennings' mantle was to fall on him. So while he lived, young Doddridge was in an ideal environment for study. Being a model student, he wasted no time in following Clark's advice:

> You have now an opportunity for treasuring up valuable knowledge under the conduct of a very worthy tutor; and as I doubt not but that you improve that advantage to the uttermost, so I am desirous it may be continued to you as long as possible: for I would have you furnished, not with a bare superficial taste of literature, but with so rich a stock of solid knowledge as may abundantly qualify you for whatever service God may call you to in his church.

Clark reminded Doddridge of the chief purpose of his education:

> Close reasoning, a perfect acquaintance with the Scriptures, and the method of applying most effectually to the consciences of men, are what I would in particular recommend to your diligent application. In order to acquire some skill in the latter, it is necessary to study the passions and the secret springs by which men are moved, and the several principles upon which they generally act, but especially your own heart; for a thorough knowledge of that will lead you the most direct way into the breast of another.[16]

Accordingly, Doddridge drew up some 'Rules for the direction of my conduct while a student'. Some edited extracts give us a glimpse of his character:

> 1. Let my first thoughts be devout and thankful. Let me rise early, immediately return God more solemn thanks for the mercies of the night, devote myself to Him, and beg his assistance in the intended business of the day...
> 3. Let me set myself to read the Scriptures every morning. In the first reading let me endeavour to impress my heart with a practical sense of Divine things...
> 4. Never let me trifle with a book with which I may have no present concern...
> 5. Never let me lose one minute of time, nor incur unnecessary expenses, that I may have the more to spend for God...
> 7. Let me use moderation at meals, and see that I am not hypocritical in prayers and thanksgivings at them...
> 11. Let me labour after habitual gratitude, and love to God and

the Redeemer...

12. In all my studies let me remember that the souls of men are immortal, and that Christ died to redeem them... [17]

Doddridge related his tutor's theological approach to Clark. Despite pursuing a radical *sola scriptura* agenda, Jennings's broad emphasis was highly controversial in some Dissenting circles:

> He does not entirely accord with the system of any particular body of men; but is sometimes a Calvinist, sometimes a Remonstrant [Arminian], sometimes a Baxterian, and sometimes a Socinian, as truth and evidence determine him. *He always inculcates it upon our attention, that the Scriptures are the only standard of orthodoxy*, and encourages the utmost freedom of enquiry.[18]

Doddridge was clearly attracted to French authors at this time, admitting that 'French is a language which I have been acquainted with for many years'.[19] He much admired the dramatist Jean Racine and Archbishop Fenelon's work on eloquence. Regarding French sermons, Doddridge considered them very much inferior to those of our English divines. Only towards the end of his life did Doddridge begin to be familiar with the Huguenot preachers of the seventeenth century. In view of the similarity in doctrine, eloquence and warmth between his own mature sermons and those of France's 'second Calvin', Jean Daillé (1594-1670), Doddridge would clearly have relished these.[20]

At this early period, Philip received some timely advice from his sister Elizabeth. She was the wife of the Revd John Nettleton of Ongar, Essex, and therefore knew well the hazards as well as the joys of the ministry:

> I pray God, that you may be made a happy instrument of His glory and the good of souls; and, as you are not insensible of the weight and importance of the work, and of man's insufficiency in his own strength for the performance of it, so I hope God will keep you humble and watchful, and entirely depending upon His Spirit for assistance; and that when you have been enabled to do any good, you will not be forgetful, but give Him all the

glory. I hope my dear brother will excuse this freedom, and my folly in advising him who knows so much better how to direct me, and will believe it to proceed from the tender love I bear him.[21]

Such faithful and loving counsel was just one example of the many influences employed by God in the formation of Philip's character. Ancestors, parents, tutors and friends were part of God's unfolding purpose in making Philip Doddridge a happy instrument of His glory and the good of souls. We must see for what purpose the God of providence and grace was preparing His servant.

2
The Road to Northampton

Doddridge's Rules indicate some of the principles by which he approached his studies in the academy at Kibworth. They reveal a spirituality that was to dominate his life increasingly. His God-centred disposition was soon to have opportunity of expression. In the year 1722, Jennings moved from Kibworth to become the pastor of the Independent church at Hinckley, also in the county of Leicester. The academy moved with him. By now, Doddridge had completed his course so, after being examined by a committee of ministers, he was licensed to preach the gospel on July 22, 1722. Thus, at the age of twenty, Doddridge commenced what was the fulfilment of his 'great desire', and what he was to describe twenty-seven years later as 'the most desirable employment in the world'.[1] - the Christian ministry. His very first sermon was preached at Hinckley. His text was 'If any man love not the Lord Jesus Christ, let him be Anathema Maranatha' (1 Cor. 16: 22). Doddridge wrote to his sister of this experience:

> It was a plain, practical discourse, and cost me but a few hours study; but as I had the advantage of a very moving subject, and a good natured, attentive people, it was received much better than I could have expected...

Possessing a 'natural gaiety of temper',[2] Doddridge continued with characteristic humour:

> There was one good old woman, that was a little offended to see such a lad get up into the pulpit; but I had the good fortune to please her so well, that as soon as I had done, she told Mrs Jennings, that she could lay me in her bosom...[3]

The young preacher was greatly encouraged to learn later that two persons were spiritually awakened as a result of this sermon.

Doddridge was to spend several years in rural seclusion before being directed to the scene of his life's work. Like Moses in the desert and Paul in Arabia, Doddridge was to live in relative isolation, virtually unknown, as the work of preparation continued. In May 1723 he was invited to consider the pastorate of the Independent church at Coventry, a large and prominent church in the Midlands. He was also approached on the possibility of accepting the pastorate of the church at Kibworth, where Jennings had been the pastor. Doddridge chose obscure and rural Kibworth in preference to attractive Coventry on the grounds of dissension and party spirit in the larger church. As is often the case with young ministers, the stirrings of ambition might tempt them to seek a large and influential church in which to commence their ministry. However, Doddridge was content with his self-imposed obscurity. Coventry was not the only church in the area in which party spirit was rife. Doddridge wrote to a friend after his settlement at Kibworth:

> As to my retirement at Kibworth, which you are pleased to enquire after, I bless God, it is upon all accounts much to my satisfaction. The people are plain, honest, intelligent Christians; perfectly free from that plague of bigotry and enthusiasm which overruns some of the neighbouring congregations.[4]

Another enquirer, one of Doddridge's fellow students, deplored Philip's rural seclusion and spoke of his friend being 'buried alive'. Doddridge made an appropriate, spirited and humorous reply:

> I live almost like a tortoise, shut up in its shell, almost always in the same town, the same house, the same chamber; yet I live like a prince; not indeed in the pomp of greatness, but the pride of liberty; master of my books, master of my time, and I hope I may add, master of myself. I can willingly give up the charms of London, the luxury, the company, the popularity of it, for the secret pleasures of rational employment and self-approbation; retired from applause and reproach; from envy and contempt, and the destructive baits of avarice and ambition. So that instead of lamenting it as my misfortune, you should

congratulate me upon it as my happiness, that I am confined in an obscure village; seeing it gives me so many valuable advantages, to the most important purposes of devotion and philosophy; and, I hope I may add, usefulness too.[5]

Surrounded by his 'country estate', master of all he surveyed, ministering to his congregation of humble farm-workers, Doddridge prayed, studied, preached and discharged his various pastoral duties. It was at this time that he began to discover the value of the great puritan authors of the previous century, whose writings were to influence him so much as he matured. To another friend he wrote:

I do not know what character my friends may have given you of my sermons; They are all upon the plainest and most practical subjects, and it is happy if they are at all calculated, as I am sure they were principally intended, to inform the judgement and awaken the consciences of the lowest of the people, In short, I am grown very familiar with the old Puritans, and consequently I am a great favourite with the old women![6]

We can be sure that others, besides the 'old women', benefited from Doddridge's early sermons! However, these 'mothers in Israel' would have remembered some of the great preachers of the late puritan era, rejoicing that one so young was declaring those same truths of the Word of God, once so mightily uttered. Response to another sermon gave a fuller hint of what was to come. On hearing it preached at Market Harborough, John Massey from London requested a copy of it:

You have my father's best acknowledgements, and my sincere thanks for the admirable sermon you sent... It was with exquisite delight that we heard it preached, and it has been with no less pleasure that we have perused it; each page commands the thoughts to soar towards the bright confines of eternal day – those regions of light and joy, where the infinite Redeemer (who is the glorious subject of the discourse) reigns in complete splendour and beatitude.[7]

In his student days, Doddridge found the theological treatises of

Dr Thomas Goodwin and Dr John Owen a little hard going, although he was to regard their practical works highly in later years. Speaking of these worthies, Doddridge wrote to his brother-in-law in 1721:

> We have some of Goodwin's works in the library, and some of the great Dr. Owen's, but you know I am not very fond of such mysterious men...[8]

Doddridge's concern throughout his life was to be in the realm of practical Christian living. As we shall see in more detail in a later chapter, he was, at this early period, particularly helped by the practical works of Richard Baxter. Three years later, in 1724, he wrote to his brother-in-law about the apostle of Kidderminster:

> Baxter is my particular favourite, and it is impossible to tell you how much I am charmed with the devotion, good sense, and pathos, which are everywhere to be found in that writer. I cannot indeed forbear looking upon him as one of the greatest orators that our nation ever produced,... I have lately been reading his *Gildas Salvianus* [The Reformed Pastor], which has cut me out some work among my people, that will take me off from so close an application to my private studies as I would otherwise covet;... [9]

We have a glimpse of the way Doddridge pursued his ministry. He learned to converse and mingle with the humbler folk in the locality, intent on applying his studies to the great concerns of practical and experimental godliness. When the time came for him to teach others, Doddridge was able to draw on a rich fund of experience. His growing compassion and pastoral skills are evident in a letter of condolence to Tommy Mitchell:

> I am not now forbidding you to mourn for the death of [your] excellent mother. God forbid! Humanity and nature require it, and therefore divine grace cannot forbid it. Only I would entreat you to take care that you do not sorrow as one that has no hope; but rather set yourself seriously to consider those things which may cheer and support you, instead of only those which aggravate your trouble... [It] should be a comfort to you

Richard Baxter
(1615 - 91)

to think that your dear mother is now with God in glory. Look over those delightful descriptions of the future happiness, which you may find in the Bible and in other good books, and then think, all this does she now enjoy... Above all, let it be a consolation to you to think that the separation between you and your dear mother will not be eternal. No; you are now left behind her in the world, but it is only for a few years, and then you must follow her to the grave, and I would hope follow her to heaven too.[10]

Doddridge lived for a while at the village of Little Stretton, about two miles from Kibworth. The contrast between the city life of his childhood and the rustic atmosphere of his dwelling must have been stimulating to his poetic personality. In another letter, we also catch a glimpse of a very human Doddridge, as he reflects on his surroundings:

You know I love a country life, and here we have it in perfection. I am roused in the morning with the chirping of sparrows, the cooing of pigeons, the lowing of kine, the bleating of sheep, and, to complete the concert, the grunting of swine, and the neighing of horses. We have a mighty pleasant garden and orchard, and a fine arbour under some tall, shady limes, that form a kind of lofty dome, of which, as a native of the great city, you may perhaps catch a glimmering idea, if I name the cupola of St Paul's. ... And then, on the other side of the house, there is a large space which we call a wilderness, a brook runs sparkling through the middle, and there are two large fish ponds at one end; both the ponds and the brook are surrounded with willows; and there are several shady walks under the trees, besides little knots of young willows interspersed at convenient distances... Here I generally spend the evening, and pay my respects to the setting sun; when the variety and beauty of the prospect inspire a pleasure that I know not how to express. I am sometimes so transported with these inanimate beauties, that I fancy I am like Adam in Paradise; and it is my only misfortune, that I want an Eve, and have none but the birds of the air, and the beasts of the field, for my companions.[11]

In the farmhouse itself, there were reminders of a different kind than his books of the Puritan past. Over the mantelpiece of the main hall was a matchlock weapon that had been used by one of Cromwell's Ironsides at the Battle of Naseby in 1645, not many miles away. Of more remote interest was a crossbow that had seen action during the Wars of the Roses.

The year 1723 brought further enquiries for Doddridge's pastoral services. In October, he was invited to consider a church at Pershore in Worcestershire, which he declined to consider on the grounds that they were 'a very rigid sort of people'.[12] In November, a large congregation in London approached him. Doddridge also declined this invitation. His reasons for so doing, stated in a letter to his brother-in-law, give us further hints that the spiritual life of the Nonconformist churches was far from healthy, about which we will discover more as we proceed. Doctrinal debates in the city had not strengthened what was already a declining influence in the land:

> I am really convinced that I am likely to do more service in the world, by spending a few years longer at Kibworth, where I have an opportunity of studying closely, and improving myself in a plain, useful way of preaching; and where I have an abundance of friends, and no enemies, than by venturing so young into that censorious, wrangling town, where I may meet with many snares, especially with regard to orthodoxy, which perhaps I may not have the prudence to avoid;[13]

Further evidence of a growing antinomian extremism among some Dissenters appears in another letter from Samuel Clark. When the Congregational church of Hertford showed interest in Doddridge as a possible successor to John Guyse, they sent two deacons to hear him. These men 'found themselves disappointed':

> It is no wonder you are thought a legal preacher when you have the Ten Commandments painted upon the walls of your chapel; besides, you have a clerk, it seems, so impertinent as to say Amen with an audible voice! O tempora! O mores! That such a rag of popery should ever be tolerated in a congregation of the faith and order of the Congregational Brethren! And, to complete all, you, the minister, conclude your prayers with a form called the Lord's Prayer! - Do you know what mischief you have done, what a blot you have brought upon yourself by such offensive practices? It is happy for you that you are not to

encounter such odd humours.[14]

Doddridge was to face 'encounters' of many kinds in his life. After visiting his sister in Hampstead, he related to her his journey back to Kibworth in graphic detail. Doddridge's account reminds us of the hazards of travel in those days:

> I know not what was the matter with my horse, but on Tuesday in the afternoon, between St Albans and Redburn, he threw me twice over his head, once on a gentle trot, the second time on a brisk pace; but a little dirt, and indeed a very little, was all the harm I then received.
>
> As we were going on Thursday morning from Newport to Bedford, I escaped a much greater danger, and desire to acknowledge it, with hearty thanks to the care of Providence which preserved me in it. We were coming along in a narrow lane and met with I know not how many waggons of coals. I was aware of the difficulty and endeavoured to guard against it; but my horse being a little frighted at the ditch on one side, started and came too near the waggons on the other. There was a sudden turn in the road which I did not observe, which just at the same time threw the waggon on towards me, so that my foot was caught in one of the wheels and whirled round with it for a part of its course, and the other came so near me after I was entangled, that all the lower part of my right side, and my horse's shoulder, were covered with its dirt; and yet, through the goodness of God, I got not the least harm, not so much as a strain or bruise.[15]

In 1725, the church at Kibworth came under the pastoral care of the Revd David Some, minister of the Independent church at Market Harborough. Doddridge became assistant to Mr Some so he moved to live at Harborough. Though licensed to preach, he was not at this time formally ordained, so Mr Some was responsible for the administration of the Lord's Supper at both churches. We have further glimpses of the spiritual pilgrimage of Doddridge, from this entry in his Diary:

> Nov. 12, 1727. I preached this day from those words, 'I know you, that ye have not the love of God in you'. I endeavoured to fix upon unconverted sinners the charge of not loving God, and

described at large the character of the Christian in the several expressions of that affection. My own heart condemned me of being deficient in many of them. I humbled myself deeply before God, and do now, in the divine strength, renew my resolutions as to the following particulars: **1.** I will endeavour to think of God more frequently than I have done, and to make the thought of Him familiar to my mind in seasons of leisure and solitude. **2.** I will labour after communion with Him, especially in every act of devotion through the week ...[16]

A few months before, a letter from Samuel Clark revealed more of the theological climate of the time. The issues raised would greatly concern Doddridge in later years:

> You have seen, I suppose, what the public prints inform us of relating to the proceedings of the General Assembly of the Church of Scotland against Patrick Simson.[17] They are going to deprive that church of one of the most valuable men it contains, because he does not think it necessary to tie himself down exactly to their Shibboleth, nor oblige himself to conform to all their scholastic ways of speaking of our Blessed Lord in points where the Scriptures are silent. By what I saw and heard of that gentleman when in Scotland, he is a much better judge of such matters than the greater part of those who presume to judge him! But his crime is that he will think for himself; - but yet he is very cautious to avoid giving offence, which I perceive is by the bigots interpreted as cunning and dissimulation.[18]

Early in 1728, Doddridge received an invitation from the Independent church at Nottingham to be their minister, which he again declined for reasons not dissimilar to those stated earlier. Concerned with training young men for the ministry, he began to express his thoughts to some friends on the possibility of becoming a theological tutor. As the result of a conversation on this subject with one individual, Doddridge drew up what he thought would be a suitable syllabus for a ministerial training course. This document came to the notice of the eminent Dr Isaac Watts, to whom Doddridge was quite unknown. Watts joined with others in encouraging Doddridge to carry out his scheme. However, Doddridge was beginning to feel diffident about the whole matter.

The turning point came in April 1729, at a special assembly of ministers held at Lutterworth. This gathering was principally convened for the purpose of praying for revival in the churches. Mr Some preached on 'Be watchful, and strengthen the things that remain, that are ready to die' (Revelation 3: 2), which deeply affected the assembled gathering. Mr Some then proposed that an academy be formed at Market Harborough, under the direction of his young assistant, Mr Doddridge! Such was the unanimity among the ministers, that Doddridge finally acknowledged this to be the will of God. This development reveals to what extent Doddridge's abilities and zeal in the service of Christ were now evident. And so, in the summer of 1729, the academy was opened with a handful of students.

No sooner than the academy was functioning at Harborough, the Independent Church at Castle Hill, Northampton, approached Doddridge with a view to calling him to the pastorate. Doddridge had preached several times at Northampton, and when the pastorate became vacant, the only man who would satisfy the zealous people of Castle Hill was Philip Doddridge. Despite the enthusiastic invitation, Doddridge was painfully unsure of the will of God. Mr Some was convinced that Doddridge should stay at Harborough, even making a journey to Northampton himself to persuade the people to withdraw their invitation.

However, when Some witnessed the hearty and unanimous resolution of the people, even he had to confess to a change of mind, urging Doddridge to accept the invitation. Yet Doddridge was unmoved. He then decided to go to Northampton in person to explain the reasons for his refusal. After preaching to them so acceptably, the people were even more determined. Doddridge was wavering indecisively. At the house where he was staying, he spent one morning in prayer over the matter. As he was leaving his room, he heard a child reading to his mother. When he heard the words, 'and as thy days, so shall thy strength be', Doddridge was deeply affected. God was speaking, yet still he refused. Shortly before he was due to return to Harborough, a great number of the younger members of the congregation came to Doddridge, imploring him to be their pastor, and promising to submit to his instruction. In the dedication to his *Sermons to Young Persons*, published in 1735,

Doddridge states that it was this particular incident that finally convinced him that the call from Castle Hill was also the call of God:

> Permit me to remind you, that, as your remarkable importunity was the consideration, which turned the scales for my coming hither, after they had long hovered in uncertainty, so you are under some peculiar obligations to study the ease and comfort of my life, which you can never so effectually secure, as by the holy regularity of your own ...[19]

With the clouds of uncertainty dispelled, Doddridge wrote, on December 6, 1729:

TO THE CONGREGATION AT NORTHAMPTON

On my acceptance of their invitation to undertake the Pastoral charge.

My dear Friends,

After a serious and impartial consideration of your case, and repeated addresses to the Great Father of Light for His guidance and direction, I can at length assure you that I am determined, by His permission, to accept of your kind invitation, and undertake the pastoral care of you, with the most ardent feelings of sincere gratitude and affection.

With a growing spirituality and deepening humility he went on to say:

> Prepare yourselves, therefore, to cover my many infirmities with the mantle of your love, and continue to treat me with the same kindness and gentleness as those dear and excellent friends have done, whom I am now about to leave, in compassion to your souls; for God knows that no temporal advantage you could have offered would have engaged me to relinquish them.

This impressive letter thus concludes:

> I shall continue to recommend you, my dearly beloved, to the Grace of Almighty God, the great Shepherd of His sheep, with that affection which now so peculiarly becomes your most devoted friend and servant, in the bonds of our common Lord,

PHILIP DODDRIDGE.[20]

On December 24, Doddridge moved to Northampton, and was ordained to the ministry at Castle Hill on March 19, 1730. Charles Stanford wrote, 'All that was especially exalted or memorable in his ministry now began. He devoted himself to the service of the Saviour with such startled energy and intense concentration, was such a wonderful and manifold worker, and seemed to live so many lives at a time, that from this point, instead of telling one consecutive story, we can only try to show what he was and what he did at the same period in different departments'.[21] Dr Nuttall sums up Doddridge's future activities in similar terms. Driven by an all-consuming desire to win souls for Christ, 'evangelism' was to be 'the thread on which his multicoloured life was strung. It was for this above all that he wrote, preached, corresponded and educated his students in the Academy'.[22]

CHRIST's *Invitation to thirsty Souls.*

A

SERMON

Preached at

NORTHAMPTON,

in the YEAR 1729.

And now PUBLISHED

Chiefly for the Benefit of the POOR, at the earnest Request of a Gentleman of the Established Church of *England.*

By *P. DODDRIDGE,* D. D.

LONDON:

Printed and Sold by J. WAUGH, *at the* Turk's Head *in* Gracechurch-Street. M.DCC.XLVIII.

[*Price* Six-Pence.]

Alexander Pope
(1688 - 1744)

3
The Spirit of the Age

Any portrait of Philip Doddridge would be incomplete without an understanding of the age in which he lived. His life spanned the first half of the eighteenth century, and the years of his maturity witnessed the beginnings of those spiritual and social changes that came with the Evangelical Awakening. In addition to the interest a student might find in the merely academic study of history, Christians are interested when they find the truths of the Word of God illustrated, demonstrated and confirmed in history. The eighteenth century is especially illuminating in this respect, in view of the immense contrasts it displays. It is a period in which the degradation of sin and the wonders of grace are to be seen, side by side. The chief value of a study of the life of Philip Doddridge lies in the remarkable similarity between our present period and the early decades of the eighteenth century. The manner in which Doddridge faced the spiritual and moral decadence of his age can inspire the mind of the dejected twenty-first century Christian to have the same trust in God and the same unwearied diligence.

It would not be inappropriate to describe the period we are discussing as the first example in modern history of a permissive society. Of course, sin has always been sin and, in this respect, society never changes. But if that society can be defined as 'permissive' which unashamedly casts off all restraint, allowing once hidden moral irregularities to be shamelessly displayed, then late seventeenth and early-eighteenth century society was permissive. In this sense, Victorian society was hypocritical rather than permissive.

Thus the age of Doddridge saw a continuing reaction to the puritan morality of the previous century, and there was little evidence to suggest that the force of Restoration permissiveness had spent itself. When Oliver Cromwell made his speech to the Major

Generals in 1656, he urged them to pursue a 'Reformation of Manners'. "Make it a shame to see men bold in sin and profaneness," said the Lord Protector, "and God will bless you."[1] In the England of the Restoration period, the court of King Charles II set such an example to the nation, inducing the common people to look upon 'sin and profaneness' as a fashion to be followed. 'Sin and profaneness' increasingly became the hallmark of English social life in the early eighteenth century, to an almost unprecedented degree.

It is no exaggeration to say that the Britain of 1720 was on the verge of moral disintegration. The first two Hanoverian monarchs could hardly claim any moral superiority over the Stuarts. Public life was unashamedly dissolute. Sir Robert Walpole, Prime Minister from 1722 to 1742, lived in undisguised adultery with his mistress. In high society, marriage was almost a mockery. Lady Mary Wortley Montagu lamented the fact that the 'state of matrimony is as much ridiculed by our young ladies as it used to be by young fellows: in short, both sexes have found the inconveniences of it, and the appellation of rake is as genteel in a woman as a man of quality'.[2] The world of popular entertainment both reflected and nurtured the prevailing moral laxity. The famous Joseph Addison, writing in the *Spectator*, remarked: 'It is one of the most unaccountable things in our age, that the lewdness of our theatre should be so much complained of, so well exposed, and so little redressed... It is to be hoped that at some time or other we may be at leisure to restrain the licentiousness of the theatre'.[3] The field of literature was also infected, so much so that Lord Jeffrey said in retrospect that 'The staple of our novel market was beyond imagination despicable, and had consequently sunk and degraded the whole department of literature, of which it had usurped the name'.[4] This was not merely 'Paradise Lost' but 'Hell Regained'.

The early eighteenth century was notorious for the 'Gin Craze'. By the year 1724, this moral epidemic had increased to such a degree that it was, in the words of W. E. H. Lecky, 'irrevocably implanted in the nation'.[5] Henry Fielding, author of *Tom Jones*, was also a magistrate, and he lamented the gin problem when he asked, "What must become of the infant who is conceived in gin, with the poisonous distillations of which it is nourished in the womb and at the breast?"[6] There was also a gambling epidemic. Sir George Otto Trevelyan says that 'society in those days was one vast casino'.[7] The Government exploited and inflamed the thirst for material wealth by sponsoring State lotteries.

The crime situation was necessarily what it was. The populace at large adopted the standards of the nobility and the gentry. With no organised police force to restrain the situation, many crimes went unpunished. Prisons were overcrowded. Gangs of hooligans roamed the streets. In these days of cock fighting and bull baiting, the statistics of violent crime showed an alarming increase. Hangings became so frequent, that the perennial wit Dr Samuel Johnson expressed his fear that the Navy might run short of ropes![8]

This reaction to puritan morality could be witnessed in every realm of life. However, the rejection of Puritanism was not only a moral one. It was also philosophical and theological in character. The development of the scientific movement, promoted by the work of Sir Isaac Newton and others, and assisted by the empiricist philosophy of John Locke, had disastrously erosive effects upon orthodox biblical Christianity. Whilst both Newton and Locke saw their enquiries to be quite consistent with belief in the personal God of Christianity, there were those who were ready to argue that a scientific view of the universe could dispense with religious ideas.

Popular with the intellectuals was 'multi-faith' Deism, a system of thought which rejected the concept of special supernatural revelation. All that is necessary for faith was basic to all religions. So the Deists replaced the study of the Bible with the study of natural theology, arguing that all that needed to be known about God could be derived from a scientific study of the created order. They viewed God like a watchmaker who, having made and wound up the watch, leaves it to run down without any further involvement on His part. Deism stood for the authority of reason at the expense of revelation, and its advocates preached morality rather than religion.

The popular current of thought was vehemently anti-Christian, a dramatic contrast to the age of Cromwell and the Puritan saints. The early eighteenth century reveals a state of affairs which is not unfamiliar to twentieth century minds. The poet and essayist Alexander Pope had his finger on the pulse of the age when he wrote his famous *Essay on Man*:

> For Modes of Faith, let graceless zealots fight;
> His can't be wrong whose life is in the right:
> In faith and hope the world will disagree,
> But all Mankind's concern is Charity:
> All must be false that thwarts this one great End,
> And all of God, that bless Mankind or mend.

With the theological values of the previous century no longer in fashion, Pope describes the virile humanism then in vogue:

> Know then thyself, presume not God to scan;
> The proper study of Mankind is Man.[9]

Churchmen were deeply alarmed at the prevailing spirit of the age. In 1738, George Berkeley, Bishop of Cloyne, reported that morality and religion in Britain had collapsed 'to a degree which was never known in any Christian country',[10] and, in the same year, Thomas Seeker, then Bishop of Oxford, lamented that 'an open and professed disregard of religion is become, through a variety of unhappy causes, the distinguishing character of the age'.[11] In 1751, Joseph Butler, Bishop of Bristol, described the climate as 'truly for nothing, but against everything that is good and sacred among us'.[12] But for the difference in style, these comments would be quite at home in the early twenty-first century. 'Sin and profaneness' are still very much with us.

Reactions to the new liberalism, incongruously styled 'The Enlightenment', were various. In the face of such a barrage upon the Christian Faith, there were three paths of retreat. The first was that taken by the Church of England into the secluded areas of 'Latitudinarianism', a viewpoint that may be described as 'broad convictions held with little emotion'. The Established Church became a haven for a quiet, unemotional theology, where orthodoxy was maintained as far as this was consistent with 'reason'. Horton Davies says that 'It was left to the Latitudinarians to conceive of a contradiction – Christianity without tears!'[13] While there were some worthy churchmen who attempted to combat the advancing infidelity of the age, they could hardly be called heroes of the faith. Their tactics were exclusively intellectual rather than spiritual – a masterly use of words without the unction of the Holy Spirit. Popular preaching had degenerated into empty exhibitionism. Displays of wit in the pulpit were thought to be more acceptable than the living utterance of a godly life. Sir Leslie Stephen portrays Hugh Blair of Edinburgh, a celebrated preacher of the period, as 'a mere washed-out retailer of second-hand commonplaces, who gives us the impression that the real man has vanished, and left nothing but a wig and gown'.[14]

There were many clergy who would rather buy their sermons than take the trouble to compose their own. Enterprising individuals with far more literary flare than religious conviction would find a very lucrative market for their pulpit products. Of this shocking situation one indignant critic wrote:

> And lo! with all their learning, when they rise
> To preach, in view the ready sermon lies;
> Some low-prized stuff they purchased at the stalls,
> And more like Seneca's than mine or Paul's.[15]

Another escape route was taken by those Dissenters who were not too worried about capitulating to the enemy; they sacrificed much orthodoxy in order to appear rational, which meant a rejection of the evangelical Calvinism of the Puritans, a declension that became Arminianism and finally Unitarianism. The Presbyterians of the seventeenth century eventually became the Unitarians of the eighteenth century. Despite the heavy artillery of the Westminster Confession of Faith, the gunners deserted their positions. The presbyterian strategy of men like Manton, Watson, Flavel and Henry did not convince the junior officers of a later generation. Writing to Philip Doddridge in 1744, John Barker (Matthew Henry's successor at Hackney) lamented that 'The dissenting interest is not like itself; I hardly know it. It used to be famous for faith, holiness and love, ... now, I hear prayers and sermons I neither relish nor understand; primitive truths and duties are quite old fashioned things. One's ears are so dinned with reason, the great law of reason, the eternal law of Reason... O for the purity of our fountains, the wisdom and diligence of our tutors, the humility, piety, and teachableness of our youth!'[16]

The third path of retreat was that made by those who claimed to be faithful to the Calvinism of the Puritans. The spectacle was a sad one indeed; men who had formerly been the crack troops of puritan Independency under Owen and Goodwin, retreated with Bibles in their hands, but with a weighty system of hyper-calvinism upon their backs. These stalwarts fled to the barren wastes of dead orthodoxy, where the watchword became 'survival'. The Independents were joined by the Particular Baptists, and they both agreed in this, that it was safest to rest their weary legs and take off their boots.

Thus the liberalism of the Presbyterians and the ultra-orthodoxy of the Particular Baptists represented the early eighteenth-century extremes of traditional Calvinistic Dissent. In a letter to Doddridge, written in 1740, the eminent antagonist of Deism, Dr John Leland of Dublin breathed a lament that could be heard on many lips:

> I wish I could say that religion is in a flourishing condition among us; but there are many sad symptoms of decay; may God awaken and revive the true genuine spirit of Christianity among ministers and people, which suffers very much from the growing looseness, and libertinism of some, and the too great narrowness of others.[17]

Describing the Particular [Calvinistic] Baptists – as distinguished from the General [Arminian] Baptists – during the period following 1689, N. B. Magruder and E. H. Overbey have written: 'The Particular Baptists, on the other hand, remained orthodox as a whole. There was among them, though, a deadness and lack of evangelistic preaching which did not bring about any significant growth'.[18] This sad state of affairs is illustrated by the famous Andrew Fuller (b. 1754) who portrayed the type of theological influences he inherited from the previous generation:

> My father and mother were Dissenters, of the Calvinistic persuasion, and were in the habit of hearing Mr Eve, a Baptist minister, who being what is here termed high in his sentiments, or tinged with false Calvinism, had little or nothing to say to the unconverted. I therefore never considered myself as any way concerned in what I heard from the pulpit.[19]

It would be wrong to suggest that the above review mirrors reality in all parts of the country in every denomination. Happily, there were some notable exceptions in Yorkshire, the Midlands and elsewhere.[20] Yet the general picture was not encouraging. The Church of England appeared like a senile old man, still revealing traces of his former glory, but now quite impotent. The Presbyterians suggest the picture of a once respectable young lady now despising the virtues of orthodoxy, a courtship which issued in the bastard of heterodoxy, while the Independents and Particular Baptists remind one of a prudish old couple with stern, joyless countenances, denouncing all this theological permissiveness with pharisaical precision. For the common people, this apparent defeat for the Christian faith only provided an excuse to live without regard for right or wrong, salvation or damnation, heaven or hell.

Whilst the spiritual, moral, social and political scene was truly critical in the extreme, it would be false to give the impression that there were no attempts to remedy the situation. As early as 1673, Dr Anthony Horneck, an Anglican clergyman in London, preached some 'awakening' sermons which resulted in the formation of religious societies. Young men gathered together for the purpose of Bible study, worship and mutual encouragement in the Christian life. These societies also engaged in philanthropic work and general acts of kindness. It was at such a Society meeting in Aldersgate Street in London that John Wesley was converted in 1738.[21]

On the wider social and religious scene, there were other efforts to redeem the situation. Hospitals were established in increasing numbers between the years 1720 and 1740 as a result of the growing knowledge of medical practice. Attention was drawn to the conditions in the prisons by a Parliamentary Committee in 1728, but something more was required to rouse the hearts and consciences of those in the chambers of power. The Gin Act was passed in 1736, but there was little sympathy to guarantee the enforcement of legislation. The early eighteenth century saw the beginnings of popular education in the Charity Schools movement. With a lack of due appreciation of the need and value of education, coupled with a shortage of competent teachers, this movement made slow progress.[22]

The prevailing moral pollution was opposed by the Society for the Reformation of Manners, which reported in 1735 that 99,380 legal actions had been taken out by the Society in the London area alone. Tracts were published by the score against drunkenness, swearing, public indecency and Sunday trading. How effective *Kind cautions against swearing* and *Kind cautions to watermen* were is difficult to determine. In this onslaught on permissiveness, Churchmen and Dissenters joined forces to disinfect society from the pollutions of the age. The most effective religious movement was the Society for Promoting Christian Knowledge, founded in 1699, but even this good work could not effectively counter the effects of theological confusion in the churches.[23]

We must now turn to consider in a little more detail the state and condition of the Dissenters at this time. This much should be clear already, that the descendants of the Puritans had largely lost the spiritual zeal of their forebears. That power for righteousness and godliness that had been so positively displayed in earlier times was now assuming a more negative character. This fact is clearly confirmed in the theological debates that dominated the life of the Dissenting congregations around the year 1719.

Theological decline chiefly began to make itself felt following the publication of works by such men as Emlyn, Clarke and Whiston. These men rejected the orthodox understanding of the Trinity, expounding views that eventually issued in Unitarianism. The new liberal ideas of the age revived the ancient heresy of Arianism. In no place did Arianism obtain a firmer grip than among the presbyterian congregations at Exeter. The managing committee of the churches in Exeter decided to refer the matter to the ministers of the London churches. A committee of the three main dissenting bodies – Presbyterian, Independent and Baptist – drew up a 'Paper of Advices' to be sent to Exeter, as a means of reconciling the contending parties. This document was discussed by an assembly of the London ministers at the famous Salters' Hall on February 19, 1719. A heated division of opinion soon followed between those advocating a more conciliatory position and those who argued for a strict prohibition of ministers advancing Arian views. This meeting brought into conflict two of the most eminent figures of the time amongst the Dissenters, the Revd Dr Isaac Watts and the Rev Thomas Bradbury. The division that came to exist between these two men of God became typical of a controversial spirit that was increasingly permeating the ranks of Protestant Nonconformity.[24]

Isaac Watts was born in 1674 of puritan parents. Around the year 1695, after criticising the somewhat dreary metrical psalmody of the Dissenters, he produced the first of a great number of hymns, which are still loved and sung by Christian people everywhere. The hymn was 'Behold the glories of the Lamb'. After a distinguished academic career, Watts became the pastor of the Mark Lane Independent Church in London, once pastored by the illustrious Dr John Owen. Watts was ordained on March 18, 1702, beginning a ministry which, though punctuated with continuous ill health, was to continue until his death in 1748. Watts was a peaceable kind of man, to whom theological controversy was distasteful. He acquired a reputation for 'moderation' and conciliation, to the point of becoming guilty of blurring necessary theological distinctions. As a preacher, Watts preferred what became known as 'experimental preaching' in contrast to the more aridly doctrinal discourses of other preachers of the period. Watts was also a prolific writer, employing his literary gift in almost every department of learning, both divine and human. His somewhat speculative turn of mind brought him into trouble with some of his Dissenting colleagues when he published certain novel views on the Trinity and person of Christ, which leaned decidedly in the direction of Arianism. Watts was unquestionably an evangelical in his emphasis on the great central truths of the Gospel, but there were certain areas of theology in which he showed questionable deviations from orthodox thinking. Anxious to avoid what they considered to be scholastic excess, the traditional emphases of puritan Calvinism were no longer to be seen in the Puritanism of 'moderate' men like Isaac Watts who, like Richard Baxter before them, sought a middle-path between High Calvinism and Arminianism.[25]

Thomas Bradbury was as different from Isaac Watts as a lion is from a lamb. The clearest picture of Bradbury is provided by Thomas Wright, who described him as 'the masterful and militant Thomas Bradbury, inspired preacher, pulpit firebrand, saint, buffoon, ogre, zealot, hard-headed, inflexible Calvinist'.[26] Bradbury was born in 1677 and he preached his first sermon in 1696. In 1707, he became the pastor of the Fetter Lane Independent Church

Thomas Bradbury
(1677 - 1759)

Dr Isaac Watts
(1674 - 1748)

and the most popular preacher in London. If Watts withdrew at the very sound of battle, Bradbury would be in the front line. He seems to have thrived on controversy, whether it was religious or political. In August 1740, Mercy Doddridge was in London when John Wesley's Arminian teachings were attracting attention. She gives us a glimpse of Bradbury's pulpit polemics in a letter to her husband:

> This morning I went to Pinners Hall, where Mr Bradbury gave us, upon the whole, a very good sermon, though not entirely free from a little of the old leaven, as it turned chiefly upon Wesley's free grace.[27]

Bradbury's patriotic fervour combined with his religious zeal every November 5th when he vented his fury upon Jacobites and Papists in thunderous and terrifying tones. After an appropriate sermon at this time, Bradbury would retire with some friends to a respectable tavern to dine. With a huge joint before them, Bradbury would break forth with his stentorian voice to sing 'The Roast Beef of Old England', a song in which, says Wright, 'it is supposed no French-loving, Pope-loving person was ever known to join'.[28] Bradbury's 5th of November sermons were published, and they are amongst the finest defences of the civil and religious liberties of this country.[29]

Bradbury's puritan patriotism is seen most clearly during the last days and death of Queen Anne. She was the last of the Stuarts, having ascended the throne in 1702. It was known that the Queen, like all the Stuarts, had sympathies with Roman Catholicism. Her ministers passed two Acts against the Dissenters, the most important one being the Schism Act of 1714. This was aimed at restoring the educational monopoly of the Church of England and destroying Nonconformist schools. The Act was to become operative on August 1, 1714, and it was generally feared that the eventual restoration of Roman Catholicism could not be far away.[30]

Many like Bradbury feared the worst. Would not the days of 'Bloody Mary' soon be upon them again? Were the Dissenters being called to suffer for the truth, as did the Protestant Reformers? On the morning of August 1, Bradbury made a journey to Smithfield, the scene of the martyrdoms of many Protestant heroes. When deep in thought on solemn things, he was interrupted by the good Bishop Burnet, who was no less concerned for the continuing establishment of Protestantism than Bradbury. The Bishop asked Bradbury why his friend was looking so apprehensive. Bradbury replied with pensive deliberation, "I have been wondering, Bishop, whether I shall have the constancy and resolution of that noble army of martyrs whose ashes are deposited in this place; for I most assuredly believe that similar times of violence and persecution are at hand, and that I shall be called to suffer in a like cause."[31] Bradbury started with amazement when the Bishop announced that the Queen was seriously ill and near the end. According to a pre-arranged plan, in which the Bishop promised to send word to Bradbury the moment the Queen's death was known, a messenger entered Bradbury's meeting house during public worship, and dropped a handkerchief from the gallery. With the greatest possible difficulty, Bradbury continued with his sermon! The congregation learned of the Queen's death during the benediction and soon the cry was heard everywhere, "The Queen is dead!" When Bradbury's congregation next met, their expectations were adequately fulfilled when 'Bold Bradbury', as the now deceased monarch had called him, gave out his text, 2 Kings 9: 34, 'Go, see now this cursed woman, and bury her; for she is a king's daughter!' Bradbury, true to form, was soon in full flight.[32]

If these events serve to illustrate the character of Thomas Bradbury, they do likewise in the case of Isaac Watts. On the occasion of Queen Anne's death, Watts preached no militant tirade, but he did compose one of the most famous hymns in the English language. It is doubtful whether Bradbury's sermon is ever read, but the Christian world still continues to sing, 'Our God, our help in ages past'.[33] With the passing of these events, August 1, 1714 was regarded for half a century by the Dissenters as the great day of deliverance – the Protestant Passover. With the ascendancy of the House of Hanover, the threat to Protestant Dissent was past: the King henceforth received unswerving loyalty from those whose liberties he promised to guarantee.

Until the Salters' Hall Conference, Watts and Bradbury had been close friends, but the first meeting saw them at odds. At the second meeting on February 24, 1719, parties became irreconcilable. Some thought that the 'Paper of Advices' should demand of the offending ministers at Exeter subscription to a Trinitarian formula. Bradbury proposed that the Advices should include the Trinitarian statements in the Thirty-Nine Articles and the Westminster Shorter Catechism. He was inflexible. "Let those who really believe the doctrine of Christ's divinity," cried Bradbury, "openly avow it. You who are not ashamed to own the deity of our Lord, follow me into the gallery!" Bradbury had scarcely mounted two steps when he was hissed at. Turning round sharply, he said, "I have been pleading for Him who bruised the serpent's head; no wonder the seed of the serpent should hiss!"[34]

When Bradbury's proposition was voted on, it was lost by a majority of four – fifty-seven against, fifty-three for. Those in favour were called the 'Subscribers', whilst those of the contrary opinion were known as the 'Nonsubscribers'. This division of opinion did not reflect any differences on the doctrines of the Trinity and the Deity of Christ, but simply whether human articles of faith should be subscribed to. As one minister present said, "It was not from any doubts in our minds as to the generally received opinions upon that subject, but from our scrupling to subscribe to any human articles of faith."[35] Despite the amount of heat dissipated, two sets of advice were sent down to Exeter.

The Salters' Hall Conference is a landmark in the history of English Nonconformity. From this time, the congregations became largely introspective, and mutual suspicion permeated the ranks of the ministers. The Conference revealed a sad anomaly, such that the eminent Presbyterian leader, Dr Edmund Calamy complained of 'a spirit of imposition'. This development was not characteristic of the Dissenters. In 1662, these men had suffered because the Act of Uniformity had been imposed on them. On the other hand, many of the Presbyterians like those at Exeter, were now claiming further liberties in rejecting their own doctrinal standards. Over-heated logic tends to push things to extremes, and what was a desire for liberty under the Gospel in 1662 was becoming liberty without the Gospel in 1719. Orthodox liberty became heterodox liberalism.

A further development following Salters' Hall was that those of the 'Subscribing' party naturally tended to question the orthodoxy of the 'Nonsubscribers', even when there were no just grounds to

Salters' Hall Conference (1719)

do so. An inquisitorial attitude was at large. Those who advocated 'charity' in disputes were automatically suspected of Arianism, while those who contended for truth were accused of bigotry. There were many cases of both liberalism and bigotry, but there were others who sought to achieve a biblical balance.

The events of the early eighteenth century fashioned the age in which Philip Doddridge commenced his ministry. The days were fraught with dilemmas. Dr R. Tudur Jones summarised the situation as follows: 'The relationships between Christian people were rendered unhappy by an exaggerated zeal for formal orthodoxy on the one hand and a cultivated vagueness about essential Christian doctrines on the other'. He then adds that 'it was of the greatness of Doddridge that he saw the need to purge the poison by combining gospel freedom with evangelical doctrine'.[36] If Isaac Watts tended towards 'cultivated vagueness', Thomas Bradbury tended towards 'exaggerated zeal'. It is not without warrant therefore, that John H. Taylor should write that 'Some men are chosen by God to work for Him in times of religious and moral depression. Such is our unenviable task today and such was that of Philip Doddridge in the eighteenth century... he piloted the churches through years of fierce and damaging theological controversy towards the goal of revival'.[37]

We must proceed to discover how Philip Doddridge dealt with the dilemmas that confronted him.

Tedious moments! ſpeed your flying,
　　Bring *Cordelia* to my arms ;
Abſent, all in vain I'm trying
　　Not to languiſh for her charms.

Buſy crowds in vain ſurround me,
　　Brighteſt beauties ſhine in vain ;
Other pleaſures but confound me,
　　Pleaſures but renew my pain.

What though three whole years are ended
　　Since the prieſt has join'd our hands,
Every rolling year has tended
　　Only to endear our bands.

Let the wanton wits deride it,
　　Huſband is a charming name ;
None can ſay, but who has try'd it,
　　How enjoyment feeds the flame.

Wives our better angels are,
　　Angels in their lovelieſt dreſs,
Gentle ſoothers of our care,
　　Smiling guardians of our peace.

Happy ſtate of mortal treaſures,
　　Circling maze of noble love :
Where the ſenſe's higheſt pleaſures
　　But the meaneſt bleſſing prove.

Dear *Cordelia !* hither flying,
　　Fold thy huſband in thy arms ;
While thus t'amuſe myſelf I'm trying,
　　More I languiſh for thy charms.

Philip's Poem on Mercy

4
Dearest Dear of All Dears

If Philip Doddridge was to distinguish himself as a man of God in things spiritual, we must never allow ourselves to forget that he was a human being. Therefore, before we see the spiritual exploits of Doddridge, we should take a glimpse at his domestic and personal circumstances. When he moved to Northampton in December 1729, he was a young man of twenty-seven years of age, and a bachelor. When he wrote in 1723 during his stay in the farm-house at Stretton that 'I am like Adam in Paradise; and it is my only misfortune, that I want an Eve', this was no isolated expression of a romantic young man. As is frequently the case with those who lose their parents at a young age, the desire for the emotional stability of marriage and home life is more pronounced than usual. Therefore, this additional element in Doddridge's spirited masculinity conspired to deepen his felt need of 'an Eve'. Doddridge's early correspondence includes many letters to young ladies, the contents of which might make the readers of Christian biography indulge in prudish censure, until they realise that he, or she, is quite as natural as Doddridge was.

The letters in question abound in witty expressions and humorous suggestions, of the kind that should only provoke a smile! In a letter to one of his female acquaintances, written in 1722, Philip revealed a secret:

> In short Madam, I - am - in - love, - and that is all. And, you will say, enough too. And yet, upon second thoughts, that is not all neither: for I am most violently in love with a charming girl that lives in the neighbourhood of Leicester, about seventeen years of age, and, to borrow an Arabian phrase, as beautiful as the moon in her fullness.

Attracted thus to Kitty Freeman, his Kibworth host's daughter,

Doddridge the young romantic clearly had difficulty in concentrating on his studies:

> I dream of her in the night; and rave of her in the day. If my tutor asks me a question about predestination, I answer him, that Clarinda is the prettiest creature in the world! Or, if I sit down to make a sermon against transubstantiation, I cannot forbear cautioning my hearers against the excesses of love.[1]

Although this youthful infatuation lasted several years, Kitty was not the 'Eve' God had planned for Philip. So he had to content himself with the metaphysical delights of predestination and other stimulating subjects a little while longer! Dr Nuttall comments that during this period of Doddridge's life, whether he knew it or not, 'he missed his mother'.[2]

Doddridge was to have a few disappointing relationships before he found the lady of his dreams. The once disappointed Isaac Watts had advised Doddridge to remain celibate, but the younger man had a more natural attitude towards marriage. In the providence of God, Doddridge met his bride-to-be on the rebound from an abortive relationship with his late tutor's daughter, Jenny Jennings. Indeed, the Lord's choice for Philip Doddridge was a young orphan girl of twenty-two years of age, a native of Worcester, Miss Mercy Maris. She was, in every respect, not only what Doddridge wanted but also what he needed. He fell deeply in love with her. He began to experience emotions he never knew existed. He was falling over backwards when he realised that what he felt was mutual. But we must let him speak for himself:

> Had I the most ample time, all I could say would be utterly insufficient to express the sense I entertain of your worth, and the warmth of my gratitude for the obliging reception you gave me. Words cannot express it; but my heart feels it so tenderly, that it often throbs with joy and fondness. Will you be mine? Methinks it is presumption to hope it ...[3]

Even in this touching letter, it is the heart of a Christian man that is in love. There to be no doubt that God was first in Doddridge's heart, with Mercy occupying her rightful, God-ordained, second place:

> I fear I shall over love you; and then perhaps God will afflict
> you. That is the only way in which I can fear being afflicted in
> you; as we must be in everything which we suffer to usurp the
> place of God in our hearts. But I hope you will rather lead me
> to Him. I am sure it ought to be so; for I am fully conscious that
> it was He, that gave you that lovely form, that intelligence, that
> wisdom, generosity, and goodness, without which your beauty
> and your wit might have tormented, but would never have made
> me happy. It was He, that opened to me a heart which the
> greatest and best of men could hardly have deserved; and kindly
> disposed events, by His Providence, in a manner favourable to
> my dearest wishes. And is He to be forgotten and neglected, and
> for this? No, my dearest, it shall not be.[4]

With the wedding only a matter of weeks away, Doddridge's honest
heart is again exposed to our view. In words that many would
identify with, he says:

> It must be your care, my dearest, to keep alive a sense of religion
> upon my heart. I am ashamed to see how soon it wears off, and
> how much more constant I am to you, than to Him, to whom I
> owe a supreme affection. Help me to conquer all the weaknesses
> of my temper, to conquer even the excess of my love to you.[5]

Ever since the death of her parents, Mercy had lived with an aunt
at Upton-upon-Severn, and it was there that the marriage was to
take place. The date was fixed for December 22, 1730. As the date
drew even closer, the young husband-to-be was irrepressible in his
letters to Mercy. One wonders if his duties as a pastor and tutor in
the Academy were suffering somewhat from distraction when, a
fortnight before the blissful day, he wrote:

> Dear Miss Maris is now receiving the last billet-doux she is ever
> to expect from her Lover! – There may possibly be a certain
> grave matron called Mrs Doddridge, who may in time, though I
> hope not very quickly, receive a letter from her husband! But
> the triumphs of the dear girl I mention are over, and her virgin
> reign, almost at an end.[6]

If Mercy was as truly feminine as she appears, she must have read these lines with the utmost delight.

At last the wedding day came, and after a brief interval, Mr and Mrs Philip Doddridge returned to Northampton to settle in their home in Marefair. It becomes clear that Doddridge the once orphaned teenager now intended to reproduce the domestic happiness he had known in childhood. He took his duties as a husband seriously, as we can see from his diary:

> As a husband, it shall be my daily care to keep up the spirit of religion in my conversation with my wife, to recommend her to the Divine blessing, to manifest an obliging tender disposition towards her; and particularly to avoid everything which has the appearance of pettishness, (i.e. sulkiness) to which, amidst my various cares and labours, I may in some unguarded moments be liable ...[7]

The happiness of this marriage made it, like Martin and Katie Luther's, a model of Christian matrimony. It was to supply much of the energy with which Doddridge applied himself to his labours. While away on his many preaching tours, Philip always found time to write to Mercy. It is obvious that he adored his wife, calling her 'dearest dear of all dears'.[8] His fond letters also exhibit his playful 'fun-loving' nature. At Wilton, on his way home from Devon and Somerset in July 1742, Philip wrote part of a letter in Dorset dialect,[9] urging Mercy to ask his pupil 'Mr [Andrew] Parminter' - son of a Bideford merchant - to translate it for her.[10] In every way, among Doddridge's voluminous correspondence, his letters to his wife are a category apart, as Dr Nuttall observes:

> [If] they were parted, as during [Philip's] annual visits to London, or because he was away *en tournée* ordaining his pupils, or when Mercy was visiting her relatives or was in Bath for her health's sake, they wrote to each other two or three times a week, sometimes oftener, and far more letters to and from Mercy are preserved than those between Doddridge and any other of his correspondents.[11]

From London in July 1741, devoted Doddridge tenderly declared that Mercy was the 'Dearest of Women dearest of Creatures my very Soul is with you by Night & Day you are my Thought my Wish my Prayer'.[12] Clearly, not only the house was empty when Mercy was absent. Writing to her at Bath in October 1742, Philip confessed that 'everything centers in you'.[13] Ever conscious of God's mercy throughout his life, Doddridge was not slow to use the *double entendre* when responding to enquiries about his health: "I am, through mercy, well!"[14] Mercy herself was just as expressive in her affection. In a letter of July 1742, her love for her husband shines through despite her famous spelling difficulties:

> I have many more mercys than afflection [affliction] & in you my dearest all I could wish or desire in any creture pray that I may not Love you to much as I think I am greatly in danger I am asham to send this sad scarwl butt as it is mine I know you will forgive it.[15]

After five letters to Mercy in the space of nine days, uninhibited Philip wrote from London that exactly a year before, he returned home from 'my Norwich journey. It was one of my wedding nights & I hope & trust that to Morrow Sevennight... will be another'.[16] Four days later he wrote:

> It is but about 108 Hours to our meeting . . . [I hope] I may never more know what it is to be another Nine Weeks together separated from you for indeed when I am not engaged in some Publick Service I seem to be but a poor Fragment of my self.[17]

The following day, Mercy confessed that her heart 'burns & throbs with love & impattiency... to see you my dear... I allmost tremble for fear any thing should prevent your coming on frday. adiu my dear charmer be asurd my ardent prayer attend you for our happy Joyfull Meeting'.[18]

Kippis quotes the following formal yet still romantic composition. Writing from London in 1733, the hymn writer sang his wife's praises:

> What though three whole years are ended
> Since the priest has join'd our hands,

> Every rolling year has tended
> Only to endear our bands.
>
> Wives our better angels are,
> Angels in their loveliest dress,
> Gentle soothers of our care,
> Smiling guardians of our peace.
>
> Dear Cordelia! hither flying,
> Fold thy husband in thy arms;
> While thus't amuse myself I'm trying,
> More I languish for thy charms.[19]

The 'charmer's' affection did not cool with the years. In August 1750 Philip related a visit to Tunbridge Wells:

> I saw the greatest number of fine young ladies that I ever met with in one place in my life but I sighed for none but you ... I think among other infirmities fondness grows upon me with age.[20]

If the Doddridge marriage was blissful, it was also fruitful. On October 9, 1731, Mercy gave birth to a baby girl. All the joys of fatherhood burst forth upon Philip. Writing to convey the happy news to Mercy's uncle, Ebenezer Hankins, Doddridge warbled away:

> It is a strange thing to me to find myself so fond of a little being who can do nothing but sleep and cry, and when it would be remarkably witty and entertaining, open its eyes and stare! ... P.S. I do not exactly know what the girl's name will be; but I imagine it must either be Ebenezer or Elizabeth.[21]

Typical of Doddridge's humour and playfulness is a letter he wrote to his sister – as if from the infant Elizabeth – from my little girl to my sister:

> I am but a little girl, and so I shall write you but a little letter. However, I could not forbear paying my respects to you, for I have heard my papa and mamma talk of you a great many times ...[22]

'Elizabeth' went on to relate the trials of infanthood:

> Even the other night my mamma was so unkind that she would not let me suck any longer than till all the milk was gone, and when I cried and bawled on, my naughty papa lay by and slept, for aught I could find, as soundly as if he had been a bachelor![23]

Elizabeth seemed particularly bright and precocious. She became a legend, and was affectionately called 'Tetsy'. Once asked why everybody loved her, 'Tetsy' replied, "Indeed, papa, I cannot think, unless it be because I love everybody."[24] The degree of spiritual understanding in the little girl was quite remarkable. On one occasion, she even attempted to teach their little dog the Catechism, but failed! The poor creature placed its tail between its legs when frustrated 'Tetsy' exclaimed, "You, Dr Doddridge's dog, and not know who made you!" On relating this anecdote, Doddridge added, 'And if so much is expected from my dog, what may be expected from my students?'[25]

In days when the rate of infant mortality was high, Christian families were not exempt from domestic loss. 'Tetsy' lived almost to the age of five, when sadly, after a long bout of tuberculosis, a grief-stricken father laid her to rest. Doddridge preached his little daughter's funeral sermon. The deeply moving discourse was published with the title, *Submission to Divine Providence in the Death of Children*.[26] After the funeral, Doddridge wrote in his diary:

> I have now been laying the delight of my eyes in the dust, and it is for ever hidden from them... Yet I bless God I have my hopes that she is lodged in the arms of Christ.[27]

Doddridge's confidence in 'Tetsy's' eternal security was well-founded. His further reflections upon this tragic circumstance are a wonderful testimony to the Gospel of the grace of God, which alone provides that balm and comfort when all else fails. Let us listen to the triumph of grace in the midst of personal grief:

> Soon after, as I came into my wife's chamber, she told me that our maid Betty, who had indeed the affection of a parent for my dear girl, had just before assured her that on the Sabbath day evening Betsy would be repeating to herself some things of what she had heard in my prayers and in my preaching, but did not

Submiſſion to Divine Providence in the Death
of Children recommended and inforced,

IN A

SERMON

PREACHED AT

NORTHAMPTON,

ON THE DEATH

Of a very amiable and hopeful
CHILD about Five Years old.

Publiſhed out of Compaſſion to mourning PARENTS.

By *P. DODDRIDGE,* D.D.

Neve Liturarum pudeat : qui viderit illas,
De Lachrymis faƈtas ſentiat eſſe meis. OVID.

LONDON:

Printed for R. HETT, at the *Bible* and *Crown,*
in the *Poultry.* M DCC XXXVII.

[Price Six-Pence.]

care to talk of it to others; and my wife assured me that she solemnly recommended herself to God in the words that I had taught her a little before she died. Blessed God, hast thou not received her? I trust that thou hast, and pardoned the infirmities of her poor, short, childish, afflicted life.[28]

How did Mercy bear up during the hour of grief? Her constancy was a lesson to Philip - and remains so to us all:

My dear wife bore the affliction in the most glorious manner, discovered more wisdom, and piety, and steadiness of temper in a few days, than I had ever in six years an opportunity of observing before.[29]

Doddridge was himself to die a premature death, from the same disease which struck down his little daughter. His final reflections are as instructive as they are touching:

Lord, I would consider myself as a dying creature. My firstborn is gone; – my beloved child is laid in bed before me... My grave is made - I have looked into it – a dear part of myself is already there; ... But, oh, let me not centre my thoughts even here; it is a rest with and in God that is my ultimate hope. Lord, may thy grace secure it to me! and in the meantime give me some holy acquiescence of soul in Thee; and though my gourd be withered, yet shelter me under the shadow of thy wings![30]

However, not all was sadness. Other children were to grace the Doddridge household: Mary (or 'Polly', b. 1733), Mercy (b. 1734), Philip (b. 1735) and Anna Cecilia (or 'Caelia', b. 1737). Others were born, including twins, but they died in infancy. Periodic sickness and sadness apart, the correspondence reveals a happy family. During a smallpox outbreak in 1740, all the children were sick. Insisting that his wife keep a safe distance from the infection, Doddridge sent her to London while the epidemic raged. He wrote to her of 'Caelia' that 'the Dear little lamb ... is exceeding patient'. She was 'exceeding ill' and 'in considerable danger'. [31] However, they all recovered. Soon little Mercy – the first to be ill - was 'so well', Doddridge told his wife, 'that she goes all over the House &

makes me a great many pleasant Visits in my Study... with her little prattle... absolutely as much a Monkey as ever'.[32] Twelve days later, we learn that 'Philly' 'is almost well, eating a Crust of Bread very heartily'.[33]

Two years later, towards the end of her husband's two-month summer vacation, Mercy wrote that their impatient children 'have made their bargain with me already, that they may sit up to see you'.[34] The mutual joy is delightfully obvious. As they grew older, the fond father brought from town 'a Fan for each of my little girls'.[35] Six years later, a homeward-bound but perplexed father wondered what home-coming gifts would be suitable for the children: 'They are too big for toys & I am not so skilled in cloaths as to know what they want or how they are to be bought'.[36] Such were the delights of Doddridge domesticity!

A few years after Doddridge's death in 1751, Mercy moved with the children to Tewkesbury where, besides travelling, she corresponded copiously with her husband's former students. Neither Doddridge nor Mercy enjoyed robust health yet she died there in 1790 aged eighty-one. There 'Polly' was married to John Humphreys; she died in 1799 in her sixty-seventh year. (A great-grandson was Richard Doddridge Blackmore (1825-1900) the author of *Lorna Doone*).[37] Doddridge hoped his son would enter the ministry but this was not to be.[38] After a law career in London, Philip also died unmarried at Tewkesbury in 1785. Mercy died unmarried at Bath in 1809 and 'Caelia' also died unmarried at Tewkesbury in 1811. The family grave may be seen behind the former Congregational Chapel in the town (now sadly a Kingdom Hall).

In making our retrospective visit to the Doddridge household, we have had a glimpse of Doddridge the husband and father. We have seen a private aspect of that total spirituality that was characteristic of Doddridge the Christian. He was no less spiritual at home than he was in the pulpit. But we can put it more strongly and say that domestic piety was the very foundation of all true religion in the puritan tradition, of which Doddridge was so distinguished a representative. We have seen what he was, and the picture is cheering, humbling and challenging. We may ask, what was the teaching behind the practice? By way of an introduction to the work of the Academy, we may profitably consider what was to Doddridge the very foundation of a true Christian education - the Christian home.

We have seen, in the previous chapter, the spiritual, moral and social conditions that prevailed in the early eighteenth century. Doddridge gave his estimate of the climate as he saw it, in *The Rise and Progress of Religion in the Soul*, a work we have already referred to. Doddridge did not rest in the cosy notion that he was living in some so-called 'Christian society':

> When we view the conduct of the generality of people at home, in a Christian and Protestant nation, in a nation whose obligations to God have been so singular, almost beyond those of any other people under heaven, will anyone presume to say that religion has a universal reign among us?... Alas! the avowed infidelity, the profanation of the name and day of God, the drunkenness, the lewdness, the injustice, the falsehood, the pride, the prodigality, the base selfishness, and stupid insensibility to the spiritual and eternal interests of themselves and others, which so generally appear among us, loudly proclaim the contrary ... [39]

However, all was not lost, and Doddridge did not exaggerate the gloomy situation when he added:

> Shamefully and fatally as religion is neglected in the world, yet, blessed be God! it has some sincere disciples, children of wisdom, by whom, even in this foolish and degenerate age, it 'is justified' *(Matt. 11: 19)*; who having by Divine grace been brought to the knowledge of God in Christ, have faithfully devoted their hearts to Him, and by a natural consequence are devoting their lives to His service.[40]

Doddridge believed that the great need was a revival of true and vital Christianity. Towards this goal he prayed as a Christian, preached as a minister, and lectured and wrote as a tutor and author. His great concern was that people might know God in Christ, and that this was the ultimate purpose of human existence.

As Doddridge viewed the situation, the essential aids to revival were education and piety. To him, these were the chief means whereby men and women are brought to God. Education without piety will produce an 'enlightened' infidelity, and piety without education could lead to superstition. In days when it is now fully realised that the content and methods of educational programmes are invariably directed by certain philosophical and ideological presuppositions, we can begin to understand Doddridge's emphasis. For him, the Christian faith supplied the very presuppositions which alone could provide a Christian ethical and social agenda. Doddridge was in a glorious tradition; he would agree with the great Christian philosopher, Augustine of Hippo who said, '...for Thou hast made us for Thyself, and our heart is restless, until it find rest in Thee'.[41] Doddridge would agree with the God-centred Calvin that 'Our wisdom, in so far as it ought to be deemed true and solid wisdom, consists almost entirely of two parts: the knowledge of God and of ourselves'.[42] There is no finer nor simpler expression of Doddridge's agreement with these illustrious precursors than that found in one of his hymns:

> What is my being but for Thee,
> Its sure support, its noblest, end,
> Thy ever-smiling face to see,
> And serve the cause of such a friend?[43]

Such are the underlying principles of a Christian education, which, for Doddridge, must begin in the home. It is not surprising to find that a number of his published works were in connection with the religious education of children and young people. *Sermons on the Religious Education of Children*[44] were published as early as 1732. Three years later, *Sermons to Young Persons*[45] were published. In 1743, a small volume appeared entitled *The Principles of the Christian Religion in Plain and easy verse for the use of little Children.*[46] Only two years before, in 1741, *Sermons on the Power and Grace of Christ, and on the Evidences of His glorious Gospel*[47] were published with a dedication to young people.

Paramount in Doddridge's thinking about the religious education of the young was the family. He gave expression to this when he published in the year 1750 *A Plain and Serious Address to the Master of a Family on the Important subject of Family Religion.*[48]

T H E

P R I N C I P L E S

O F   T H E

Chriſtian Religion,

Expreſſed in

Plain and Eaſy V E R S E,

And divided into ſhort L E S S O N S for
the Uſe of little C H I L D R E N.

By P. DODDRIDGE, *D. D.*

JESUS *ſaid unto* Peter,——*Loveſt thou me?*——*Feed
my Lambs.* John xxi. 15.

L O N D O N:

Printed and Sold by M. FENNER, at the *Turk's
Head* in *Gracechurch-ſtreet.* M DCC XLIII.

[Price 4 *d.*]

A

PLAIN and SERIOUS

ADDRESS

TO THE

Master of a Family,

ON THE

Important Subject

OF

FAMILY-RELIGION.

By *P. DODDRIDGE*, D. D.

LONDON:

Printed and Sold by J. WAUGH, at the *Turk's Head* in *Lombard-street.* M DCC L.

However, it was in another work in which he firmly establishes his point. When we realise that the humanism of the Deists descended like an avalanche on the domestic piety of the age, it was essential to lay the foundations well. One of the advocates of Deism was Henry Dodwell, who, in 1742, published a pamphlet entitled *Christianity not Founded on Argument*, a work to which we will refer later. In 1743, Doddridge answered Dodwell in three separate letters published at intervals. With the role of parents in mind, Doddridge wrote:

> ... the father and mother concur in a wise and conscientious care, to keep their dear offspring, as far as possible, out of the sight and hearing of everything profane, cruel, and indecent; and 'whatsoever things are true, whatsoever things are venerable, whatsoever things are righteous, whatsoever things are pure, whatsoever things are lovely, whatsoever things are of good report, if there be any virtue, if there be any praise' [Phil. 4: 8], the child will be taught, by the force of precept and daily example, to think on these things, and to pursue them. The consequence of this, under those influences of Divine grace which may be cheerfully expected in the way of duty, will probably be an early sense of decency, virtue and piety. The growth of those seeds of corrupt nature, which will in some instances discover themselves in the most amiable children, will in a great measure be suppressed; religion will grow familiar and pleasant, under the smiling aspect it will appear to wear; and the Bible, which our little disciple will early have been taught to read, will soon become a most delightful book.[49]

It is clear in Doddridge's thinking that the parents' duty is to provide an environment in which a child finds it natural to be a Christian. Deism attempted to create a climate in which the seeds of piety could not long survive. Doddridge believed that church and family could provide an effective antidote to the virus of unbelief and scepticism. There was nothing new in what Doddridge advanced, but in his day, it appeared to be radical thinking, when personal and family religion were becoming unfashionable. As Doddridge surveyed his 'foolish and degenerate age', he was advocating eternal truths – the health of society depends on the health of the home; the health of the home depends on the health of the church; the health of the church depends on the Gospel of Jesus Christ. To parents of his and every age, this Christian pastor and father says with regard to children:

> Consider, that the world, into which you have been the means of bringing them, is a place in which they are surrounded with many temptations, and in which, as they advance in life, they must expect many more; so that in plain terms, it is on the whole much to be feared, that they will perish in the ignorance and forgetfulness of God, if they do not learn from you to love and serve Him. For how can it be expected they should learn this at all, if you give them no advantages for receiving and practising the lesson at home?[50]

We may be sure that many others besides Tetsy Doddridge have reason to bless God that such teaching fashioned the home life in which they found the Saviour who said, "Suffer the little children to come unto me,...for of such is the kingdom of heaven" *(Matt. 19: 14)*. Six years after Tetsy's death, Doddridge wrote lines which doubtless were instrumental in awakening many a child to its eternal concerns in his day:

> How shall a young immortal learn
> This great, this infinite concern,
> What my Almighty Maker is,
> And what the way this God to please?
>
> Shall some bright angel spread his wing
> The welcome message down to bring?
> Or must we dig beneath the ground,
> Deep as where silver mines are found?
>
> I bless his name for what I hear;
> The word of life and truth is near,
> His gospel sounds through all our land;
> Bibles are lodg'd in every hand.
> That sacred book inspired by God
> In our own tongue is spread abroad:
> That book may little children read,
> And learn the knowledge which they need.
> I'll place it still before my eyes,
> For there my hope and treasure lies.[51]

5

The School of Christ

One autumn morning in the year 1733, a letter was delivered at the Doddridge residence in Marefair, Northampton. It was addressed to 'Philip Dotteridge of the Parish of All Saints in the town of Northampton in the County of Northampton Gentl'. An expression of surprise soon gave way to one of indignation, as the recipient read the imperious communication:

> By virtue of a Citation under seal herewith shewn unto you I Cite you to appear personally before the Reverend George Reynolds, Doctor of Laws, Vicar General, Commissary General, and Official Principal in Spiritual Matters of the Right Reverend father in God, Robert, by divine permission Lord Bishop of Peterborough, and also official of the Reverend the Archdeacon of the Archdeaconry of Northampton, or his lawful Surrogate, or some other competent Judge in his behalf, in the Consistory Court adjoining to the Parish Church of All Saints in the same town of Northampton, on Tuesday the Sixth day of November 1733, at the usual time of hearing causes there, then and there to answer to certain Articles, or interrogatories to be objected and administered to You concerning Your soul's health and the Reformation and Correction of Your manners and excess, and especially Your teaching and instructing Youth in the Liberal Arts and Sciences, not being Licensed thereto by the Ordinary of the Diocese ...[1]

This was not the first time that an academic institution in the borough of Northampton was threatened with dissolution. In the year 1260, during the reign of King Henry III, the University of Northampton was founded by the granting of a royal license. Northampton might have been as famous as Oxford and Cambridge as a centre of learning, but for the turbulent political

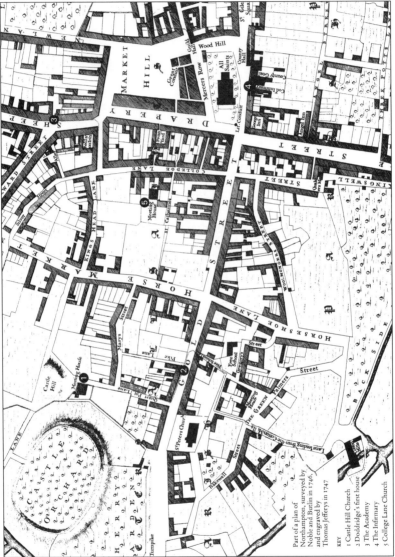

Map of Northampton (1746)

Part of a plan of
Northampton, surveyed by
Noble and Butlin in 1746,
and engraved by
Thomas Jefferys in 1747

KEY

1 Castle Hill Church
2 Doddridge's first house
3 The Academy
4 The Infirmary
5 College Lane Church

events of the time. The reign of Henry III (1216-1272) was characterised by weakness and incompetence, and the King gave the country neither strong government nor popular control. The royal policies brought the King and his barons into conflict, and civil war was inevitable. The barons were led by the father of English democracy, the famous Simon de Monfort, Earl of Leicester, whose brief year of power following the Battle of Lewes in 1264 laid some of the foundations of England's parliamentary institutions. Earl Simon could lay claim to popular support, and the students of Oxford were not slow in espousing the Barons' cause. Northampton had also declared itself to be in sympathy with the Barons, so when the King drove the masters and scholars from Oxford, many of them fled to Northampton. The King then marched on Northampton, which was stormed and taken. The borough of Northampton, now firmly established in the beginnings of its long republican tradition, was duly chastised for its insolence. On February 1, 1264, a writ was issued forbidding the Mayor and citizens of Northampton to have a university. The charter was never renewed.[2]

Events in the Middle Ages may have little direct relevance to Philip Doddridge and his academy, but there are some interesting similarities. As the suspension of the University was a direct consequence of the conflict between the King and his Barons, so the threat to Doddridge's Academy was a reflection of the uneasy truce that had existed between the Church of England and the dissenting bodies since 1688, the year of the 'Glorious Revolution'. In Hanoverian England, where enlightened legislation guaranteed the right of the Nonconformists to dissent from the established Church, bitter emotions frequently prevailed. Happily however, the differences were to be more important than the similarities, for whereas the University had to wait over seven centuries to be 're-established' (since 1999, Nene College has become the University College of Northampton), the Academy was to survive, albeit with some difficulties.

The circumstances which led to Doddridge being cited to appear before the diocesan court are important as well as interesting. In accordance with his wider public ministry, Doddridge preached occasionally in the villages around Northampton. In the year 1731, he preached to a company of Dissenters in a barn at the village of Kingsthorpe, now a northern suburb of the borough. Such an incident came to the notice of the curate-in-charge of the parish, 'the Revd Mr Wells'. The curate's wrath was so stirred that he wrote a letter of admonition to Doddridge, denouncing his behaviour on the grounds that he alone was the sole custodian of the spiritual welfare of those within his parish. Mr Wells also reported the incident to his vicar, the non-resident 'The Reverend George Reynolds, Doctor of Laws, Vicar General, etc...'

The non-residence of incumbents of the Church of England was one of the scandals of the age; parochial revenue would be received on the basis of 'The living', irrespective of any services rendered. 'Pluralism' was rife, where a man would receive the benefits of two or more parishes, leaving a poor curate to cope with all the day to day responsibilities in return for a meagre salary.

The debate, which ensued between Doddridge and Wells, was common in the previous century, when the rights and liberties of the Nonconformists were continually in question. It hinged on the exclusive right of the Church of England 'by law established' *versus* the liberty of the Dissenters to worship according to their understanding of the New Testament. James Wells was of a generation of clergy who not only poured scorn on nonconformist worship but who also questioned the validity of non-episcopal ordination. However, Doddridge had his wits about him. Writing to Wells, he said:

> As for my preaching occasionally at Kingsthorpe, and the neighbouring villages, I know it is a liberty which the law permits, and I cannot imagine that either you or any of your brethren can reasonably resent it. If the doctrine we preach be the same with yours, as I am sure it is, if you adhere to the articles of your church, methinks you should be pleased to reflect, that any of your people, who may chance to drop in amongst us, may be confirmed by observing this mutual agreement. ...

Doddridge went on to affirm that it was his policy to treat the clergy of the Established Church 'not merely with decency, but with sincere and respectful friendship', adding with careful deliberation:

... yet you must pardon me, Sir, if I tell you that I dare not compliment him (i.e. Mr. Wells) or them, at the expense of those truths of God, which I am sure scripture plainly reveals, and on which I apprehend the life of religion, and the welfare of immortal souls to depend.[3]

If Doddridge was a friend to all, he was an even greater friend to truth. He was not a Dissenter for nothing. In vain did Wells bring to bear on Doddridge all the ecclesiastical artillery at his disposal. In a manner that would have thrilled grandfather Doddridge and his noble colleagues of 1662, the puritan grandson replied with polite tenacity:

Notwithstanding your letter, my visits to your parish will be continued as before; since I cannot apprehend any one man to be so exclusively the proper teacher of any prescribed district, as to exclude any other minister, whom the people may choose either stately or occasionally to hear.[4]

Doddridge was sure of his ground. When Wells drew attention to the claims of episcopal authority, Doddridge – with a typical touch of ingenuity and gaiety – denied the validity of diocesan bishops. Having read the early-church fathers Clement of Rome (d. c. 100) and Ignatius (d. c. 108) as requested, he replied:

In Clemens I find nothing at all of bishops, and though the word often occurs in Ignatius, and their power be magnified as divine in a very unscriptural strain, yet a spiritual lord must pardon me, if I say that I apprehend the persons there spoken of were just such parochial bishops as yourself![5]

It was this controversy that occasioned the attack on Doddridge's Academy after his activities became more widely known. The debate over the lawfulness of the institution lasted nine months before the situation eased. Doddridge had friends in high places such as Lord Halifax who was able to enlist the services of the Solicitor General to stop proceedings against his Academy. Doddridge firmly refused to take out a license, arguing his right to teach without one. Foul means as well as fair were employed to suppress the Academy before its continuity was finally guaranteed. One winter's night, a mob stoned the house, possibly at the instigation of the disgruntled Mr Wells and his imperious master Dr Reynolds. Although a prohibition was granted on the case by the Solicitor General, the case was renewed six months later. The threat to the Academy was only finally removed when the whole proceedings were stopped by a message from the King, George II, who insisted 'That in his reign there should be no persecution for conscience' sake'.[6]

We have seen in an earlier chapter how the academies came into being, and the purpose they were intended to serve. When we read the opinion of one nineteenth century writer, who said that Philip Doddridge gave 'the mightiest impulse to the work of rearing an educated Nonconformist ministry in England',[7] it is not difficult to see why the Northampton Academy became the most famous of its kind. We may add here that the original inspiration for these institutions was found in the Academy of the great Protestant Reformer John Calvin at Geneva. It was therefore fitting that the Dissenters should call their institutions 'academies' since they regarded themselves as the true custodians of the Protestant Reformed cause in England. We have already observed the broad-based curriculum of the academies in which philosophy, literary and scientific subjects were taught. Calvin's Academy also taught philosophy besides theology, Hebrew and Greek. Such was the prestige gained by Calvin's religious and educational reforms that the great Scottish Reformer John Knox described Geneva as the most perfect school of Christ since the days of the Apostles.[8] If Doddridge's Academy became famous, there are those who would question whether Knox's words could ever be used of the Northampton Academy. We will see the significance of such a remark as we proceed.

The eighteenth century world of Doddridge was as different from the sixteenth century world of Calvin as the age of Concorde is from the age of the stagecoach. Doddridge had to contend with forces inside as well as outside the church which were hardly known in Calvin's day. However, the two periods are linked. The Protestant doctrine of private judgement gave birth to a liberal attitude which in the days of Roman Catholic tyranny was a blessing, but in the days of the Enlightenment was to prove a curse. If the right of private judgement gave birth to a legitimate heir in *liberty* to follow the Scriptures, it also gave birth to the bastard *liberalism*. If Reformation Protestants cast off the yoke of papal infallibility, many Enlightenment Protestants cast off the yoke of biblical infallibility. Doddridge and his colleagues had to breathe an atmosphere infected with Deism and Arianism, as well as the general air of scepticism which came with the rise of the scientific movement. Doddridge's dilemma was clearly defined: how to remain faithfully biblical without becoming irrelevant to his age. We see the way he faced the problem in the work of the Academy.

We have already observed that religious qualifications required for entry into the universities of Oxford and Cambridge proved an obstacle to those Dissenters who desired a higher education. The Dissenting Academies provided an education for both ministerial and non-ministerial students, even though their primary purpose had been to prepare men for the ministry. When Doddridge drew up his plans for his Academy, his intention was to educate men exclusively for the ministry. When this became known, he was advised to accommodate the two categories of students. A minister in London, the Revd David Jennings (brother of Doddridge's Kibworth tutor), argued the point with him:

> You will remember that the support of our interest comes from the laity, and that they will not be constrained to bring up all their sons either as ministers or as dunces! Should we attempt to oblige them to send their sons, who are designed for physicians, lawyers, or gentlemen, to Oxford, or Cambridge, or to make them rakes in the foreign universities? - judge you, how prudent that would be![9]

This argument convinced Doddridge to broaden the student intake. Thus his Academy pursued 'sacred' and 'secular' agendas (a fact not realised in Professor Donald Macleod's recent criticism[10] of Doddridge's educational method). But it was a decision that he seemed to have regretted later. Even though the rules of the Academy applied equally to all students without exception, the ministerial students suffered a certain amount of distraction from those whose callings did not appear to demand so deep a spirituality. Although all students had to provide sufficient evidence of their spiritual conversion, there were those who had to be expelled as a result of 'unbecoming behaviour'. That said, during his student days 'when [the] academy was in a very flourishing state' (1741-5), Andrew Kippis did 'not recollect that any of the theological students were corrupted by the others'.[11]

It is unfortunate that separate academic institutions of a non-ministerial nature were unavailable at this time. This would have been a solution to the problem of education facing the Dissenters. However, there was a shortage of tutors (and doubtless funds too), and those who were most qualified to teach were ministers. To some extent therefore, the problems of a mixed student body were forced upon men like Doddridge. Of course, the situation was not without its compensations. The non-ministerial students came under a spiritual as well as an academic discipline which otherwise they might not have had. If the solution to the Dissenters' educational dilemma was unsatisfactory, it is certainly unjust to blame Doddridge for all the weaknesses of the situation he found himself in.

The course of study at the Academy was both long and exacting. Ministerial students studied for four or five years, the non-ministerial for three. Even those students who were studying with some profession other than the ministry in view had to study some theology. A wide variety of subjects were taught besides theology and its allied subjects, Greek, Hebrew and church history. Philosophy in all its branches (metaphysics, ethics and logic), the classics, civil history, geography and law were all part of the basic curriculum. The reason for such a 'liberal arts' curriculum was not simply to accommodate the non-ministerial students but to provide a basic awareness of the entire spectrum of human learning from a Christian perspective. It was an attempt to demonstrate a 'Christian worldview'. This was the policy of John Jennings at Kibworth where Doddridge received his higher education; it was Jennings who inspired Doddridge's attitude to education. In an age when science and theology seemed in the eyes of many to be mutually exclusive, such a policy was an attempt to prove that human and divine learning were not necessarily inconsistent.

The eighteenth-century mind was beginning to be acquainted

with the rapid advances in science and discovery, and Doddridge was concerned to keep abreast of all these developments. Lectures were also given on natural philosophy (or physics), including mechanics, optics, hydrostatics, pneumatics and astronomy. Mathematics was taught, including algebra and trigonometry. Doddridge thought that an acquaintance with history gave the students an opportunity of surveying the providence of God in human affairs, and that the study of mathematics and science demonstrated the rationality and wisdom of God. Anatomy was also taught. Apart from any medical benefits, the subject provided evidence for God's amazing handiwork in the design and functioning of the human body. It was 'well calculated to inspire the young men with the sentiments of veneration and love for the supreme Artificer'.[12] The Academy could also boast in having a good selection of scientific equipment including a microscope. Thus the students were encouraged to take an interest in experimental science. Living a whole century before Charles Darwin, one may surmise that the theory of evolution would never have appealed to Doddridge. Its highly speculative and non-empirical (as well as atheistic) character[13] would have made it invalid in his eyes.

The centrepiece of Doddridge's course was published in 1763 with the title *A Course of Lectures on the Principal Subjects in Pneumatology, Ethics and Divinity*.[14] Many of the lectures are now only of interest to the student of the history of education since one of the Academy's aims was to be topical and contemporary. Yet, while the sciences have made immense strides since his day, Doddridge's introductory methodological observation remains valid:

> As these sciences do insensibly run into each other, I judged it not proper to treat of each separately, but have chosen to consider them in such a connected view as might convey to the mind ... the principal truths relating to each.[15]

This sums up Doddridge's 'cosmological' outlook; he saw knowledge as a whole. He had a co-ordinated approach to learning, viewing all areas of knowledge as parts of that totality of which God was the author. The editors of Doddridge's complete works (published 1802-5) said of the lectures that, compared with similar works, they could claim more originality of design , adding that 'we presume it is the most complete syllabus of controversial theology, in the largest sense of the term, ever published in the English language'.[16]

It could not be claimed that Doddridge was entirely original in regard to his educational philosophy. What is of particular interest is a further link with John Calvin. It has often been remarked that one of the essential differences between Luther and Calvin is that whereas the German reformer's wider thinking was still medieval, Calvin's was progressive and modern. T. H. L. Parker says of Calvin:

> We may observe, in this connection, that Calvin, as an educated gentleman... was no mere theological specialist. Besides his competence in the humanities, he was obviously interested in the sciences – in medicine, in natural history, ... in astronomy. Particularly in astronomy.[17]

The same could be said of Philip Doddridge. He was surely in the Reformed tradition, in the highest possible sense of the term.

What is most incredible is that the Academy lectures were all given under Doddridge's own personal supervision. He had two assistant tutors however. Doddridge himself had an enthusiastic interest in scientific questions, his contributions extending beyond the confines of the Academy. We find three papers of his in the *Transactions of the Royal Society*.[18] The society's secretary Henry Baker was sure of Doddridge's interest when he related some early experiments with electricity in 1747.[19] Doddridge was also an active member of the Northampton Philosophical society, consisting of medical and other professional gentlemen in town and county, and before whom he read two papers on Applied Mathematics.[20] On one of these occasions, one of his students propounded a theory for travelling to the moon. This was too much, even for the scientific Doddridge! With scepticism mingled with humour, he indulged in this piece of poetic protest:

> And will Volatio leave this world so soon,
> To fly to his own native seat, the moon?

'Twill stand, however, in some little stead,
That he sets out with such an empty head![21]

As has been hinted at already, Doddridge's method of tuition in the Academy has been severely criticised by many, both in his day and subsequently. Adverse reflections were made by Doddridge's friend Joseph Williams of Kidderminster who wrote in his diary: 'I don't think even Dr Doddridge's [academy] was strictly enough governed... It is certain many under his tuition have run into the scheme of the Remonstrants [Arminians]'.[22] Half a century later, in 1805, the following conversation was reported to have taken place aboard a Northampton stagecoach. A Particular Baptist and another passenger were discussing Dr Doddridge, when the Baptist commented:

> ... a great and good man, but a very bad tutor ... he gave both sides of the question ... Doddridge knew the truth, and all besides is damnable heresy. What better proof can you have of his pernicious mode of tuition, than that most of his divinity students turned out Arians or Socinians? [23]

Six years later, Joseph Kinghorn of Norwich added his own similar criticisms. Writing to William Newman, the president of the Stepney Academy, Kinghorn said 'I believe it is sufficiently plain that very many of Dr Doddridge's students imbibed opinions very contrary to his own; and surely this was in part owing to an error in their education'.[24]

Whether or not the number of deviant students has been exaggerated - Nuttall's index indicates 3 Arians, what of the supposed 'error' in Doddridge's educational method? He would have vigorously defended his policy of giving both sides of the question, and not only because non-ministerial students were present at the lectures. He regarded it as a necessary part of preparation of the minister's mind. When John Wesley asked Doddridge for a suggested reading for his local preachers in 1746, Doddridge's reply reveals the purest academic integrity. At the same time, he could hardly be accused of indifference to truth:

> I dare say, Sir, you will not by any means imagine that I mean to

recommend the particular notions of all the writers I have here mentioned, which may, indeed, sufficiently appear in a multitude of instances; but I think that in order to defend the truth, it is very proper that a young minister should know the chief strength of error.[25]

Doddridge's policy was thought to be dangerous because an acquaintance with both sides of an argument increases the possibility of doctrinal 'contamination'. Such a method of tuition might at least promote a gradual erosion of orthodox convictions. It cannot be denied that several students became 'infected' with Arianism and Socinianism, a fact which Doddridge deeply lamented. After expressing his concern to his friend Nathaniel Neal, Doddridge received some realistic reflections on his work. Neal evidently felt quite confident regarding Doddridge's method and, to encourage the tutor, he declared:

> I perceive [the subject] sits heavier on your mind than, I think, there is occasion for ... I have no conception that you can, by any sensible men, be deemed responsible for the tenets of your pupils, farther than your lectures, or instructions, may be supposed to have favoured them; ... and if your Academy produces none whose sentiments differ from your own, you are a tutor without parallel.[26]

The policy with which Doddridge lectured could hardly have been otherwise. He believed that the orthodox Christian faith could withstand all the attacks of scepticism and unbelief, and so he regarded free enquiry to be an asset to a Christian understanding. Also, the Reformation tradition which bequeathed the right of private judgement to subsequent generations of Protestants demanded a freer and more open method of imparting truth even if there was the risk that liberal views of truth might result in some cases. In his method of education, Doddridge was applying one of the foundation principles of the Protestant Reformation, and the Enlightenment era demanded that Christians come to terms with some of the implications of that principle.

Doddridge argued his position in his debate with the Deist Henry Dodwell whose tract *Christianity not Founded on Argument* we noted in the previous chapter. Dodwell argued that the truths of the Gospel lacked adequate rational justification. This was the attitude of Enlightenment thinkers in general. The main thrust of this view was that ultimately, Christians are quite irrational in their beliefs. The problem of the age was therefore one of authority, and Doddridge was anxious to establish the point that truth is self-authenticating, and not dependent on the authority of the Pope, the scholars of Protestantism, or himself. In the first of his letters in reply to Dodwell, Doddridge said:

> I would not represent Christianity to my catechumens, or my children, nor indeed to the most intelligent and judicious of my hearers, as a dubious uncertain thing ... yet I may in perfect consistence with this persuasion, and with the declaration of it, recommend it to others, not as on my own authority, but with the force of reasons, concerning the strength of which they are to judge for themselves; though I am ever so earnestly solicitous, that they may judge aright.[27]

A measure of the success of Doddridge's reply to Dodwell is seen in a letter from his friend, Dr Oliver of Bath:

> Your answer to the artful author of the pamphlet *Christianity not Founded on Argument*, gave me a great deal of pleasure. You effectually pluck that snake out of the grass, under which he endeavoured to conceal himself; you dispel the mists and fogs with which he hoped to obscure the truth; and you plainly prove that the religion of Jesus is founded on the immutable basis of the eternal difference between right and wrong, – confirmed and propagated by the most solid arguments and therefore highly worthy to be embraced by all reasonable creatures.[28]

Doddridge's criterion for judging 'aright' was not open to discussion, even if the entire field of intellectual enquiry was. For Doddridge, the standard of truth was neither reason, nor experience; it was the Word of God. Accordingly, his biblical convictions were by no means suppressed. Indeed, he countenanced

THE
Perfpicuity *and* Solidity
OF THOSE
EVIDENCES
OF
CHRISTIANITY,
TO WHICH THE
Generality of its Profeffors among us may attain,

ILLUSTRATED and VINDICATED;

In a LETTER to the AUTHOR of a late Pamphlet, intitled, *Chriftianity not founded on Argument, &c.*

By P. DODDRIDGE, *D. D.*

WE *alfo believe, and therefore fpeak.* 2 Cor. iv. 13.
An High-way fhall be there;—it fhall be called THE WAY OF HOLINESS;—*the way-faring Men, tho' Fools, fhall not err therein.* Ifa. xxxv. 8.
Quis non contemplatione—concutitur ad requirendum quid intus in re fit? Quis non, ubi requifivit, accedit? ubi acceffit, pati exoptat? *Tertull. Apolog. cap. ult.*

LONDON:
Printed for M. FENNER, at the *Turk's Head* in *Grace-church-ftreet*; and J. HODGES, at the *Looking-Glafs* over-againft *St. Magnus* Church, *London-Bridge.*
MDCCXLII.

no 'take it or leave it' indifference to truth. Let us hear two of his students speak. Job Orton, Doddridge's pupil, colleague and first biographer, described the lecturer's method of tuition:

> He never concealed the difficulties which affected any question, but referred them to writers on both sides, without hiding any from their inspection. He frequently and warmly urged them not take their system of divinity from any man or body of men, but from the Word of God. The Bible was always referred and appealed to upon every point in question to which it was supposed it could give any light.[29]

However, a rather less-favourable impression is created by the recollections of Andrew Kippis, one of Doddridge's more critical pupils:

> Having laid a firm foundation in so ample a statement of the evidences of Christianity, he entered into a copious detail of what were, or, at least, what appeared to him to be, the doctrines of Scripture. In so doing, though he stated and maintained his own opinions, which in a considerable degree were calvinistical, he never assumed the character of a dogmatist. He represented the arguments, and referred to the authorities on both sides. The students were left to judge for themselves; and they did judge for themselves, with his perfect concurrence and approbation; though, no doubt, it was natural for him to be pleased when their sentiments coincided with his own. Where this was not the case, it made no alteration in his affection and kind treatment, as the writer of the present narrative can greatly witness.[30]

Was Doddridge then as seemingly indifferent to truth as Kippis implies? Only if we neglect what he adds several pages later, a statement which instantly confirms Orton's own recollection:

> Dr Doddridge...allowed and encouraged [his pupils] to propose any objections, which might arise in their own minds, or had occurred in the authors they perused. If, at any time, their objections were petulant or impertinent, he patiently heard and mildly answered them; for he put on no magisterial airs, but

always addressed them with the freedom and tenderness of a father. He frequently and warmly urged them not to take their system of divinity from any man or body of men, but from the Bible. It was the Bible that he always referred and appealed to, upon every point in question, to which it could be supposed to give any light.[31]

What then should Doddridge have done? What alternative was there? Simply presenting an uncritical orthodox curriculum would have been mere propaganda. Would it have been more commendable to browbeat the liberal students? In refusing to do so, was Doddridge as indecisive as many suppose? For those who still question his essentially orthodox instincts and theological integrity, Kippis himself supplies a decisive item of information:

> How sincerely Dr Doddridge detested the want of integrity in character, was displayed in the following fact. One of his pupils was in the habit of making a jest of what is called orthodoxy, and ridiculing those who adhered to it; and this he continued to do, up to the time in which he began to preach. Then, to the no small surprise of his intimate acquaintance, it was rumoured, that in the congregations where he had officiated in the neighbourhood of Northampton, he had appeared highly calvinistical, and indeed much more so than almost any other of his fellow-students. For obvious reasons he declined ever preaching at Northampton. At length, the affair was brought before the Doctor; and both parts of the charge having been proved by decisive evidence, the young man was dismissed.[32]

Indeed, the tutor's lot was not always a happy one. An incident occurred in August 1740 which was doubtless upsetting. Philip wrote thus to Mercy (then in London):

> I was last night expounding the first of John in the family & insisting on the importance of remembering & maintaining the Deity & Satisfaction of Christ when some of our good preaching Seniors were pleased to express their Contempt of what they heard by laughing & almost making Mouths.[33]

This was clearly not typical of the situation. Three years later,

Doddridge assured the mother of one of the students that he desired 'that my House may be filled with sound & serious & evangelical Youths & those of another stamp seldom stay long in it'.[34] By 1747, he reported happily to Samuel Clark: 'I think I never knew more regular diligence & piety among a set of pupils & so little Matter of complaint among them in my life'.[35] Then, in the final year of his life, Doddridge rejoiced: 'Nor did I ever know a finer class of young preachers, for its number, than that which God has given me this year, to send out to the churches'.[36]

The academy course itself has also been criticised. The first half of its ten parts deal with 'natural religion' (the human mind, the being and attributes of God, ethics, the soul's immortality and the possibility of revelation). The second half covers 'revealed religion' (the Bible, God and the Trinity, sin and redemption, church order and sacraments, and eschatology). Some have even criticised the lecture format itself. The entire course of two hundred and thirty lectures is cast in a quasi-Euclidian logico-mathematical form, viz. *'definition'* (a formulated idea), *'proposition'* (the statement to be considered), *'demonstration'* (arguments supporting the proposition), *'axiom'* (a self-evident truth), *'lemma'* (an assumption), *'scholium'* (further explanation with objections and answers) and *'corollary'* (additional inferred conclusion). This pattern is imposed throughout. Besides being a useful teaching aid, Doddridge believed the logical structure would facilitate an objective presentation of truth, independent of the personal convictions of the lecturer. Thus it has been suggested that, for some of the students at least, the 'rationalistic' structure of the course could have lessened their respect for special revelation, leading them to believe that they were competent to judge even the Scriptures by their own reason. But did Doddridge assume the priority of reason over revelation?

On the place and use of reason, Doddridge was being biblical when he observed that 'when Paul was addressing the Athenians [Acts 17], he argues upon principles of natural reason, and [then] from the resurrection of Christ from the dead'.[37] However, Doddridge did not hold that 'reason was king'. Indeed, he wrote: 'That our minds are naturally so dark, and our hearts so hard, is indeed a matter of the justest lamentation'.[38] Consequently, he insisted:

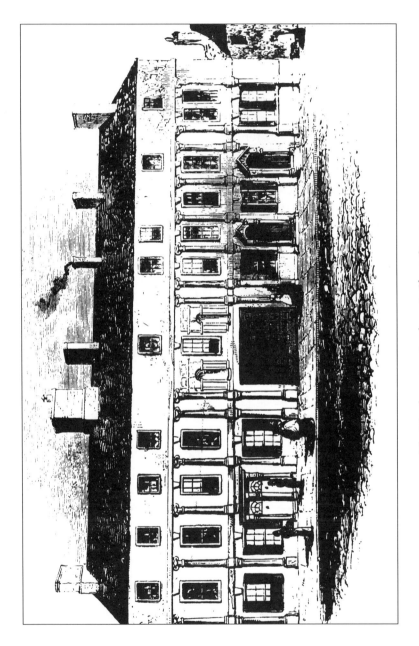

The Northampton Academy in Sheep Street, 1751

As for dependence on Divine grace and influence, it must be universal: and since we always need it, we must never forget that necessity. A moment spent in humble, fervent breathings after the communications of the Divine assistance, may do more good than many minutes spent in mere reasoning: and though indeed this should not be neglected, since the light of reason is a kind of Divine illumination, yet still it ought to be pursued in a due sense of our dependence on the Father of lights, or where we think ourselves wisest, we may become vain in our imaginations, Rom. 1: 21.[39]

It is thus more accurate to say that Doddridge's lectures are 'rational' rather than 'rationalistic'. In the tradition of Baxter (and even Owen), Tillotson and John Locke, Doddridge occupied the middle ground between the anti-rational subjective pietism of some and the anti-supernatural rationalism of others. As both Orton and Kippis made clear, Doddridge did not downplay the necessity of revelation or the centrality of the Scriptures. For him, the Bible itself is above theology. In his intelligent Christianity, the Word of God always had 'the last word'. When discussing Doddridge's skills at theological analysis, Kippis makes the same point:

Perhaps there were few men who had more carefully studied the different systems of theology, or who could point out their several defects with greater accuracy and judgement. While he was not one of those who affect to treat with contempt the labours of the wise and the learned who have gone before them, but was always ready to receive whatever light they could afford him, nevertheless, without a slavish regard to human schemes, he took the sacred oracles for his guide, and always referred to them for the proofs of the doctrinal sentiments which he maintained.[40]

It becomes evident that Philip Doddridge is one of those unique individuals who saw intellectual enquiry to be not only consistent with, but necessary for, a faithful and effective proclamation of the Christian faith. This much must be emphasised, that Doddridge's attitude to learning was not conditioned by a desire for intellectual respectability, a charge that may be levelled against some nineteenth-century Nonconformists. Like the Apostle Paul in his debate with the Athenian philosophers, Doddridge endeavoured to deflate the arrogance of the learned infidel, as a prelude to exhibiting the glorious Gospel of the God of Truth. His lectures, and the replies to Dodwell, reveal a Christian mind, working out the philosophical implications of biblical truth, whilst at the same time making a vital contribution to the spread of the Gospel during the great Evangelical awakening. Failing to recognise this, Colin Brown's book *Philosophy and the Christian Faith*, provides a highly doubtful assessment of the eighteenth-century evangelical scene:

> As with Luther, so with Wesley and the many who had similar experiences of God in the Evangelical Revival, this meant that the whole of life must be looked at in the light of this continued experience. The guide to life was the Word of God. Philosophy was set aside. There were more important things to do. No doubt this was true. All the same, it was a pity that no one in the Evangelical Revival attempted to work out the philosophical implications of their faith (a notable exception was Jonathan Edwards (1703-58) in America).[41]

But Jonathan Edwards of Northampton, New England was not the only exception. The Northampton of Old England could also claim to have a champion in the conflict between Orthodox Christianity and Enlightenment secularism. However, like Edwards, Doddridge was primarily a man of God, and he never lost sight of his goal. If Doddridge was seeking to provide a decidedly Christian education, his primary purpose was still to train men for the Christian ministry. We must never lose sight of the fact that this educator was a minister of the Gospel of Jesus Christ, and he was clear in his task:

> It is my heart's desire and prayer to God that not one [student] may go out from me without an understanding enlightened from above, a heart sanctified by Divine grace, quickened and warmed with love to a well-known JESUS, and tenderly concerned for the salvation of perishing souls. What are all our studies, labours and pursuits, to this?[42]

When we consider the work of the Academy, it is noteworthy that such high standards of academic attainment were not regarded as inimical to true piety, for the personal godliness of the principal tutor filled this seat of learning with spiritual devotion. The students were able to see the character of Christ shining brightly in one whose literary achievements sparkle before our eyes. Even in the pursuit of learning, Doddridge warns his students in the introduction to the course of lectures:

> Let the great vital truths of Christianity taught in Scripture be constantly regarded. As to matters of controversy, let them be referred to their proper place, without any eagerness to anticipate them, which often produces great bigotry and error. ... and may it never be forgotten that matters of abstruse speculation and laborious enquiry, are not, even to theological students, the one thing needful, though they may be important in subordination to it. ... I would beseech and charge you, ... that it be your daily and governing care, after having solemnly devoted your soul to God through Christ in the bonds of the Christian covenant, to live like his servant, to keep yourself in the love of God, and to endeavour in all things to adorn His Gospel.[43]

A failure to heed this faithful exhortation, no doubt often stated from pulpit and lecture rostrum, is the explanation for the students who lapsed into Arianism and Socinianism. Significantly, some of the most noted evangelical ministers of the later eighteenth century received their tuition under Philip Doddridge. Risdon Darracott of Wellington in Somerset, and Benjamin Fawcett of Kidderminster are worthy of special mention. Doddridge described these men as 'persons of eminent piety'.[44] Both of them were associated with the early Methodists, and Darracott was described by George Whitefield as the 'Star of the West'.[45] Shortly after Doddridge's death in October 1751, Darracott wrote to a friend:

> O what will the society of heaven be! ... What will it be to sit down with Abraham, and Isaac, and Jacob, with Moses, David, Paul, Peter, John, Baxter, Doddridge, the general assembly and church of the first-born in the kingdom of our Father![46]

Dying in 1759 at the age of forty-one, his last words included:

> Blessed be God, all is well, all is well. I am now going to see
> dear [Joseph] Williams [of Kidderminster], Doddridge, and the
> rest of the glorified saints. Farewell, my friend, a goodnight to
> you.[47]

Richard Denny, one of Doddridge's last surviving students, faithfully reflected his tutor's outlook. In 1763 he became the pastor of the Independent church at Long Buckby, Northants. After a long ministry of nearly forty years, he died in 1813 at the age of ninety. Thomas Coleman wrote:

> Though there was a great disparity between him and his tutor in
> talents and acquirements, yet there was a great resemblance in
> Christian affection, holy zeal, and ardent piety; and such was his
> regard to the 'dear doctor', as he generally styled him, that he
> often mentioned his name and his excellencies with the tear
> glistening in his eye. ... In his last hours he said, "I shall soon
> see the blessed, blessed Redeemer, and the dear Doctor
> Doddridge."[48]

On a more mundane note, how was Doddridge's Academy administered? While the rules were strict, they were not imposed unilaterally by the principal and his colleagues. Some *Constitutions, Orders and Rules*[49] were drawn up in 1743 by both staff and students. The average day, for all students, commenced with rising at 6 am in the summer and 7 am in the winter. Names were called in the great parlour at ten minutes after the hour of rising. Private prayer was expected of every student and, at 8 am, everyone would assemble for 'Family Prayer'. A chapter of the Old Testament was read in Hebrew by one of the students. This was then expounded by Doddridge. They sang a psalm, followed by prayer. Breakfast lasted from the end of prayer to 'five minutes before ten'. Evening prayer took place at 7 pm, when the New Testament would be followed in Greek, one of the students taking the prayer.

Lectures were held only in the mornings, with the exception of

Thursday which was free time all day. There were personal tutorials conducted by Doddridge and his assistants. Doddridge was progressive in his day in a number of respects. For example, lectures were given in English, rather than the customary Latin, and he introduced the system of shorthand of Jeremiah Rich, modified by himself.[50] Every student was expected to master the shorthand in his first year (see p. 296).

The *Constitutions, Orders & Rules* of the academy convey something of the daily regime operated by Doddridge. Regarding strictly educational activities, the following were expected of final year students (Section I. 10, 11):

> Four classics, viz. one Greek and one Latin poet, one Greek and one Latin prose writer as appointed by the tutor, are to be read by each student in his study, and observations are to be written upon them to be kept in a distinct book and communicated to the tutor whenever he shall think fit.
>
> Each student of the upper class may be allowed to propose a difficult scripture to the principal tutor every Thursday morning to be discussed and examined by him the next Thursday morning. But it will be expected that the person proposing them write some memorandum of the solution to be afterwards subjected to review.

The library seems to have functioned efficiently. According to its Rules (Section VI. 2, 3):

> Every one that takes a book out of the library is to make a distinct entry of it in the library book prepared for that purpose, adding his name at length and is in consequence of that entry to be accountable for the book while it stands under his name.
>
> When he brings in the book (which he is always to do at three a Clock every Saturday in the afternoon if not before, references excepted) he is to return it to its proper place in the library blotting out the entry he has made of it. And in case either of these rules are neglected 1/2d is to be forfeited for each book.

There were rules in connection with the daily meals. Dinner was served 'precisely at two'. In every age, inflation always seems to hit a student's pocket! In section III. 7, we read:

> As making toasts & butter & toasting cheese has been found to
> be more expensive than can conveniently be afforded on ye
> usual terms here, that custom is to be disused except by ye
> parlour borders.

In this respect, care had to be taken as much in the event of a
student's irregular eating habits, as in the case of his piety! Section
III. 9 reads:

> That ye servants may not be hindered in their business, none of
> ye students are, on the penalty of forfeiting an half penny each
> time to be in the kitchen before morning prayer, nor from twelve
> at noon till ye dinr is served up. ... And during these seasons of
> exclusion, the kitchen door shall be bolted whenever the cook
> shall think fit.

There were strict rules regarding a student's 'retirement at night'. In
Section IV. 1, we find that

> The gate is to be locked every night when ye clock strikes ten &
> the key is to be brought to the tutor ... every pupil who comes
> in after that time is to forfeit two pence for every quarter of an
> hour that he hath exceeded ten.

When students were away from the Academy, or visiting friends in
the town, they were reminded, in Section VIII. 1, 'Rules Relating to
Conduct Abroad', that

> No student is to go into a public house to drink there on penalty
> of a public censure for ye first time, & ye forfeiture of a shilling
> the second time; unless some particular occasion arise which
> shall in ye judgement of the tutor be deemed a sufficient
> reason.[51]

No doubt there were those who always found mitigating
circumstances, especially in view of such impoverishing fines!

In this highly industrious institution, care was taken to avoid 'all
work and no play'. An area behind the Academy was used for
football by the students. Sadly, one 'match' produced a fatal injury.

Doddridge reported to Henry Baker of the Royal Society in London that young William Worcester wounded his toe on a bone frozen into the ground 'while exercising himself with some of his companions within my walls at football'.[52] The injury led to lockjaw and death.

While the Academy's government might be regarded as somewhat severe by today's standards, it is obvious that a warm relationship existed between the tutors and the students in this institution, judging by a letter written by one of the students to his father, dated November 12, 1750:

> Dr. Father, I should esteem it not only as a great favour, but as a great honour paid to me, if you would be so good, as it is for my interest, to make a present to the doctor of a couple of Cheshire cheeses, not strong, but mild and fat, which will be very acceptable to the doctor, as he provided me a tutor last year, and I do not know whether he will be paid for it, and likewise if you please, that I should make a present of something, about a crown value, to the Drs. assistant, who, when he should have been taking recreation, has been instructing me, so that it would be a means of my further improvement.[53]

We can only trust that father rose to the occasion!

The fame of the Academy spread far and wide, even recruiting students from the Netherlands[54] as well as all parts of the United Kingdom. During his twenty-two years at Northampton, about two hundred students passed through Doddridge's hands, of whom about one hundred and twenty became ministers. Professor McLachlan was surely correct in saying that the Northampton Academy was 'in many ways the most famous of the nonconformist seminaries'.[55] Doddridge's institution, with its open method of instruction, its interest in scientific enquiry and well-ordered administration revealed an attitude towards education which was far ahead of its time. In the opinion of Irene Parker, 'Doddridge was great, not only in his own academy at Northampton, but in his influence in the country generally. In his day, to mention Northampton Academy was not merely to speak of the best educational centre in the country, it was also to speak of a new education'.[56] Doddridge's labours did not go unrecognised in his day, for in the year 1736, the University Colleges of Aberdeen (Marischal and King's) conferred upon him the honorary degree of Doctor of Divinity.[57] Doddridge's standing was such that in 1744 he was sent a pre-publication copy of the Statutes of Hertford College, Oxford (then newly incorporated) by the Principal Richard Newton who also requested to see Doddridge's method of education.[58]

Not surprisingly, many preferred to study under Philip Doddridge at Northampton, rather than go to either Oxford or Cambridge, such was the quality of the education. The list of Doddridge's students contains the names of many gentlemen and noblemen's sons. These include the Earl of Dunmore, Lord William Manners, Sir Henry Houghton and many others who became merchants, barristers, officers in the army and members of parliament. More was at stake than mere academic prestige, a point made clear in a letter from Lord Kilkerran (Sir James Ferguson) to Doddridge:

> As the education of my children in a right way is what I have much at heart and that I foresee many dangers attending the usual method of sending young gentlemen to the Universities, I have been long of opinion that the better way is to send them to an academy under virtuous people who will be no less watchful over their morals than over their literature.[59]

Since the year 1741, the seat of the Academy had been a large residence in Sheep Street, Northampton, formerly the town house of the Earl of Halifax. There Doddridge and the 'family' – as the entire company under his roof was affectionately known – lived and studied. Following Doddridge's death in 1751, one of the assistant tutors, Dr Caleb Ashworth assumed the principalship. Since Ashworth was not called to succeed Dr Doddridge as the minister of Castle Hill Church, the Academy moved to Daventry when Ashworth was called to the pastorate there. So opened a less glorious chapter in the history of the Academy, but that is another story.

6

Pastor and People

The principal of the Academy at Northampton was first and foremost a minister of the Gospel of Jesus Christ. Philip Doddridge was a minister training ministers, which gave him the advantage of combining theoretical instruction with practical example. In Dr Doddridge, the students observed a model pastor, whose ministry has continued to be a spur and encouragement to subsequent generations of ministers. In his classic work *The Christian Ministry*, Charles Bridges includes the life and ministry of Philip Doddridge amongst those whom he judges to be 'of the highest value and consideration', adding that 'More lessons of practical detail and encouragement may be learnt from this branch of study, than from whole treatises of abstract theology'.[1]

Philip Doddridge always had a consciousness of the exalted nature of the Christian ministry. He rejoiced in the privilege of having been called to such a work and office. In all the varied activities in which he was constantly occupied, Doddridge never lost sight of his priorities. A typical example of his entire outlook can be seen in an entry in his diary on the occasion of his thirty-seventh birthday. On June 26, 1739, he wrote:

> I have been praising, and would praise Him that made me a man, a Christian, and a minister; an author and a tutor; and has heaped, numberless blessings on me under all these characters; and as a husband, a father, and a friend. Late mercies, by no means to be forgotten, are great assistances in the ministry; wonderful communications of light and love have been made to my soul, in some instances of secret meditation far beyond what I have commonly known.[2]

We should note the sequence: 'a man, a Christian and a minister'.

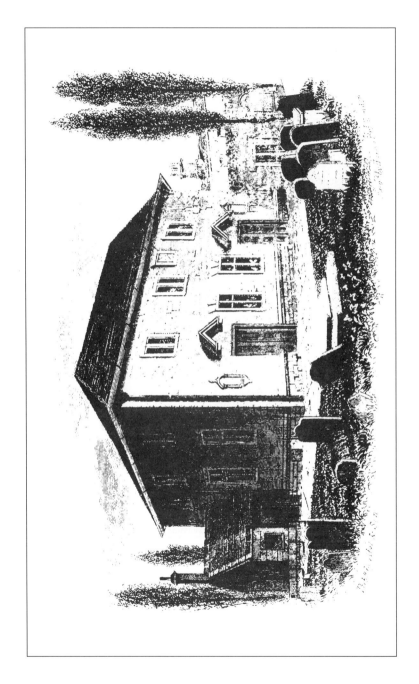

Castle Hill Meeting House in Doddridge's day

Doddridge was the minister he was because of the kind of Christian he was. There was no false 'professionalism' with this minister. As we can see from this diary entry, the piety displayed by Doddridge in his ministry was fashioned at the throne of grace, and nurtured by prayer in total dependence on the Holy Spirit.

Whilst Doddridge was not a 'professional' in the odious sense of the term, he was very businesslike in his work. Shortly after his settlement at Northampton, he drew up 'An imperfect scheme of business' as a self-imposed guide. In considering himself 'in the treble view, of a Pastor, a Tutor, and a Student', he outlined a rigorous and exacting programme. Coming to his pastoral duties, he says:

> As a Pastor, I will visit my people, both in town and country, throughout the whole congregation, allowing ... the afternoon for that purpose, and generally going into the country on Thursdays. I will have a peculiar regard to the young people, for whom I propose to draw up a catechism; I will expound on Friday nights at the vestry; perhaps I may also expound before the morning service, and catechise before that of the afternoon.[3]

With all the requirements of Doddridge's work, he never considered himself to have stopped learning. His student days did not end at Kibworth. Towards the end of his 'scheme' we see some of the authors who influenced his maturing thought:

> Besides others, I hope to dispatch Mr. Philip Henry's *Life*; Dr Owen on the *Mortification of Sin in Believers*; Tillotson to page 620; Howe's *Carnality of Religious Contention*, and *Discourses of Union among Protestants* ...; Baxter of *Making light of Christ*; of *Faith and Judgement*; of *Repentance and Right Rejoicing*; besides his review of his *Gildas Salvianus* [the *Reformed Pastor*]; Burnet's *Pastoral Care*; Chrysostom on the *Priesthood*; ...[4]

One of the distinctive features of Doddridge's ministry was the intense energy and determination with which he carried it out. When one remembers the time and energy that the work of the Academy would have demanded, his application to pastoral work appears all the more remarkable. His pastoral visits usually took place in the afternoons. He frequently preached several days in a week in the villages around Northampton in the evenings. When his health permitted, Doddridge would preach on average five times a week, including the services at Castle Hill. During his annual vacation, he would spend one of the two months making pastoral visits, besides engaging in itinerant preaching and personal study. Doddridge was a model of diligence and industry in the service of his Master. In addition to these regular labours was Doddridge's constant stream of correspondence. This was not only numerous but extensive. He had contacts and friends throughout the entire Christian world. His correspondents were to be found among the Protestant churches of Europe and America as well as the British Isles. This fact reveals Doddridge's standing internationally as a divine; his opinions and judgements were sought on a wide variety of issues, both academic and spiritual. He was in touch with not only some of the brightest ornaments of the Christian Church, but with men of stature in the world of learning and wider society.

With regard to his pulpit ministry, Doddridge never confused lecturing with preaching; their functions are different and he was careful to distinguish them. Doddridge gained a reputation for fervent preaching and a concern with experimental (or experiential) Christianity. He had a clear understanding of the place and purpose of preaching as well as the state and condition of his hearers:

> While I have any reverence for scripture or any knowledge of human nature, I shall never affect to speak of the glories of Christ, and of the eternal interests of men, as coldly, as if I were reading a lecture of mathematics, or relating an experiment in natural philosophy! It is indeed unworthy the character of a man and a Christian to endeavour to transport men's passions, while the understanding is left uninformed and the judgement unconvinced. But so far as is consistent with a proper regard to this leading power of our nature I would speak and write of divine truths with a holy fervency.[5]

It would be discouraging as well as misleading to give the impression that Doddridge was always consistent with his own ideal. At one time his sermons became second-rate and unedifying, to the extent of provoking a protest from some of his students. The lectures were excellent at the expense of the sermons. As a result of this, Doddridge, never averse to gentle admonitions, took more pains to improve his preaching. Kippis tells us that, at his best, Doddridge's sermons 'were often excellent in a high degree'. A more detailed account shows the power of Doddridge the preacher:

> I remember a remarkable instance of his power in extemporaneous speaking. Akenside the poet, who in early life was settled, for a short time, at Northampton, being visited by some relations from Newcastle upon Tyne, who were Dissenters, came with them, unexpectedly, one Sunday morning, to Dr Doddridge's meeting. The subject he preached upon was a common orthodox topic, for which he had scarcely made any preparation. But he roused his faculties on the occasion, and spoke with such energy, variety, and eloquence, as excited my warmest admiration, and must have impressed Dr Akenside with a high opinion of his abilities.[6]

That said, Doddridge did not set out to 'impress' his hearers. Stoughton rightly summarises Doddridge's aims as a preacher: '[he] entered the pulpit not to dazzle, but to teach; not to amaze but to convince; not to gratify, but to reform; not to be thought great, but to do good'.[7]

The Diary also reveals an honest heart grappling with the problems of maintaining a constant level of spirituality. Doddridge speaks for many when he confesses his spiritual backslidings:

> The Bible has been to me as a sealed book. I have seen no beauty, I have felt no energy in it; and all the respect I have paid to it has been a form rather than a reality. I have been under great temptation to doubt the truth of Christianity itself...The Spirit of God seems to have deserted me, and to have left me under blindness and hardness...I resolve against it. But these are operations of the understanding rather than of the heart...I am like a block or a stone. Lord, I am weary of such a frame. O that my heart were enlarged! O that it were melted under a sense of sin! O that it were drawn out in desires after Thee![8]

Like the psalmist, Doddridge was able to say 'For His anger

endureth but a moment', finding by his own happy experience that 'weeping may endure for a night, but joy cometh in the morning' (Psalm 30: 5). At a later date, we find Doddridge in jubilant spirit:

> My God, I own Thy goodness; I record it that I am Thine; and thou knowest my heart, knowest that Thy service is the delight of my days. Whom have I in heaven but Thee? and what on earth do I desire in comparison with Thee? [9]

Here we see the source and secret of Doddridge's life. It was rooted in a vital knowledge of the living God. To Doddridge, religion was life, and he lived in God. Indeed, he 'enjoyed' God, as another diary entry shows. On New Year's Day 1745 he wrote:

> I must not forget, in reviewing the mercies of the last year, that sweet and joyful experience which I had on Sunday, December 2nd, when I was meditating alone in the morning before I set to any other business. Breathing out my soul in love to God; – I then waited in a kind of silent, but lively ecstatic expectation, when these words came down, as it were from heaven to my soul, in such a manner as almost to overwhelm me with delight. "Because he has set his love upon me, I will deliver him. I will set him on high, because he has known my name. He shall call upon me, and I will answer him. I will be with him in trouble. I will deliver him and honour him. With long life will I satisfy him, and show him my salvation" (Psalm 91: 14-15).[10]

We will have occasion to see more of Doddridge's pastoral labours as we proceed. Let us take a look at the church by which, under God, he was called to minister in Northampton.

It is important to recall that the town has a long and distinguished nonconformist history. Not many miles from John Wycliffe's Lutterworth, Northampton witnessed considerable Lollard activity during the fifteenth century. After the Reformation, Puritanism had a strong presence. An English translation of John Calvin's Genevan Catechism was first used during the 'prophesyings' at All Saints Church Northampton in 1571. Robert Browne of 'Brownist' fame had local connections and was buried in St Giles' churchyard in 1633.[11] However, the church meeting at

Doddridge's vestry may still be seen, arranged exactly as it was when he used it.

CASTLE·HILL

DR DODDRIDGE'S VESTRY

Drawn by - W.J.Pash.

Castle Hill Vestry

Castle Hill, Northampton has an origin somewhat shrouded in mystery. Unlike most of the old Dissenting congregations in England which came into being after the Act of Uniformity of 1662, Castle Hill Church appears to have emerged along with other churches in Northamptonshire after the Battle of Naseby in 1645. At the time Doddridge settled in Northampton, the church was Independent or Congregational in character. In the beginning however, it appears to have been Presbyterian. Following the Act of Indulgence of 1672 when Charles II granted certain liberties to the nonconformists, several preachers in Northampton received licenses to preach, and five 'meeting houses' were licensed for worship. These churches were Presbyterian, one of which became Castle Hill when a chapel was erected in the year 1695.

It has been thought that Castle Hill Church originated from the labours of the ejected Vicar of St Giles, Northampton, the Revd Jeremiah Lewis. Mr Lewis died within a few months of his ejection, so this is unlikely. It is probable that nonconforming members of St Giles joined the congregation at Castle Hill since St Giles had been a Presbyterian church during the Commonwealth period.

The first pastor of Castle Hill Presbyterian Church was the Revd Samuel Blower, one time fellow of Magdalen College Oxford. According to some accounts, he became the minister of Castle Hill in 1674. In the year 1698, the pastorate was offered to the Revd John Hunt, who 'embraced ye call' on February 25, 1699. Mr Hunt was a vigorous and controversial preacher who set himself to solve all the knotty theological problems of the day. These were days in which congregations were being disturbed by fierce debates about Calvinism and Arminianism, paedo-baptism and believer's baptism, and other theological issues. Hunt was a rather over-zealous Calvinist, flaying his opponents with his orthodoxy, yet comforting the godly with deep pastoral earnestness. These were days which required firm leadership and Mr Hunt provided it. However, he appears to have been rather too controversial in his ministry and too autocratic in the oversight of the church. A significant change took place in the church order of Castle Hill Church during this man's ministry.

After the Great Ejection, the synodical assemblies of the Presbyterian churches became less prominent in the affairs of the local church. Linked together instead in County Associations, the churches tended to function more like Independent churches.[12] However, these congregations still had, besides deacons, ruling elders who assisted the pastor in his duties. This form of church government – pastor, elders, and deacons – had been common to all Presbyterian and Independent congregations until this time. However, on May 7, 1707, at Castle Hill Church, the following resolution was passed at a church meeting:

> It was agreed upon by the whole church assembled at a public church meeting for weighty reasons that for the time to come the church shall be governed without ruling elders. [13]

What these 'weighty reasons' were is impossible to determine. They could be a reflection on the rigid autocracy of John Hunt or the aspirations for power entertained by the ruling elders. Whatever were the facts of the situation, it is clear that the 'whole church' was in agreement on the matter. From this time, the basis of church power passed from ruling elders to a democratic majority. Whilst this change was to have dangerous consequences in the life of Congregational churches of later generations, it served a warning to the overseers of the churches not to 'overlook' the fact that pastoral rule should never exclude consultation and fellowship.

It may be noted here that in early life, Doddridge himself was a Presbyterian, but advancing years brought a change of opinion. Speaking of independency in the year 1723, he said he was 'moderately inclined' towards it.[14] In later years, when telling his students to 'encourage meetings of ministers', he warned them to be careful that 'they do not grow up into authoritative synods'.[15] However, Doddridge was far from being an isolationist. Indeed, towards the end of his life, one may detect at least a restored respect for Presbyterianism, as we will see in the last chapter. That said, Doddridge frequently spoke not of 'Presbyterian' or 'Independent' but 'Gospel' ministers to demonstrate that however important differences in church government might be, the concerns of the Gospel were paramount.

The Revd John Hunt was succeeded by the Revd Thomas Tingey

in the year 1709. This worthy man ministered the Word of God for twenty years at Northampton, during which time he gained a reputation as an affectionate and zealous servant of God. Tingey's ministry was a necessary complement to Hunt's; in many respects, both men paved the way for Doddridge's own ministry in which both soundness of head and warmth of heart were to be seen. If Hunt's ministry provided an orthodox foundation, Tingey ensured that truth blended with warmth of piety. It was both these features that the zealous people of Castle Hill saw in young Mr Doddridge. Thus they invited him to settle amongst them, which he did in 1729.

When Philip Doddridge commenced his pastoral labours at Northampton, he could claim to be blest with one of the wisest and warmest congregations in England. A strong and cordial bond was soon established between pastor and people which was to continue throughout Doddridge's remaining years with them. The membership of the church was 342 in the year 1730 and Doddridge had the joy of regular additions as the years went by. It was with ever increasing responsibilities that Doddridge proposed to the church that they choose 'such persons as they should think proper' to assist him in the oversight of the church. And so in 1740, the office of elder was restored at Castle Hill Church. However, these elders were not to be the ruling elders discontinued in 1707 (since church power remained congregational) but pastoral overseers, assisting the pastor in his work.

The elders of the church asked Doddridge to outline the particular duties and functions that were required of them, which he did in a letter to them. The entire membership was divided into classes, and one elder was assigned to a class. Regular visitation was urged with a view to ensuring that family worship was observed:

> ... take the heads of families apart to learn how it fares with them and their families religiously, and exhort, instruct, and admonish them, as judged fit; engage them to a strict observance of family worship and the spiritual care of their children and servants.

Provision was made for discipline, in which Doddridge was careful to follow the directions of the New Testament:

> Apply directly to those whom you hear behave disorderly, and when any come to you with complaints of offence by others do not engage in the quarrel, but, according to the Lord's command, bring them together, and let the offended tenderly expostulate with the offender; but, if he will not hear, let him take two more and repeat the admonition, and let these be persons of discretion, humility and tenderness. But does he still refuse, let the elder state it to the church. And as debates in church meetings are dangerous if not managed with prudence, the elders and pastor ought to be made acquainted with the facts, to take counsel together, and to pray for further counsel and guidance of the Lord. When the scandal is public, the offender should be publicly admonished and his repentance publicly confessed.

It would be necessary for a harmonious church that the pastor and elders be in harmony with each other. With this in mind, Doddridge says:

> The Elders should cultivate an intimate friendship with each other, so that they may be prepared to act together for the good of all.

Although Doddridge believed the Pastor to have a unique role as the shepherd of the flock, his wisdom and humility are very evident in the following paragraph:

> As the Pastor watches over the Elders, admonishes and exhorts them, so ought they, in humility and love, to watch over him in the Lord. And I do hereby entreat and charge you, my brethren, that if there be anything in my temper and conduct which appears to you to give just and reasonable offence, you would remind me of it, plainly and faithfully, and I hope you will always find that I shall receive advice with meekness, and endeavour to be an example to others, of a readiness to reform as God shall enable me.[16]

Despite its flourishing state, the church had its problems. Thus the Elders, sad to say, had opportunities of fulfilling their office. In April 1741, the church was acquainted with seven offenders. Three members were guilty of drunkenness, one of whom was expelled, the others being cautioned. Two other members were found guilty of bankruptcy, both being excluded from Communion 'till they gave the church those evidences of humiliation'. Two other members had disputed with one another, but were reconciled and re-admitted to communion. The cases of bankruptcy were not isolated instances of 'imprudence'. Furthermore, one of the offenders arrogantly challenged the church for its attitude. The following order reveals an unfortunate state of affairs:

> It is the unanimous Judgement of the Church that frequent Acts of Bankruptcy which have happened in Dissenting congregations as well as elsewhere have brought so great dishonour on Religion and occasioned so much mischief and reproach that we think ourselves obliged in duty to enter our public protest and caution on this head. And we do hereby declare that if any person in stated communion shall become a bankrupt or as it is commonly expressed, fail in the world, he must expect to be cut off from our body unless he do within two months give to the church by the Elders either in word or writing such an account of his affairs as shall convince us that his fall was owing not to his sin or folly but to the afflicting hand of God upon him. In which case far from adding affliction to the afflicted we hope that as God shall enable us we shall be ready to vindicate, comfort and assist him as his friends and brethren in Christ.
>
> Signed in the name and presence of the Church this first day of May, 1741.
> P. Doddridge, Pastor
> J. Orton, S. Haworth, John Brown, John Evans, Elders.[17]

The manner in which these cases of discipline were handled is both instructive and impressive. We see gentleness tempering severity, and compassion mingled with justice. Furthermore, Doddridge and his Elders were not motivated by a cold pharisaism in seeking to purge the poison but a concern lest the godless should pour scorn upon the name of Christ. This was Puritanism at its best.

Doddridge's sacramental meditations indicate that the monthly communion services were seasons of immense joy to both pastor and people. Here vows were renewed and love to God rekindled. These times were more than mere memorials of a crucified Saviour; they were further tastes of His undying love. In one such meditation, we hear Doddridge the devoted pastor:

> Why have we the power of remembrance, if not to remember Christ? ... Better, O blessed Jesus, a thousand times better, were it that we had neither eyes to see, nor ears to hear, nor tongues to speak, nor power to breathe, than that our hearts should not be filled with love to thee, our tongues employed in thy praises, and all our powers both of soul and of body for ever devoted to thy service.

Even at the Lord's Table, Doddridge was a pastor with an evangelist's heart. In anticipation of the next chapter, we here observe the 'Baxterian Calvinist' theology that directed all his concerns:

> *In pouring out the cup* I said, "Behold the Lamb of God that taketh away the sins of the world!" [Jn. 1: 29]. ... *When the communion was over, observing some of the elements remain. –* This is an emblem of the provisions of the Gospel. Here is bread and wine enough and to spare. Enough for all; enough for more than are here; and if any perish, it is not for want of a sufficiency of grace, but for want of a heart to use it.[18]

As with all faithful ministers of Christ, Doddridge had his encouragements and his discouragements. It would appear from memoranda in the Church register that, on an average, he received between sixteen and twenty members per year throughout his entire ministry at Northampton. Doddridge wrote in the Church book:

> May 2 1748 I reviewed the List of the Church from the Beginning & found that from 1694 when it was gathered i.e. within the compass of 54 years 784 members have been admitted i.e. one year with another more than 14 members each year of which 240 only continue alive & reside still among us of which 58 were admitted before my Settlement with the Church

FAC-SIMILE of the Hand Writing of the Rev.ᵈ Dᴿ DODDRIDGE,

(in a letter to the Baptist Church at Northampton)

Whereas the Deacon here of Hannah Barret hath been for some time a Member of the Church of Christ under my Pastoral Care & hath now signifies her Desire of removing from our Communion chiefly because there are those among us that practise Infant Baptism, who we cannot condemn our selves so far as to think this Reason sufficient yet we pretend not to judge her Liberty & Conscience & think our selves bound it Duty to bear our Testimony to her orderly walking amongst us & to declare our Affection to her in our common Lord & our hearty Desire that where ever she may settle the or Keep in Fellowship with her, however in their Judgment different from any of us may enjoy that Presence & Blessing of Christ & attain to growing Edification in knowledge Faith Hope & Love & every other Grace which may conduce to the Glory of God & their own everlasting Felicity

Signed in the name & by the Direction of the Church at their late Meeting

P. Doddridge Pastor

North. Dec. 29. 1739

& as I have admitted 299 that shows that 117 who have been admitted since that Time are either removed or dead; besides many others who were admitted before N.B. 78 have been my Pupils.[19]

In the year 1749 twenty-two members had been admitted, while exactly the same number had died. This fact serves to illustrate the absurdity of counting heads as an indication of spiritual success, and Doddridge was concerned not so much with quantity as quality. In 1747 the Moravians had founded a cause in Northampton, the effects of which gave Doddridge cause for alarm. The early Moravians tended to despise all order, claiming a spiritual superiority over other Christians. Doddridge lamented that Moravianism had 'infected several weak but affectionate people' of his flock. Besides becoming morally lax they had expressed 'a contempt of almost all external ordinances'. The novelty and excitement of this 'charismatic' movement had a detrimental impact on the Castle Hill congregation. Some of them left, reducing the membership to 239 in 1749. In a letter to the Revd John Ryland (snr) we see a discouraged pastor:

> I have been much afflicted by the breach made in our Church by the Moravians, who have got from us a little congregation. The affliction has been increased by the death of some very promising and hopeful persons, ... so that it is one of the greatest blows of that kind that I have received since I came hither. My spirits are much grieved and oppressed; pray that I may be enabled to wait on the Lord with quiet submission and humble hope.[20]

Like a good soldier of Jesus Christ, Doddridge persevered in his course. The Lord sanctified his distresses to him, so much so that we never find this saintly pastor becoming either inflated with success or despairing in failure. To the end of his days, Doddridge had abundant cause to praise God, accompanied by a mature understanding in all his experiences:

> God hath sanctified all these grievances to me; hath made me more humble, more watchful, more mortified to this vain world, and its interests and enjoyments, than I ever remember to have

found myself. He has visited me from time to time with such strong consolations, with such delightful effusions of His love, that, in this connection, I am His debtor for all these afflictions; and from this growing experience of His goodness, I am encouraged, and have determined, to leave myself with Him, and to have no will, no interest of my own, separate from His.[21]

The stresses and strains of the ministry make sympathetic friends all the more necessary. Doddridge had several, among whom Samuel Clark, John Barker of London, Colonel James Gardiner and Thomas Scott of Norwich may be mentioned. However, Doddridge's closest 'bosom friend' was former pupil and Scott's successor at the Old Meeting House in Norwich, Samuel Wood. In April 1748, busy Doddridge wrote to his friend:

Let twenty affairs lie by neglected – sermon, Family Expositor, letters, visits, the care of our nearly approaching and warmly contested election – I will write to my dear friend, Mr Wood; ... Your letters always delight me.[22]

A year later, before rushing off to give a lecture, the obviously-agitated tutor wrote to Wood, 'Oh that I could unbosom a little of my heart to you'.[23] But what other burdens did he bear? Not least among the pressures Doddridge suffered was incessant criticism, as we shall see later. Judging by the correspondence, the Northampton-Norwich connection provided much needed encouragement, and Wood knew how to comfort his weary friend:

But, as Providence has called you to such distinguished services, God has given you equal furniture of mind, and made his grace sufficient for you. In this I greatly rejoice, for notwithstanding your own humility, your friends know of how great importance your life and labours are to the world; a [Matthew] Henry, a[n Isaac] Watts, and a Doddridge, are not found in every age to bless the Church. I will not say how much we have of the two first eminent ministers in our dear Doddridge, but I am sure of this, that while he lives we shall not very sensibly know their loss or that of any other eminent divine; I know it will give your heart uneasiness to be mentioned with such company, and yet I cannot help saying what I do: I am sorry that a treasure of so much importance to religion depends upon the uncertain life of one dear gentleman, and sometimes the thought overpowers me till I can gain respite enough to derive consolation from the perpetuity and all-sufficiency of a glorious Redeemer, who is compassionately concerned for his own interest, and is able to carry it forward as seems good to his infinite wisdom. ...

Wood obviously felt keenly the losses of his predecessor Thomas Scott who died in 1746 and of Isaac Watts who died in 1748. Thus he valued Doddridge all the more:

... I say, dear Sir, the loss these and other ministers of celebrated note has frequently made a painful impression upon my heart, and, in such gloomy moments, my thoughts (whether I would or not) have immediately gone to Northampton. Oh! my dear friend, may the God of Heaven bless you in all that variety wherein you want the blessings of the Almighty! May your health be continued, may your happy family be blessed, may your academy be prospered, may your ministrations among the people be succeeded, and may all your labours be crowned abundantly, to the enriching the souls of many thousands in these and other countries.[24]

Indeed, Doddridge's standing among his brethren and the churches was evident wherever he went. A summer visit to the West country in 1742 involved him in the ordination of Benjamin Fawcett at Taunton. He reported thus to Mercy:

Your delightful letter reached me on Monday night, just after I was returned from the polite and religious family of the Welmans, the glory of the dissenters in these parts. ... Their only fault was, that they received me with almost a princely elegance and magnificence at a table much fitter for an archbishop than a poor country minister, which confounded me not a little.

Besides relating the ordination itself, Doddridge reveals the demands made upon him:

Yesterday I preached and prayed over Mr Fawcett. We had, I suppose, near two thousand persons present; of whom forty were ministers. I was treated by them with a deference of which I was quite unworthy; and forced by them to submit to honours which I should rather have bestowed on the least of my brethren, and bless God, I went through my work with cheerfulness, though I had no sleep the night before.

All this morning I have been receiving visits; and as I slept near seven hours on the stretch, and so rose late, I cannot enlarge. I set out this evening for Wellington. ...[25]

Next to his regular sermon preparation, Doddridge mentioned to Wood his *Family Expositor*. This was one of the permanent literary fruits of his numerous pastoral activities. It actually extended his ministry way beyond the boundaries of Northamptonshire both in his day and for generations to come. Besides the constant stream of published sermons, Doddridge published the first volume of his *magnum opus* in 1739. He had projected the work during his days at Kibworth[26] and it occupied all the years of his Northampton ministry. The manuscript was completed only two years before His death. The purpose of the *Family Expositor* can be deduced from its title; it was designed to form a basis for family worship, being a paraphrase of the entire New Testament including a new translation of the original Greek. The four Gospels were woven into a harmony showing the inter-relations between the four evangelists. The whole work was reduced to sections and each one is followed by a devotional and practical comment called the 'Improvement'. This work can also claim to be the first of its kind to encourage a popular critical understanding of the text; it abounds in critical notes, either on the text itself or on theological points. There was no work on which Doddridge spent more time and energy than the *Family Expositor*. It enjoyed great popularity for over a century and even to this day, it is not without its usefulness.

We will have occasion to observe the contents and theology of the *Family Expositor* in the next chapter. For now, there is an interesting circumstance in connection with the work that is worthy of note. One June evening in the year 1750, a fire started in Doddridge's study when a candle used for sealing letters continued to burn after he thought he had blown it out. The fire had lasted for about fifteen minutes when a neighbour across the street noticed the flames and sounded the alarm. Let Doddridge continue the

THE

FAMILY EXPOSITOR:

OR,

A PARAPHRASE AND VERSION

OF

THE NEW TESTAMENT;

WITH

CRITICAL NOTES,

AND

A PRACTICAL IMPROVEMENT OF EACH SECTION.

VOLUME THE FIRST;

CONTAINING THE FORMER PART OF

THE HISTORY OF OUR LORD JESUS CHRIST,

AS RECORDED BY

THE FOUR EVANGELISTS.

DISPOSED IN THE ORDER OF AN HARMONY.

BY P. DODDRIDGE, D.D.

THE EIGHTH EDITION.

TO WHICH IS PREFIXED,

A LIFE OF THE AUTHOR,

BY

ANDREW KIPPIS, D. D. F. R. S. and S. A.

Ει δε τις υπο τειων μη πασχη των λογων, υπο μονων αν των εν αδυ δικαϛηριων υπευθυνθειη. SIMPLIC. in EPICTET. Proem.

LONDON:

PRINTED BY H. BALDWIN AND SON,

FOR G. G. AND J. ROBINSON; R. BALDWIN; C. DILLY; F. AND C. RIVINGTON; J. MATHEWS; W. OTRIDGE AND SON; J. SCATCHERD; DARTON AND CO.; C. LAW; LONGMAN AND REES; J. WALKER; VERNOR AND HOOD; D. OGILVY AND SON; T. HURST; J. CUTHELL; LACKINGTON AND CO.; AND J. WALLIS.

M DCC XCIX.

story in a letter to Benjamin Fawcett:

> When I came up, I found my desk, which was covered with
> papers, burning like an altar; many letters, papers of
> memorandums, and schemes for sermons, were consumed. My
> book of accounts was on fire, and the names at the top almost
> burnt through, a volume of the *Family Expositor*, the original
> MSS from Corinthians to Ephesians, surrounded with flames,
> and drenched in melted wax; . . . and yet, so did God moderate
> the rage of this element, and determine in His providence the
> time of our entrance, that not one account is rendered uncertain
> by what it suffered, nor is one line which had not been
> transcribed destroyed in the MS . . . all my sermons and MSS
> intended for the press, and among the rest and remainder of the
> *Family Expositor*, were all in such danger, that the fire, in
> another quarter of an hour, had probably consumed them.
> Observe, my dear friend, the hand of God, and magnify the
> Lord with me.[27]

This event had far reaching consequences since the *Family
Expositor* had, in the providence of God, important work to do.
The great missionary movement, in which Doddridge had a
pioneering interest, will demand some attention later. But we may
conclude this chapter by remembering that when William Carey
translated the first Bengali version of the New Testament from the
Greek, the only English commentary used was the *Family Expositor*
of Dr Philip Doddridge.[28] There is surely no doubt that many Indian
Christians as well as others have cause to thank God that a major
part of the *Family Expositor* was not destroyed in that
Northampton inferno.

7
Truth and Charity
I

Whereas a certain amount of interest in Doddridge has been generated in recent years, more attention has been paid to the man than to his beliefs. This is understandable, since Doddridge was an attractive personality by any standard. However, it is also unfortunate, since for Doddridge personally, his faith and his life were of a piece: what he was, was due, in great measure, to what he believed and thought.

At least two reasons can explain the deficiencies in current Doddridge interest. *First*, Doddridge is not regarded in the same 'league' as Augustine, Thomas Aquinas, Luther, Calvin or Barth, although his contribution remains highly significant. That said, after describing Doddridge as 'a very great man', a contemporary Dutch pastor said: 'Happy land, where such lights of the world shine'.[1] Although Doddridge undoubtedly had the intellectual capacity to 'shine' at a scholastic level, he deliberately refused to do so. For him, doctrine was designed for the purposes of practical piety rather than intellectual entertainment and stimulation. Thus one may call Doddridge a practical rather than a theoretical intellectual who combined an eclectic genius with a brilliant 'user-friendly' skill of communication. Endowed with a sharp and highly retentive brain, he possessed a phenomenal ability to soak up information and use it to good effect. No moment was lost in acquiring knowledge. Kippis tells us that 'one of his students generally read to him when he was shaving and dressing'.[2] *Second*, the late twentieth century is little interested in the kind of theological convictions held by Doddridge and his generation. This was stated quite explicitly in the bicentenary celebrations of Doddridge's death in 1951, when the Unitarian Roger Thomas said, "The important thing for us, however, is not Doddridge's theological opinions ..."[3]

Renowned as Doddridge was for his gracious and charitable disposition, it has become necessary to dispel the myth that truth and conviction were unimportant to him. His daughter Polly's oft-quoted retort to a critic of her father's theological views, ["Sir, the orthodoxy my father taught his children was charity."][4] has reinforced the fact that, in his lifetime, Doddridge was accused of being indifferent to theological convictions. The truth, however, is otherwise, although in an ecumenical and post-modern age, one is not surprised to find that the myth is preferred to the reality. Whilst Doddridge always lectured, preached and wrote according to the apostolic maxim of 'speaking the truth in love', it must never be forgotten that it was undiluted biblical truth which he attempted to proclaim. We must not allow Doddridge's charm to seduce us into neglecting Doddridge's theology.

The task before us is to allow Doddridge the theologian to speak to us. It is perhaps much more entertaining to dwell upon the purely biographical and anecdotal details of this godly man's life, but we must be concerned, not so much with entertainment, as with instruction. My desire is to complete the picture, to correct any misconceptions, and to justify a continuing study of the life and work of Dr Philip Doddridge. What we are doing needs little justification. Serious Christian people are aware that important issues demand our attention. The Christian Church is a restless institution, uncertain of its message, and doubtful of its relevance or place in the modern world. Whilst Philip Doddridge is no infallible guide, he did at least address himself to issues very similar to those which face us today. Since these issues are of eternal significance, we are not being retrogressive in considering some of his views, although they were uttered 250-80 years ago.

We have seen in an earlier chapter, that the theological atmosphere in which Doddridge lived and ministered was one of extremes. On one hand, there was an 'exaggerated zeal for formal orthodoxy' and, on the other, a 'cultivated vagueness about essential Christian doctrines'. We may surely ask, "Are things very different in the early 21st century?" Doddridge could be sure of one thing: wherever a man stood on the theological spectrum – left, centre or right – he would incur the censure of someone. As he stated in a late sermon, the dilemma that faced Doddridge was how to contend 'in the name of the God of truth' in 'a manner which may not offend Him as the God of love'.[5] To proclaim the truth without being branded as a bigot, and to show charity without being accused of compromise, was almost impossible in the eighteenth century. Indeed, this is a problem that has faced Christian people in every age and generation.

In the confusion of Enlightenment theology, the chief problem was one of authority. Those who contended for biblical orthodoxy sought to buttress their position by appealing to confessions of faith as standards of orthodoxy, while those of a liberal cast of mind rejected not only man-made confessions but also cast doubt on the Bible itself. If the orthodox High Calvinists gave the impression that authoritative Scripture was insufficient for the defence of its own truths, the Arians employed the very words of Scripture to oppose the Trinitarian orthodoxy of the confessions of faith. This state of affairs is reflected in a sermon preached by Doddridge in August 1742 at the ordination of his pupil John Jennings, son of his own tutor at Kibworth. Doddridge advised young Jennings to pursue the following course:

> You have ... I hope taken your religion from the Word of God, and not from any human system or composition whatever. Go on to act upon this maxim. I dare not say, like St. Paul, Continue in the things thou hast learned, and been assured of by me, knowing of whom thou hast learned them (2 Tim 3: 14). It rather becomes me to say, examine all I have taught you, and *Search the Scriptures daily whether these things are so* or no (Acts 17: 11). You will not, I am persuaded, run the matter to extremes, and imagine, like some half-thinkers, that liberty consists in boldly daring to decide against received opinions, as soon as some new difficulties are discerned; and confidently venting raw and undigested notions, however noxious, without fearing any of the consequences.[6]

Doddridge was anxious to be a biblical Christian without being guilty of either 'exaggerated zeal' or 'cultivated vagueness'; he regarded it as his duty to avoid the extremes of the age. In his view, truth demanded the middle course. It was in the application of his principles that Doddridge attracted criticism. As with theological extremism in general, denominationalism or 'party spirit' was repugnant to him. If he argued for truth with regard to opinions, he pleaded for charity with regard to persons. As a consequence, Doddridge did not confine his acquaintances to those whose views corresponded exactly with his own. He was, in the best sense of the phrase, blessed with a 'catholic spirit'. As the logical Calvin has been denigrated as heartless, so the cordial Doddridge has been condemned as devoid of doctrinal principle.

Yet Doddridge was, pre-eminently, a biblical theologian in the Reformed tradition. He believed in the full divine inspiration and authority of the Bible (despite the reactionary nineteenth-century criticisms of the Louis Gaussen school).[7] As with Luther, Doddridge's 'conscience was captive to the Word of God'. In his *Dissertation on the Inspiration of the New Testament*, he tackles the issues which still trouble biblical scholars. His view of inspiration does not lead him to deny that the human instruments – albeit superintended by the Holy Spirit – sometimes employed their own choice of words: he is not therefore committed to a crude mechanical dictation theory of inspiration. Whilst denying that the original documents had any errors, he does not concede that the cause of truth is lost in admitting the possibility of minor errors in copies. Doddridge emphasises the relationship between inspiration and authority:

> Nothing can be more evident, than that a firm and cordial belief of the inspiration of the sacred scripture is of the highest moment; not only to the edification and peace of the church, but in a great measure to its very existence. For if this be given up, the authority of the revelation is enervated [weakened], and its use destroyed: The star which is to direct our course, is clouded; our compass is broke to pieces; and we are left to make the voyage of life in sad uncertainty, amidst a thousand rocks, and shelves, and quicksands.[8]

For Doddridge, the Bible itself is above theology. It tests and regulates our thinking:

> Let us therefore always remember that & we are indispensably obliged to receive with calm and reverend submission all the

dictates of Scripture; to make it our oracle; and, in this respect, to set it at a due distance from all other writings whatsoever; as it is certain, there is no other book in the world, that can pretend to equal authority, and produce equal or comparable proofs to support such a pretention. Let us measure the truth of our own sentiments, or those of others, in the great things which Scripture teaches, by their conformity to it.[9]

The student of church history cannot but be sad when he surveys the many inconsistencies of God's people. The disarray of the professed disciples of Jesus Christ often prejudices some against the truth of the Word of God until they realise that the church militant will never be free from the influences of human corruption and frailty. What can be even more alarming is the discovery that greater degrees of theological purity do not necessarily imply greater degrees of holy living amongst Christian people. Thus Doddridge lamented in the *Rise and Progress*:

> Yet there may be a great deal of speculative knowledge, and a great deal of rapturous affection, where there is no true religion at all ... The exercise of our rational faculties upon the evidences of Divine revelation, and upon the declaration of it as contained in Scripture, may furnish a very wicked man with a well-digested body of orthodox divinity in his head, when not one single doctrine of it has ever reached his heart.[10]

It was all too easy in the eighteenth century to make such observations as these. And there was no one more aware of the difficulties then prevailing in the Church of Christ than Philip Doddridge. Thus he warned young Jennings against the evils of the times:

> We must be cautious lest the old serpent find out a way of brooding over our hearts, and diffuse his venom there, while we mistake the fermentation it occasions to be only a warmth of zeal for Christ, and so do the work of His enemy in His name. I cannot, for my part, apprehend satire to be an ordinance of Christ; at least I believe, He will be more ready to excuse those who have erred on the tender, than on the severe extreme, ... nevertheless it is a sin that easily besets young divines, who, as I

suppose, with their wits and passions warm about them, have had the chief hand in bringing theological fury into a proverb.[11]

If these words provided Mr Jennings with some useful directives for his ministry, they also give us a clear picture of Doddridge's mind. However, it was sentiments such as he expressed that were to cost him his reputation in the eyes of some. Notwithstanding the biblical basis of Doddridge's thinking, there have been those who traced both the declension among his students and his catholicity of heart to serious deviations in his theology. This has been the true focus of attention of Doddridge's critics for more than two centuries.

Probably the most strident criticism of Doddridge was expressed in a letter dated December 8, 1908 from William Robertson Nichol, the one-time editor of the *British Weekly*, to James Denny:

> As for Doddridge, he was virtually, I think, an Arian. At least he recognised the Arians as brothers, though he admitted some modifications. Principal [Alexander] Gordon, who is biased but well informed, says that the majority of Doddridge's students became Arians, and he is rather disposed to think that Doddridge himself was.[12]

This is an extraordinary statement (see appendix). Even if journalists are less inclined to be sure of their facts than scholars, a little acquaintance with the sources would have saved the author from such an embarrassing blunder. Principal Gordon was also ill-informed, as Article 17 of Doddridge's ordination confession (1730) makes clear:

> I believe [Christ] is possessed not only of [his] humane and created nature in which he conversed amongst the children of men, but that He is also in a sense common to no other, the Son of God, the brightness of His Father's glory, and the express image of His person [see Hebrews 1: 3], and so partaker of all divine attributes and perfections as to be really one with the Father and, Himself, God over all, blessed for evermore.[13]

As his writings bear constant witness, this remained Doddridge's conviction throughout his life. His paraphrase on Hebrews 1: 3 in the *Family Expositor* – actually written three years before his death – surely confirms this:

> I speak of that great Emanuel, whom we have so long been taught to know and adore; *who being the effulgent ray of [his, i.e. the Father's] glory, and the express delineation of his person,* on whom his likeness is instamped in living characters in a manner which no created nature can admit, and *upholding the universe* which he hath made *by the* efficacious *word of his* Father's *power,* which is ever resident in him, as his own, by virtue of that intimate though incomprehensible union which renders them one. (John 10: 30); ...[14]

There's no Arianism here! Yet even a confession like this has failed to silence completely the suspicions of others. Charles Haddon Spurgeon, writing in his famous 'Downgrade' article in the *Sword and Trowel* in 1887, was both unbiased and better informed, when he wrote:

> Doctor Doddridge was as sound as he was amiable; but perhaps he was not always judicious; or more probably still, he was too judicious, and not sufficiently bold and decided ... his amiable disposition permitted him to do what men made of sterner staff would not have done. He sometimes mingled in a fraternal manner, even exchanging pulpits, with men whose orthodoxy was called in question. It had its effect on many of the younger men, and served to lessen in the estimate of the people generally the growing divergence of sentiment. No one, however, could, and certainly the present writer will not, insinuate even the suspicion of heresy against the author of 'Jesus, I love thy charming name'.[15]

Even if Doddridge might have been mistaken over the orthodoxy of some preachers, it is hard to imagine that the orthodox though charitable members of Castle Hill would fail to detect the serious doctrinal divergences of the day. After all, Doddridge – by word and example – taught his people well. While Spurgeon endorses Doddridge's personal theological integrity, he is possibly not in possession of all the facts. A case in point, of which neither

Principal Gordon nor Spurgeon seem to be aware, concerns the heterodox London preacher, James Foster. In his earlier years, probably during the Kibworth period, Doddridge had invited this man to preach for him. In 1737, Foster came to Northampton, only to find Doddridge refusing him his pulpit. Whereas Doddridge was ·of an amiable disposition, even his catholic spirit could say 'thus far, and no further'. Doddridge could be firm as well as friendly. This incident brought a remonstrance from his friend and benefactor, Samuel Clark of St Albans, with the implicit charge that Doddridge was 'countenancing a narrow spirit'.[16] Poor Doddridge! One cannot please everybody.

This incident also serves to answer Professor Macleod's criticism that Doddridge lacked 'theological proportion' (see appendix). His decision to reject Foster yet invite Wesley (in 1745) to lecture to his students accords with Macleod's own generous concession that, unlike Arianism, Wesley's Arminianism was not 'life-threatening to the body of Christ'. But Doddridge was clearly aware of the dangers of Arian error judging by his reply to an accusation that he had 'trimmed a little with the gospel of Christ'. While he admitted that his refusal to engage in 'heresy hunting' was wrongly construed as sympathy for 'the Arian scheme', his position was unambiguous:

> I had infinitely rather the [*Family Expositor*] should perish than advance anything contrary to the tenor of the Gospel, and subversive to the souls of men. I guard against apprehending Christ to be a mere creature, or another god, inferior to the Father, or coordinate with Him.[17]

It is true, Doddridge did not have the natural constitution of a man like Thomas Bradbury. Neither does such a comparison imply that Doddridge was devoid of courage. It would not even be doing justice to the man to say that at times he may have appeared a little naive. However, there were times when he could be over concerned in his attempt to avoid censure. But even his fear of giving offence had some justification. In an era when orthodox zeal could be excessive and when party spirit divided many sincere Christians, Doddridge had something useful to say, even in this humble confession in a letter to a friend in London:

The apprehensions of wise and good men are so different, that I am sometimes confounded amidst the variety of their opinions and counsels; and often think of the grey headed man and his two wives. But, if I err, I would choose to do it on the side of modesty and caution, as one who is more afraid of doing wrong than of not doing right. But when the world is to be remarkably reformed, God will raise up some bolder spirits, who will work like your London firemen and I pray God it may not be amidst smoke, and flames and ruin.[18]

When the time came for God to 'raise up some bolder spirits', it was soon found necessary to heed this gentle warning.

Doddridge was quite deliberate in his attitude, even if he confesses to the possibility of error. However, the caution with which he speaks was not a negative thing. In another ordination sermon, the humble Doddridge speaks with courage: 'I hope we shall never practise so dangerous a complaisance to unbelievers of the present age as to waive the Gospel that we may accommodate ourselves to their taste ...'[19] For Doddridge, these words sound like a healthy intolerance! But for those who might be tempted to think this was only 'paper courage', a public incident shows otherwise. In December 1742, he attended a banquet at which Sir John Robinson used some 'dreadful expletives'. Doddridge promptly rose and left in personal protest. The following day, Sir John was kindly but firmly admonished by letter for having blasphemed 'the venerable name of the ever-blessed God in so light a manner'. Doddridge's courageous but gracious actions greatly impressed the Earl of Halifax who said, "Ah, there goes a Christian and a gentleman."[20] Indeed, Doddridge was not for 'accommodating himself to public taste'.

So, in preaching and 'living out' the Gospel, Doddridge clearly saw the issues of the day, and he stood his ground with conviction, even when much opprobrium was poured upon him. In another letter he wrote:

Indeed the Gospel is a great thing, or it is nothing. I am more and more convinced of the importance of keeping to the good old evangelical and experimental way of preaching; and look on most of the new fashioned divinity, of which some persons in different extremes, are so fond, as a kind of quackery, which bodes ill to the health of the soul, and of the church in general. You know how cautious I am of troubling the church with disputes; but my faith in the doctrines I preach is more and more confirmed by studying the Scriptures, by experience and observation. What I have wrote concerning them proceeds not from any sourness of temper, or any want of charity for, or love to, persons of a different opinion; though some of them have, as you well know, laid me under strong temptations to it, by exercising as little charity towards me, as if there had been no common bond of Christianity or even humanity to unite us.[21]

If we still have not grasped the true character of Philip Doddridge, or have difficulty in understanding his motives, let one of Doddridge's closest friends add his impressions. The Presbyterian minister John Barker wrote:

I love you beyond expression, and admire your abilities, furniture and spirits, more than you imagine; and not a man in the world rejoices more in your usefulness than I do, and yet I often make myself merry with your character and conduct. I will give you a sketch of it. You are so entirely devoted to God, to truth and holiness, that it is very easy to impose upon you under the appearance of any of these; and are so perfectly made up of candour and good nature, that a pious enthusiast or a godly dunce, or an upright Arian &c is welcome to your table and heart. You are so good yourself that you think everybody else ten times better than they are; see merit in the darkness of midnight; cannot see faults without a noonday sun; forgive injuries before they are confessed; confer favours as a reward for affronts, and never will believe but that all who are in good earnest in religion, and enter into the belief, practice, life and spirit of it, are to be embraced by you, because Christ receives them, let their opinions or denominations be what they will; now how should you be a party man, or be likely to have your academy supplied by people who live upon notions, phrases, and external forms.[22]

Doddridge could thus be attractively and even pardonably naive. However, faced by a soundly-orthodox but loveless (and possibly-unregenerate) Calvinist on one hand, and a kind, peaceable (and possibly-regenerate) Arian on the other, there's no doubting where

Doddridge's sympathy would lie. Clearly, there were critical Calvinists and kind Calvinists, attractive Arians and awkward Arians in his day. In both respects, some would have better hearts than heads, depending on their spiritual development. Thus, on one occasion, Doddridge allowed an Arian whom he considered 'to be a real Christian' to partake of the Lord's Supper. Although he was criticised by some of his congregation, this was a judgement of charity not an endorsement of error.[23]

One can hardly question whether the attitude of Doddridge is right. This much must be emphasised, that Doddridge did not seek peace at any price; it would be an insult to his Christian mind to suggest that his kind of catholicity resulted from an indifferent attitude to truth. Indeed, he had theological reasons for his policy. He was concerned as much for true Christian charity as he was for biblical orthodoxy; indeed, as Doddridge saw orthodoxy, charity was a necessary ingredient of it. It is evident that Doddridge was consistent with his own teaching, for in commenting on the incident recorded in Mark's Gospel where the disciples tried to silence others not of their immediate company Doddridge says:

> It is sad that the spirit, which remains in so many Christians, and in this instance appeared even in the beloved Saint John, should (as the Apostle James expresses it) lust unto envy (Jas. 4: 5); How ill does that spirit become a disciple, and much more a minister, of the benevolent Jesus! The Apostle Paul had learnt and taught a better temper, when he rejoiced, that Christ was preached, even by those who were his personal enemies (Phil. 1: 18). To seek our own glory, is not glory (Prov. 25: 27), and to confine religion to them that follow us, is a narrowness of spirit which we should avoid and abhor *(Improvement on Mark 9: 38)*.[24]

So, if Philip Doddridge was no Arian, where do his other doctrinal sympathies place him? The sometimes-critical Kippis stated that his master's 'sermons at Kibworth had less of the Calvinistical dress of expression than was adopted by him after his settlement at Northampton'.[25] The nonconformist historians, David Bogue and James Bennett record a similar verdict on Doddridge:

To us it affords pleasure to reflect that he was more Evangelical and Calvinistic as he advanced in years; and the regret which some have expressed at his orthodoxy, will serve to reconcile others to what they had blamed as not sufficiently decided.[26]

Despite his various misgivings, Professor Macleod also has no doubts that Doddridge was a Calvinist. However, these votes of approval are more generous than accurate if they imply that Doddridge was a theologian in the mould of Dr John Owen and the Westminster (and Savoy) divines. Judging by a letter as early as [March] 1721, Doddridge the young Presbyterian clearly expected his tutor's teaching to be 'conformable to the Calvinistic system'.[27] As we saw in chapter two, about a month before, he wrote enthusiastically, 'Tillotson is my particular favourite', adding significantly that 'We have some of Goodwin's works in the library, and some of the great Dr Owen's, but you know I am not very fond of such mysterious men'.[28]

After receiving a gift of Richard Baxter's works in March 1724, Doddridge's preferences suddenly changed. A month later, he wrote of 'Mr Baxter's incomparable writings'[29] which during May he continued to study 'with an abundance of pleasure'.[30] By October, Doddridge's enthusiasm showed no sign of waning: 'I am going on with Mr Baxter's works, which I cannot sufficiently admire'.[31] By December, Tillotson had to take second place to his puritan friend, as Doddridge declared to his brother-in-law:

Baxter is my particular favourite ... he appears to have been so far superior to the generality of those whom we must charitably hope to be good men, that one would imagine God raised him up to disgrace and condemn his brethren, by showing what a Christian is; and how few in the world deserve the character.[32]

Thus Baxter became the chief – though not the only – influence in Doddridge's life and ministry. However, only a month before he wrote this eulogy on Baxter, he declared defensively to a critical acquaintance: 'I am in all the most important points a Calvinist'.[33] Thus Doddridge's settled place on the theological spectrum may be stated accurately. He penned this interesting self-assessment in December 1726:

I have lately preached twice at Northampton, and have the character of a very orthodox divine; but to my great mortification, I hear from another quarter, that my sermons are all Do, Do, Do! To speak my sentiments without reserve, I think the one too favourable, and the other too severe.[34]

This was Doddridge's way of saying that he was neither an antinomian High Calvinist nor a legalistic Arminian. Following his settlement in Northampton three years later, his 'middle-way' theology was expressed in his ordination Confession of Faith. Although he came to lament the 'listing of ourselves under the *name* of this, or that man, how wise, how good, how great soever ,[35] as late as October 1748 – just three years before his death – he said to his close friend Samuel Wood of Norwich that 'Baxterian Calvinist' was 'a very proper expression'.[36] By this he meant, among other things, that he was a 'four-point Calvinist'. Like Baxter (and Calvin), Doddridge believed – together with predestination and election – that the Bible teaches that Christ died sufficiently for the whole world but effectually for the elect. Although he came to admire John Owen's practical works, Doddridge's view of the atonement was to be Baxter's rather than Owen's (see appendix).

II

Doddridge did not hide his theology under a bushel. According to his confession of faith, his lectures and the *Family Expositor*, so he preached. In the year 1741, he published two sermons entitled, *The Scripture-Doctrine of Salvation by Grace through Faith*. In the dedication, after lamenting the fact that in his day, 'the credit of many evangelical truths' had fallen very low, he speaks thus of the doctrine of 'Salvation by Grace': 'This glorious doctrine has been the joy of the church in all ages on earth; and it will be the song of all that have received it in truth throughout the ages of eternity, and be pursued in the heavenly regions with ever-growing admiration and delight'.[37] Let us hear how Doddridge speaks of the function and origin of faith as he expounds his text, Eph. 2: 8:

Faith receives our Lord Jesus Christ; it is its great office, and its great glory to do it. But how could it have received him, unless

THE

Scripture-Doctrine

OF

SALVATION by GRACE
through FAITH,

Illuftrated and improved in

Two SERMONS:

The Subftance of which was Preached at

ROWELL in *Northamptonſhire.*

By P. DODDRIDGE, *D. D.*

Publiſhed, with ſome Enlargements, at the
earneſt Requeſt of the Congregation there.

I am not aſhamed of the Goſpel of Chriſt ; *for it is
the Power of* GOD *unto Salvation to every one
that believeth.* Rom. i. 16.

LONDON:
Printed, and Sold by M FENNER, at the *Turk's-
Head* in *Gracechurch-ſtreet* ; and JAMES HODGES,
at the *Looking-glaſs* over-againſt *St. Magnus* Church,
London-bridge. MDCCXLI.

[Price Eight-pence.]

he had been given? And how could he have been given in this view, but by the appointment of the Father, in concurrence with his own free and most gracious consent? – Faith apprehends and submits to the gospel plan of salvation by the obedience and sufferings of the Son of God; yea, it not only submits to it, but rejoices and glories in it. But who could have exhibited, who could have contrived, who could have executed such a plan, unless it had been formed and determined in the counsels of eternal love? – Admit faith to be ever so voluntary, and so far as is possible to a creature, ever so independent an act, can we any of us say, that there was so much merit and excellency in that act, or in any of its subsequent fruits, that God upon the foresight of it should say, "These creatures, guilty and condemned as they appear, will be so ready to receive the intimations of my will, that they will fully deserve that I should save them at any rate; they will deserve even that my Son should become incarnate, and die as a sacrifice, to make way for their happiness." Can any of you, Sirs, imagine this to have been the case? Or can you hear it even supposed, without finding something shocking in the very representation of it? The Blessed Paul, I am sure, had very different views, when he said God *hath predestinated us to the adoption of children by Jesus Christ to himself, according to the good pleasure of his will, to the praise of the glory of his grace, wherein he hath made us acceptable in the beloved* (Eph.1: 5, 6). And the Apostle John had other notions of it, when he said, full as his gracious heart was of the most lively sentiments of gratitude and zeal, *Herein is love, not that we loved God, but that he loved us. And sent his Son to be the propitiation for our sins* (1Jn. 4: 10).[38]

Does predestination mean that hearers of the Gospel can only sit and do nothing? Not according to Doddridge, who urges his hearers to examine themselves:

It is a melancholy, but most obvious truth, that *All men have not faith* (2 Thess 3: 2). There are thousands and ten thousands under the gospel, with regard to whom its ministers have reason to complain, *Who hath believed our report, and to whom hath the arm of the Lord been revealed?* (Isa. 53: 1) On whom has its power been so exerted, as to conquer the natural incredulity and obstinacy of their hearts? Are you, Sirs, of that number, or of the number of those, who, as the Scripture expresses it, *Have believed through grace?* (Acts 18: 27) It is the question on which your eternal state will turn at last; and therefore you would do well to examine it now.[39]

To say that predestination makes humans mere automatons, or that evangelism is unnecessary, is to abuse the doctrine and fly in the face of God's Word. Thus in his *Practical Discourses on Regeneration*, Doddridge is careful to safeguard the relationship between divine sovereignty and human responsibility. After citing quotations which speak of God 'hardening' the human heart (see John 12: 39-40; Romans 9: 18), he then remarks:

> These, to be sure, are very emphatical Scriptures; and though it is necessary to understand them in such a qualified sense as to make them consistent with other Scriptures which charge men's destruction, not on any necessitating decree of God, but upon themselves, and the abuse of their own faculties; yet still these expressions must stand for something; and in the most moderate sense that can be put upon them, they directly confirm what I have here brought them to prove. So that on the whole, the matter must come to this, "That the cause of men's final and everlasting ruin may be referred, in one view of it, to God's withholding those gracious influences, which if they had been imparted, would indeed have subdued the greatest perverseness: but his withholding these influences is not merely an arbitrary act, but the just punishment of men's wickedness, and of their obstinate folly in trifling with the means of grace, and grieving his Spirit till it was provoked to withdraw." This thought which I might largely prove to you to be a compendium of the Scripture-scheme, reconciles all; and any consequences drawn from one part of that scheme to the denial of the other, how plausible soever, must certainly be false.[40]

Observing the biblical balance of 'the Scripture-scheme', Doddridge refused to 'particularise' universal atonement texts in the manner of John Owen. As his exposition makes clear, Paul's compassionate mission to the world is something Doddridge shared. Without introducing dubious qualifications, he weaves the Apostle's own words (2 Corinthians 5: 14-15) into his own without tampering with the text :

> The Apostle ... was transported to such a zeal for Christ, and
> the souls of men, that some thought him beside himself; and no
> doubt many would represent him as the greatest enthusiast
> upon the face of the earth. But as it was a very small thing to
> him to be judged of man's judgement, he calmly vindicates
> himself, by declaring that there was a cause for all this warmth,
> as the honour of God, and the Redeemer, and the eternal
> salvation of men, were so intimately concerned in the affair:
> *The love of Christ*, says he, *constrains us*, or (as the word
> properly signifies) it bears us away with it, like a mighty
> torrent, which we are not able to resist; *because we thus judge,*
> *that if one died for all, then all were dead*, under the sentence
> of God's righteous law, or they would not have needed such an
> atonement as the blood of his Son, and we farther judge, *that*
> *he died for all, that they who now live*, only in consequence of
> his dying love, *should not henceforth live unto themselves, but*
> *unto him that died for them* ...[41]

In a communion discourse, Doddridge reminded his hearers of the
limitless provision of redeeming mercy:

> *Behold the Lamb of God, that taketh away the sins of the world*
> [John 1: 29]. He is the Lamb. He is the Lamb of God; sent,
> appointed, approved by him. And he takes away sin; - not only
> some little slight offences, *but all sin*: he has merit enough to
> take away those of the whole world![42]

Accordingly, in the *Family Expositor*, we read:

> Let our faith daily behold Jesus under the character of the Lamb
> of God ... As such let us humbly apply to him to take away our
> sins, and rejoice that (as the apostle John elsewhere expresses it)
> *he is the propitiation, not for our sins only, but also for the sins*
> *of the whole world*; all ages and nations being interested in the
> benefit of his atonement (1 John 2: 2) *(Improvement on 1 John*
> *2: 1-17)*.[43]

Doddridge descants on 1 John 2: 2 with the heart of an evangelist:

> While we joy in [Christ] as the *propitiation for our sins*, let it

comfort our hearts to think, how wide the efficacy of his atonement extends. O, that *all the world* might be engaged to apply to him under this important consideration! *(Improvement on 1 John 2: 1-17).*[44]

Consistent with the Baxterian emphasis of his lectures (see appendix), Doddridge evidently saw a correlation between the universal availability of the atonement and the free offer of the gospel. In his sermons on the *Power and Grace of Christ*, he says:

> And as the apostle argues, that *if Christ died for all; then were all dead* [2 Cor. 5: 14], all were in a state of death, or they would not have needed such an expiatory sacrifice; so we may assure ourselves, that if Christ is to be offered to all as a Saviour, then were all in a state of ruin.[45]

Thus Doddridge had no inhibitions about being evangelistic as a result of the Bible's teaching about election. As an advocate of the 'middle way' of 'authentic' or 'Baxterian Calvinism', he was able to preach the Gospel with great eloquence:

> It is an advice of the highest importance, that "whoever you are, you should immediately fly to Christ, and repose the confidence of your souls upon him." Observe that I urge you, WHOEVER YOU ARE, to fly immediately to Christ: and this I do, to guard against a strange notion which some are ready to entertain, as if we were to bring something of our own righteousness and obedience to him, to render us worthy of being accepted by him. But this is a grand mistake. The blessings of the Gospel are not to be considered as matter of bargain and sale: no, if we come to buy wine and milk, it must be without money and without price (Isa. 55: 1); and whoever will take of the water of life, must do it freely (Rev. 22: 17). If he pretends to offer an equivalent, he forfeits his share in the invitation; and must be made to know, that the price he offers is a great affront to the value of the blessings for which he would thus barter. – Let this then be your language, "Lord, I have undone myself, and in me is no help: I see nothing in myself which makes me worthy of thy regard; but this I know, that where sin has abounded, grace does much more abound, and reigns through righteousness unto eternal life by Jesus Christ (Rom. 5: 20-1); through whom thou

hast assured me in thy word that eternal life is the gift of God (Rom. 6: 23). As such let me receive it: and by how much the more undeserving I have been, by so much the more will I celebrate the riches of thy grace in making me a vessel of mercy, and a monument of love throughout all eternity. – Blessed Jesus, thou hast said, that him who comes unto thee thou wilt in no wise cast out (Jn. 6: 37): behold, I come, and cast myself at thy feet; receive me, and put me among the children (Jer. 3: 19), though I deserve not the very crumbs that fall from thy table (Matt. 15: 27). [46]

Yet, in the final analysis, Doddridge believed that the success and efficacy of the atonement was guaranteed by election; this was where his 'Baxterian Calvinism' differed from the universalist view of the Arminians. Accordingly, he says in his *Lectures*:

... there (is) a sense, in which Christ might be said to die for all; as all men partake of some benefit by his death, and such provision is made for their salvation, as lays the blame of their ruin, if they miscarry, entirely upon themselves: but it was in a very peculiar and much nobler sense, that he died for the elect, intending evidently to secure for them, and only for them, the everlasting blessings of his Gospel. ... John 10: 15, 16, 26; 17: 2, 9, 16. [47]

Not surprisingly, Doddridge the 'middle-way' Calvinist was attacked by 'extremists' on both sides. Job Orton tells us that 'some charged him with being too loose in his sentiments; others with being too strict'. [48] Besides accusations of Arianism, Doddridge was also suspected of Arminianism. He says himself that he 'was censured by the High Calvinists on this side, and some of the friends of liberty and catholicism, as by a strange catachresis [= misuse] they call themselves, on the other'. [49] After preaching in London, Doddridge painted a colourful picture of the High Calvinists in this amusing comment to his wife:

I had several orthodox spies to hear me this morning, and they observed, with great amazement, that I urged my hearers to endeavour to get an interest in Christ. This, it seems, is Arminianism. [50]

John Brine, the Particular Baptist and friend of Dr John Gill, was a savage critic of Philip Doddridge. In *The Certain Efficacy of the Death of Christ* (1743), Brine criticised Isaac Watts' *The Ruin and Recovery of Mankind* (1740) in which the author endorsed Baxter's views of universal redemption and justification. In passing, Brine criticises Doddridge's exposition of the imputation of Christ's righteousness to the believer; he accuses Doddridge of following the Socinians and the Arminians, all because Doddridge says that the believer is declared righteous in the sight of God the moment he trusts Christ for his salvation. Lurking in the background is Brine's hyper-Calvinist dogma of eternal justification, and he fears that Doddridge's free offer of the Gospel will militate against the certain efficacy of Christ's death. Brine is unmerciful:

> The churches of Christ in Northamptonshire may expect to soon hear the universal extent of Christ's death in express words asserted, when they are sufficiently prepared for it, by such artful and sly insinuations of it.[51]

As for the theory of justification from eternity, Doddridge dismisses it with biblical simplicity:

> Some have inferred, that [the elect] were actually justified from eternity, and consequently are in a justified state, even while they are going on in a course of unrepented sin: but this seems most directly contrary to the whole tenor of Scripture; and it is certain, that on the same principles on which they may be said to be justified, they may also be said to be glorified from eternity [Rom. 8: 30]. If the expression be intended to signify no more, than that God *purposed* to justify them, it is not denied; but it is a most improper way of speaking, and the arguments drawn from thence in favour of any kind of licentiousness are utterly inconclusive.[52]

On the Arminian side, Doddridge was regarded as insufferably orthodox. In 1737, Samuel Bourne, a prominent figure in the cause of theological liberalism, wrote to his friend George Benson in connection with the Rotherham Academy, saying that 'we want a man to be a balance to that Northampton tutor'.[53] Andrew Kippis reported that 'Many judicious persons have wished that his devotional treatises had been more accommodated to universal use, by a less Calvinistical turn of opinion and language'.[54]

Whatever criticism Doddridge had to suffer from his fellow-countrymen, encouragement was found elsewhere. After reading the Dutch translation of the sermons quoted above, a pastor of the Reformed Church at Amsterdam, Wilhelmus Peiffers declared to the printer:

> Herewith I gratefully return you the work of Dr Doddridge, concerning the New Birth, Salvation by Grace, &c which I have read more than once with such uncommon pleasure, that I long to see all that excellent author has published. I did not know him by name; but from this incomparable masterpiece, in which the oratory of the ancients seems to be revived, he appears to be a very great man.[55]

Peiffers is very specific in his commendation:

> Here orthodoxy reigns with moderation, zeal with meekness, deep hidden wisdom with uncommon clearness: Here simplicity shines without coldness, elegance without painting, and sublimity without bombast. Here one is equally charmed with reason without pelagianism, and heavenly mindedness without enthusiasm.[56]

With such a testimonial before us, it is hardly surprising to find Doddridge's position abundantly confirmed in his published works. In his magnum opus, *The Family Expositor*, precise faithfulness to the text is a notable feature. What Spurgeon said of Calvin applies also to Doddridge:

> In his expositions he is not always what moderns would call Calvinistic; that is to say, where Scripture maintains the doctrine of predestination and grace he flinches in no degree, but inasmuch as some Scriptures bear the impress of human free action and responsibility, he does not shun to expound their meaning in all fairness and integrity. He was no trimmer of texts.[57]

Not surprisingly, Spurgeon – though mildly critical – *actually* says of Doddridge's commentary:

> It is worthy of a far more extensive reading than is nowadays accorded to it. ... The notes are very good and reveal the thorough scholar. Our Authorised Version is placed in the margin, and a new translation in the paraphrase... The practical improvements at the end of each chapter generally consist of pressing exhortations and devout meditations, suggested by the matter under discussion. ...[58]

This verdict is fully justified. The manner in which Doddridge handles the difficult passages, those guaranteed to be an occasion of controversy, reveals a spiritual mind, avoiding the quicksands of legalism on one hand and the rocks of antinomianism on the other. For Doddridge, grace never cancelled duty, and obedience was all of grace. Doddridge the faithful exegete studied the divine chart well, which enabled him to set sail for heaven with a heavenly mind. When discussing the merits of Bible commentators, Spurgeon adds this amusing testimonial to Doddridge's orthodoxy:

> I have placed next to Gill in my library Adam Clarke, but as I have no desire to have my rest broken by wars among authors, I have placed Doddridge between them.[59]

Spurgeon described John Gill as the 'Coryphaeus of hyper-Calvinism', and so Doddridge's 'Baxterian Calvinism' provided some theological insulation between Gill and the Wesleyan Arminian, Adam Clarke.

Those who know Doddridge's most popular work, *The Rise and Progress of Religion in the Soul*, and have sung his hymns, which were but a fraction of his literary output, will not be surprised to know of his great admiration for the Puritans. When the tide was against Puritanism, even within the ranks of their lineal heirs, the Northampton tutor was guiding the reading of his theological students in the 'old paths':

> I recommend to you, first, to form some acquaintance with the Puritans, though they are too often despised. There was good

sense and learning in those days, as well as ours. Our grandmothers had real beauty, though the change of fashions has made their dress ridiculous to us.[60]

In a sequence of remarks in his *Lectures on Preaching*, Doddridge then proceeds to recommend such famous 'practical writers' as Robert Bolton ('excellent both for conviction and consolation'), Bishop Joseph Hall ('the most elegant and polite writer of his age'), Richard Sibbes ('his style is pathetic and tender'), John Owen and Thomas Goodwin ('Both highly evangelical, but both very obscure, especially the latter ... Owen's style resembles St Paul's ... *His Exposition of the 130th Psalm* is most excellent'), Richard Baxter ('He discovers a manly eloquence, and the most evident proofs of an amazing genius ... See his *Saint's Rest*, ... especially his *Call to the Unconverted* ... Few were ever instrumental of awakening more souls'), Thomas Manton ('he has many judicious remarks on scripture ... His chief work is on the 119th Psalm'), William Bates ('charming and elegant, ... read his *Harmony of the Divine Attributes*'), John Howe ('The truest sublime is to be found in his writings ... His best pieces are, *The Blessedness of the Righteous*, *Redeemer's Tears*, and *The Redeemer's Dominion*'), John Flavel ('Not deep, nor remarkably judicious, – but plain, popular, tender') and Stephen Charnock ('On the Attributes he is deep and sublime') to mention but a few.[61]

Doddridge clearly admired the works of Archbishop John Tillotson ('There is such an easiness in his style, and beautiful simplicity of expression ... He had some puritanical expressions'[62]) and Matthew Henry ('perhaps the only commentator so large that deserves to be entirely and attentively read through'[63]). Among sixteenth-century authors, Doddridge commends John Calvin ('[He] has a multitude of judicious thoughts ... His two best [volumes] are, I think, that on the *Pentateuch*, and on the *Harmony of the Evangelists*').[64] However, Doddridge reserved his highest praise for the writings of the Scottish Archbishop Robert Leighton, an edition of whose works he prepared for publication in 1748. Not even Richard Baxter received the unqualified admiration that Doddridge had for Robert Leighton:

One of the most eminently devout and pious writers his age has

Robert Leighton
(1611 - 84)

produced... His works [notably the *Commentary on 1 Peter*] ought to be reckoned among the greatest treasures of the English tongue. They continually overflow with love to God, and breathe a heart entirely transformed by the Gospel. ... Few uninspired writers have a greater tendency to mend the world.[65]

Doddridge's lengthy preface to his edition of Leighton's *Works* reveals something of the editor as well as the Archbishop:

The delight and edification which I have found in the writings of this *wonderful man*, for such I must deliberately call him, would have been a full equivalent for my pains, separate from all prospect of that effect which they might have upon others. For truly I know not that I have ever spent a quarter of an hour in reviewing any of them, but even amidst that interruption which a critical examination of the copy would naturally give, I have felt some impressions which I could wish always to retain. I can hardly forbear saying, as a considerable philosopher and eminent divine [Dr Henry Miles, FRS], with whom I have the honour of an intimate correspondence and friendship, said to me in a letter[66] long ago, and when my acquaintance with our Author's works was but beginning, "There is a spirit in Archbishop Leighton I never met in any human writings; nor can I read many lines in them without being moved."[67]

With such a persuasive array of evidence before us, whence the suspicion which has surrounded the memory of this saintly 'Baxterian Calvinist'? For the answer, we need look no further than the passage quoted earlier in this chapter from the *Rise and Progress* (where Doddridge laments that through mere rational activity 'orthodoxy' can coexist with 'wickedness').

It is sad to relate, that in Doddridge's day, there was much orthodoxy mingled with much wickedness. Doddridge himself had to suffer on account of this and he knew keenly the significance of the Apostle Paul's warning to Timothy, 'Yea, and all that will live godly in Christ Jesus shall suffer persecution' (2 Tim. 3: 12). In a letter, Doddridge wrote of resentment among some students:

Some have thought themselves injured, because I cannot oblige them, at the expense of my conscience, by granting them testimonials, which I know they do not deserve; or by helping them into settlements, which would be unhappy to themselves and the congregations which refer their case to my advice. For this reason, imaginary injuries, never complained of to me, were talked over and aggravated. My conduct was continually watched over for evil: my writings, my lectures, sermons, letters, words, everything, were compared to find out imaginary inconsistencies, and to charge them, as instances of dishonesty, partiality and what not? When they went abroad, they talked of these things; and there were those, in both extremes, who were ready to lay hold on any story to my disadvantage. [68]

It is a credit to the godliness of Philip Doddridge that he did not indulge in meting out to others the kind of treatment he himself received. It is the logic of iniquity that condemns a man, in the name of orthodoxy, for being charitable and honest. They are the tactics of Satan that call a scriptural catholicity of heart, a compromise of truth. In a letter to Doddridge in 1746, John Wesley asked, among other things, whether letters should be signed with the writer referring to himself as 'Faithful, humble servant'. In his reply, after rejecting the proud implications of claiming perfect humility, Doddridge declared:

> In what can I say I have already attained? Only in that I love my Divine Master. I would not have a thought in my heart that He should disapprove. I feel a sweetness in being assuredly in His gracious hand, which all the world cannot possibly afford; and which I really think would make me happier in a dark dungeon than ten thousand worlds could render me without it; and therefore I love every creature in the earth that bears His image; and I do not except those who through ignorance, rashness or prejudice, have greatly injured me.[69]

Doddridge's 'catholic spirit' created a wide circle of acquaintance. In his concern for unity, he had discussions with the Archbishop of Canterbury Dr Herring as well as Baptist pastors; he was a friend of Methodist revivalists as well as more traditional Dissenters. However, it is obvious from his correspondence and writings that he was concerned with *Protestant* Unity, in days when no one doubted that the Church of England was a Protestant Church.

If he could not justify perpetual divisions between the Protestant bodies, he had no doubts about the duty of separation from the Roman Catholic Church. In his sermon on the *Iniquity of Persecution*, he starts with this forthright statement:

> If Popery be considered in a religious view, it must appear the just object of our contempt, as well as our abhorrence.[70]

Doddridge was not unaware of the political dimension of Roman Catholic influence. Speaking of 'papists amongst us', he observes:

> They are under such obligations in conscience to obey the pope, and to submit themselves to whatsoever prince he shall see fit to establish here, that they are at best but very precarious subjects to that royal family which the gracious providence of the Almighty has been pleased to fix on the throne of these nations; especially while there is a pretender ['Bonnie Prince Charlie'] to that throne devoted to the see of Rome, and espoused by it.[71]

Comparing the persecuting tendencies of Roman Catholicism and Islam, Doddridge is careful to observe a significant difference:

> A [Muslim] may perhaps prove from his [Qur'an] (see Suras 2, 4, 5), that the true faith is to be propagated by the sword, and that heretics and unbelievers are to be cut off or made tributary; but if a Christian plead in favour of persecution, while he has his New Testament in his hand, in an intelligible language, he must be condemned out of his own mouth. It is condemned by the example of Christ, *Who went about doing good* [Acts 10: 38], *who came not to destroy men's lives but to save them* [Lk. 9: 56].[72]

In another sermon, he explains his protestant position very clearly:

> My brethren, pardon the freedom of my speech. I should have thought it my duty to have separated from the Church of Rome, had she pretended only to determine those things which Christ has left indifferent: How much more when she requires a compliance with those, which he hath expressly forbid? & You

The Abſurdity and Iniquity of PERSECUTION *for Conſcience-ſake, in all its Kinds and Degrees.*

CONSIDER'D in a

SERMON

PREACH'D at

NORTHAMPTON.

By P. DODDRIDGE, D. D.

Publiſhed with ſome ENLARGEMENTS.

Recommended by the Reverend Mr. *SOME,* as a proper APPENDIX to the late LECTURES at *Salters-Hall.*

Δεῖ γὰρ ἕκαςον κα]ὰ]ὴν ἑαυ]ῦ προαίρεσιν
Θεον εὐσεβεῖν ἀλλὰ μὴ με]ὰ βίας.   JOSEPH.

It were Inhumanity to ſtand on the Shore, and ſeeing Men ready to periſh in a Storm at Sea, to ſtorm at them our ſelves, or to ſhoot them to death, or to caſt Fire into their Veſſel, and burn them, becauſe they are in danger of being drown'd. Yet thus do we deal with thoſe whom we perſecute, becauſe they miſs of the Truth; and, it may be, raiſe a worſe Storm in our ſelves, as to our own Morals, than they ſuffer in their Intellectuals.
Dr. OWEN, of Underſt. Script. p. 138.

LONDON:

Printed for R. HETT, at the *Bible* and *Crown* in the *Poultry;* and ſold by Mr. FOWLER, at *Northampton;* and Mr. RATTEN, at *Market-Harborough.* M.DCC.XXXVI.

(Price 6 d.)

shall not only bow at the venerable name of our common Lord, but you shall worship an image: You shall not only kneel at the communion, but kneel in adoration of a piece of bread: You shall not only pronounce, or at least appear to pronounce, those accursed, who do not believe what is acknowledged to be incomprehensible, but those who do not believe what is most contrary to our reason and senses. When these are the terms of our continued communion, the Lord judge between us and them! Had nothing but indifferent things been in dispute, we should have done, as we do by our brethren of the Church of England, taken our leave of them with decency and respect: We should have loved them as our brethren, while we could not have owned them as our Lords. But when they require us to purchase our peace, by violating our consciences and endangering our souls, it is no wonder that we escape as for our lives.[73]

For Doddridge, the position and power of the Pope, the doctrine of the Mass and transubstantiation, worship of the Virgin Mary and priestly celibacy were major issues at stake. On papal power and influence, he says:

(Above all that is called God, &c.) The usurpation of the papacy in Divine things is so unequalled, that if these words are not applicable to it, it is difficult to say, who there ever has been, or can be to whom they should belong. The manner in which the Pope has exalted himself above magistrates (civil governments) is equally remarkable and detestable *(Note on 2 Thessalonians 2:4)*.[74]

The scandalous and extravagant pretences which the followers of the papacy have made to miracles, exceeding in number, and some of them in marvellous circumstances, those of Christ and his apostles, plainly display the energy of Satan, that father of frauds, pious and impious. And the most incredible lies, which they have, by solemn and irrevocable acts, made essential to their faith, shew the strength of delusion *(Improvement on 2 Thessalonians 2:1-12)*.[75]

For Doddridge, the doctrine of transubstantiation was as ridiculous as it is unbiblical:

(This is my body) When I consider that (as a thousand writers have observed) on the same foundation on which the papists argue for transubstantiation from these words, they might prove, from Ezekiel 5:1-5, that the prophet's hair was the city of Jerusalem; from John 10:9 and 15:1 that Christ was literally a door and a vine; and from Matthew 26:27,28, and from 1 Corinthians 11:25, that the cup was his blood, and that Christ commanded his disciples to drink and swallow the cup; I cannot but be astonished at the inference they would deduce from hence (Note on Matthew 26:26).[76]

Prayers to the Virgin Mary were a failure to grasp the nature of our Lord's authority as well as a denial of the direct access we have to the throne of grace:

If his mother met with so just a rebuke for attempting to direct his ministrations in the days of his flesh, how absurd it is for any to address her as if she had a right to command him on the throne of his glory (Improvement on John 2 :1-11).[77]

Besides being a happily married man, Doddridge had no doubts about the evil of Rome's requirement of obligatory priestly celibacy:

Marriage has been forbidden, while the pardon of fornication, adultery, and incest, have been rated at a certain price by that grand merchant of the souls of men, who hath ventured to call himself the vicar of Christ upon earth (Improvement on 1 Timothy 4: 3).[78]

It is plain, therefore, that Doddridge was far from being indifferent to doctrine. It was clearly of the greatest importance to him. Indeed, his views on Roman Catholicism will cause disappointment to some who have viewed him as an ecumenical prophet, and yet reassurance for others. However, it must be said in all truth that he clearly drew a distinction between Roman Catholicism and Roman Catholics, between the system and its blind devotees. Nowhere is this more perfectly illustrated than in the 'Connell Affair'. One Bryan Connell was found guilty of murdering a man at Weedon, near Northampton. Doddridge befriended the poor man, who pleaded innocence, and Doddridge believed that he was not guilty. Despite an appeal, Connell was executed on April 3, 1741.[79] Now Connell was a Roman Catholic, and Doddridge's concern for him even led many to suggest that the Reformed pastor had inclinations towards Roman Catholicism! In a letter to Connell, written only two days before the execution took place, Doddridge pleads with the condemned man to seek salvation in Christ. The letter also tells us a great deal about Doddridge – the Protestant, the Evangelical, the spiritual and truly Christian man that he was:

> I beseech you by the worth of your precious and immortal soul! that in these solemn moments, you guard against every false dependence. You well remember how frequently and how earnestly I have repeated this caution. I rejoice in finding you so often declare, that you put no confidence in the power of a Priest to forgive sin; nor in the efficacy of sacraments to save an impenitent sinner; nor in the intercession of saints and angels; nor in the value of your own blood, supposing it, in this respect innocent, to make satisfaction to God for the sins of your life; but that you desire to trust in the mercy of God, through the blood and intercession of our Lord Jesus Christ alone. Whatever your opinion of the church of Rome may be, which this is not a time to debate, you are in all these things a very good Protestant in your notions; but let me remind you, Sir, that we cannot be saved by the soundest notions, but must feel their power to change our hearts, and must act upon them. I do therefore again, that I may deliver your soul and my own, solemnly exhort you most earnestly to seek the renewing influences of Divine grace, to change your sinful heart, and to fit you for the presence of God.
>
> Pray that God may give you repentance unto life, not merely a grief for temporal ruin, and a dread of that future punishment which the worst of men must desire to escape, but a repentance arising from the love of God, attended with a filial ingenuous (or sincere) sorrow for the indignity and dishonour which your sins have offered to so excellent and so gracious a Being. Oh! while there is yet hope fly to the blood and the righteousness of Christ, and to the free grace of God in the Gospel which is manifested to the greatest of sinners, and shall be manifested in you, if you sincerely believe. I am glad I have seen no crucifix near you, but in a spiritual sense to lie at the foot of the cross,

and to look by faith unto him that died upon it, is the safest and best thing you can do. Pardon and grace, help and happiness must be sought here, not only by you, my friend, but by the most upright and virtuous man upon the earth, or he will appear a condemned sinner before God. God is my witness that this is my refuge: let it be yours, and we may have a happier meeting than we have known upon earth.[80]

Of course, in the eighteenth century as now, Baptism was a contentious issue. The catholic spirit of Philip Doddridge is no more clearly seen than in his relationship with the nearby College Lane (now College Street) Baptist Church. Although Doddridge strongly believed and taught Reformed covenant baptism (believers and their infants), several of his members at Castle Hill were Baptists by conviction. In Doddridge's day, the candidates from College Lane were baptised in the nearby River Nene (pronounced 'Nen'), just two hundred yards down the hill from Doddridge's chapel. Doddridge usually made his vestry available for the use of the Baptists. (It was from Castle Hill vestry that William Carey walked down to the banks of the Nene in 1783, to be baptised at the hands of the then minister of College Lane, the Revd John Ryland, Jnr).[81] On one such occasion, Doddridge – who believed a good biblical case could be made for either 'immersion' or 'sprinkling'[82] – was actually present at a baptismal service. When Mr Rodgers the Baptist pastor came out of the water, Doddridge took off his Geneva gown and placed it round his brother's shoulders. Such conduct was typical of Doddridge who was anxious that the essential unity of the Dissenters – Presbyterians, Independents and Baptists – should be visibly evident.

A final thought: one wonders if Mr Rodgers would have comfortably reciprocated the gesture by attending the baptism of an infant at Castle Hill? This much is certain, Doddridge's Reformed view is in no way opposed to believer's baptism, even if Baptists reject infant baptism. So, in the best biblical sense, Doddridge's position has a clear ecumenical advantage! Thus he endeavoured to unite 'truth and charity'.

8

The Great Awakening

In the early decades of the eighteenth century, the Christian church seemed to be in her death throes. The Dissenters, despite their virile puritan legacy, were hardly to be distinguished from the Church of England. Spiritual paralysis was everywhere evident. As we saw in Chapter 3, an air of spiritual unreality could be sensed as much in the Meeting House as in the Parish Church. In vain did both Churchmen and Dissenters attempt to stem the ever-advancing tide of spiritual and moral darkness.

Consistent with Philip Doddridge's concern for vital godliness was his concern for revival. After preaching a communion sermon on the text, 'But ye have profaned it, in that ye say, the table of the Lord is polluted; and the fruit thereof, even his meat, is contemptible' (Malachi 1: 12), Doddridge and his congregation sang his now famous communion hymn, the last verse of which reads:

> Revive Thy dying churches, Lord,
> And bid our drooping graces live;
> And more that energy afford,
> A Saviour's blood alone can give.[1]

In the year 1730, Doddridge published his concern for revival in a tract entitled, *Free Thoughts on the Most Probable Means of Reviving the Dissenting Interest*. His first published work, it was a reply to an anonymous attack on the Dissenters by Strickland Gough, an ex-Dissenter who had recently conformed. The title was very specific. It is doubtful whether anyone believed that the Established Church of the 1730s would ever experience revival. If preaching was generally cold amongst the Dissenters, it was little more than a tiresome exercise within the Church of England.

FREE THOUGHTS

ON THE

Moſt Probable MEANS of Reviving

THE

DISSENTING INTEREST.

Occaſion'd by the late

ENQUIRY

INTO THE

Cauſes of its DECAY.

Addreſs'd to the Author of that ENQUIRY.

By a MINISTER in the Country.

P. Doddridge, V. D. M.

——*Quem te DEUS eſſe*
Juſſit, & humanâ qua Parte locatus es in Re,
Diſce.———Perſ.

Interdum VULGUS rectum videt. Hor.

LONDON:
Printed for RICHARD HETT, at the *Bible* and
Crown in the *Poultry*, near *Cheapſide.*
MDCCXXX.

(Price Six-pence.)

Doddridge exposed this unhappy state of affairs as follows:

> And I cannot but believe, that if the established clergy, and the
> Dissenting ministers in general, were mutually to exchange their
> strain of preaching, and their manner of living but for one year,
> it would be the ruin of our cause, even though there should be
> no alteration in the constitution and discipline of the Church of
> England.[2]

Doddridge believed that preaching was the means that God
employed to awaken people's hearts and consciences – God-
anointed and God-honouring preaching. But what were the marks
of such preaching? What kind of preacher did Doddridge have in
mind? He was certain that 'he who would be generally agreeable to
Dissenters, must be an evangelical, an experimental, a plain and
affectionate preacher'.[3]

What would be the manner of the preacher? How should he
deliver his message? Doddridge had his answer. The pattern was to
be the Prince of preachers himself:

> Our Lord Jesus Christ is a most amiable and wonderful example
> of a plain, familiar, and popular preacher. When we come to
> peruse those divine discourses, which extorted a confession
> from His very enemies that He spake as never man spake, we
> find neither a long strain of abstract reasonings, nor a
> succession of laboured periods, adorn'd with an artificial
> exactness; but the most solid and important sense, delivered in
> an easy, natural way, illustrated by similes taken from the most
> common objects of life, and enforced with lively figures, and the
> strongest energy of expression; ...[4]

The remedy which Doddridge had the spirituality to see was the
very one that God Himself was about to apply in sovereign power.
Quite unknown to Doddridge, a movement was taking place in
Oxford, just forty miles from Northampton that was destined to
shake the world. A group of students at the University calling
themselves the 'Holy Club' were gathering regularly for prayer, the
reading of the Scriptures and self-examination. The leaders of the
group were John and Charles Wesley. In 1732, these 'Methodists'

as they were nicknamed, were joined by a young man from Gloucester named George Whitefield who was destined under God to be the leading preacher of the movement. In 1735, after a long period of painful conviction of sin and hungering after righteousness, George Whitefield found in Christ the salvation and peace that he longed for. In his *Journal*, the exultant Whitefield wrote:

> I found and felt in myself that I was delivered from the burden that had so heavily oppressed me. The spirit of mourning was taken from me, and I knew what it was truly to rejoice in God my Saviour; and for some time, could not avoid singing of Psalms wherever I was; ...[5]

Soon he was engaged in an astonishing itinerant ministry not only in England but also in America. The first of thirteen voyages across the Atlantic, Whitefield set sail from Deal on January 30, 1738, the very same day that John Wesley arrived back from Georgia disillusioned and heavy in spirit. Then in the month of May 1738 the Wesley brothers joined their Holy Club colleague in singing the song of the redeemed. The doctrines of the new birth, justification by faith in Christ alone and assurance of sins forgiven began to echo in the churches of London. Although they were ministers of the Church of England, pulpits were rapidly closed to these 'enthusiasts'. So they turned to the fields, the market places and the commons. The nation was being set alight for Christ.

Having recently read Whitefield's *Sermons and Journal*, Doddridge clearly rejoiced at this 'explosion' of gospel grace. Learning of the evangelist's return from America in November 1738, Doddridge wrote to him in mid-December 'Though personally unknown yet being cordially united to you in spirit'. Anticipating charges of 'enthusiasm', Doddridge continued (in this recently discovered letter): '[If] this be madness I do from my soul emulate those that are most transported with it as the happiest of mankind'. He longed to hear 'how our Moravian brethren fare, how the mission to the Negroes succeeds, and what prospect there may be of the Indians receiving the Gospel'.[6] Doddridge was 'refreshed and delighted' by Whitefield's rapid reply, revealing in a further letter of December 23 the impact of these developments. He declared that

> ... by a secret but powerful kind of magic it conveyed something of that spirit of piety and love that ever seems to burn in your own bosom and by which so many hearts have been warmed and raised ... My very soul is with you and I rejoice in all your success ... Oh what little things are those that divide us when compared with the great things that unite us.[7]

Looking forward to the continuation of Whitefield's *Journal*, Doddridge also asked him to pay his respects to John and Charles Wesley.

In the spring of 1739 George Whitefield was on a preaching tour in Hertfordshire, Buckinghamshire, Northamptonshire and Bedfordshire. On May 23 Philip Doddridge and George Whitefield met for the first time. Whitefield recorded in his *Journal*:

> Reached Northampton about five in the evening, and was most courteously received by Dr Doddridge, Master of the Academy there.[8]

That same evening, Whitefield preached on the racecourse (... on a common near the town, from the starting post...) to some three thousand hearers. In the morning, he preached at eight o 'clock to a 'much larger audience'.

A friendship rapidly developed between Doddridge and Whitefield which only death was to bring to an end. Whitefield's visit seemed to have had a quickening effect upon Doddridge; he himself seemed to be experiencing the refreshing breeze of the Holy Spirit. On his birthday, June 26, 1739, with his heart overflowing with praise to God for 'late mercies' not to be forgotten, Doddridge wrote in his *Diary* that he had received

> ... great assistances in the ministry; wonderful communications of light and love have been made to my soul, in some instances of secret meditation far beyond what I have commonly known.

We find him thanking God

George Whitefield
(1714 - 70)

... for adding to me the friendship of some excellent persons, among whom I must mention Mr Whitefield and Colonel Gardiner; and giving me to see the prosperity of the Gospel in some remarkable instances, both at home and abroad. These things impress my heart. Oh, may they melt it more and more![9]

Although Whitefield was the first of the Methodist leaders to make Doddridge's acquaintance, it was not in fact Doddridge's first contact with Methodism. Two years before, he met the Revd Benjamin Ingham, a former member of the Holy Club at Oxford. It is evident that Doddridge was not only deeply interested in the new movement. Indeed he was powerfully stimulated by it. His *Diary* records his first meeting with Ingham, on September 10, 1737:

I had this day the great pleasure of beginning an acquaintance with Mr. Ingham, a clergyman of the Church of England, in whom I think I saw as much of God as in any person that in the whole period of my life I have ever known. He was one of those who went over to Georgia to propagate the Gospel there ... He told me also that God was beginning His work not only at Oxford, where it was advanced, but likewise in many other parts; and indeed expressed such a sense of divine things in his own heart, such dependence upon the Spirit, such deep and experimental religion, that it was almost unparalleled. ... I must say, I hardly know any conversation or any occurrence, that has brought my soul nearer to God, or has ever made me fit for my everlasting rest.[10]

Ingham had accompanied the Wesley brothers on their mission to Georgia in 1735, but he returned to England early in 1737. Whitefield soon heard of Ingham's home-coming, describing his impressions of his Holy Club colleague in the same enthusiastic manner in which Doddridge had recorded his:

I had the pleasure of seeing my dear friend, Mr. Ingham, lately returned from Georgia; and perceiving him as I thought remarkably grown in grace, I longed still more to be sent to the same school, hoping to catch some of that holy flame with which his soul was fired.[11]

It is hardly surprising that men like Doddridge and Whitefield should be drawn together. Indeed, it was predictable. However, it must be realised that the friendship that developed between Anglican Methodist Mr Whitefield and Dissenting Tutor Dr Doddridge became a unique source of embarrassment. Relations between the established church and the dissenting bodies had been, generally speaking, icy. In the early stages of the revival, the heirs of the Puritans resisted co-operation with the new Evangelicals. Methodism was viewed with much suspicion by the nonconformist leaders. However, it was Philip Doddridge who was responsible - more than any other Nonconformist – for erecting a bridge between the old evangelicalism and the new. With a close similarity in theological convictions and an experimental emphasis, the association between Doddridge and Whitefield had an almost symbolic significance. It was the meeting of two traditions. The grandson of the Puritans had met the father of the Evangelicals.

The friendship between these servants of the Lord became a more public matter. On July 28, 1743, Doddridge took part in one of Whitefield's services at Moorfields. Heavy censure was inevitable. The eminent Dr Isaac Watts took the matter in hand, writing thus to Doddridge:

> I am sorry that since your departure I have had many questions asked me about your preaching or praying at the Tabernacle, and of sinking the character of a minister, and especially of a tutor among the Dissenters, so low thereby ...[11]

The storm became a hurricane when, in October of the same year, Whitefield preached for Doddridge at Castle Hill, Northampton. On this occasion, the windows behind the pulpit were removed to allow the great concourse of people to hear. Even Doddridge's close friend John Barker expressed his fears for Doddridge's reputation in a letter written in November:

> I was troubled to hear of the late intercourse that happened between you and Mr Whitefield, the consequence of which, with respect to the Church, it is easy to foresee ...[13]

The situation was further aggravated when some dissenting ministers in the west of England, formerly students of Doddridge, had openly received both Whitefield and Wesley. Even this rebounded on poor Doddridge. Nathaniel Neal, son of Daniel Neal the historian of the Puritans, remonstrated with Doddridge after certain complaints about these former students had reached London:

> ... These letters likewise mention that some ministers there, who were your pupils, have given them countenance; and you can hardly conceive the disrespect this has occasioned several ministers and other persons in town to speak of you with ...[14]

These reactions to Methodism are a sad comment on the staid respectability of eighteenth-century Dissent. They were over-sensitive about their reputation. They could not imagine that the Holy Spirit might bless the church of their persecutors. So was God confined to the dissenting denominations? Alas, the descendants of the noble and courageous men victimised with persecution in the years following 1662 had lost their glory and their vision. They forgot that God was sovereign. However, Doddridge thought differently. Criticised by his fellow Dissenters, he was suffering for 'nonconformity' all over again!

It is worthwhile pausing to consider who these ministers were who were supporting the Methodists, since it provides further evidence of the spiritual bond existing between Doddridge and Whitefield. Indeed, we've met them before! They were Risdon Darracott of Wellington in Somerset and Benjamin Fawcett of Taunton in the same county. As we have seen, Doddridge always had a special regard for these two men. Darracott's ministry at Wellington had almost as profound an effect on the people there as Baxter's ministry had at Kidderminster in the previous century. We have already noted that Whitefield called Darracott the 'star of the west'. Fawcett later moved to Kidderminster where he exercised a powerful ministry like Baxter before him. In addition, he edited the 1758 edition of Baxter's *Saints' Everlasting Rest*. The tender love that Doddridge bore towards his former pupils is also witnessed in Whitefield. In a letter he wrote:

> On Saturday last, when I came to Wellington, the Revd Mr Darracott persuaded me to stay there, because the country

John Wesley
(1703 - 91)

people had come from all quarters several times to hear me and had been disappointed. ... The Revd Mr Fawcett, formerly pupil to Dr Doddridge, came there and stayed all night. The Blessed Jesus gave us much freedom in conversation ...[15]

Replying to Nathaniel Neal, Doddridge was not deterred by the pressure of criticism. Since some of his other students had disappointed him, he made clear his position with respect to Darracott and Fawcett:

I am sure I see no danger that any of my pupils will prove Methodists: I wish many of them may not run into the contrary extreme.[16]

Although sensitive Doddridge was doubtless disturbed by the reaction of his dissenting critics, he was not to be moved. He viewed Whitefield as a 'flaming servant of Jesus Christ' and he was prepared to stand by him. Shortly after this, Doddridge was dining with Lady Huntingdon and others when the conversation turned to the remarkable religious movements of the day. With glowing face and ardent tone, Doddridge gave his view of the 'wonderful works of God':

Such are the fruits that will follow the faithful proclamation of Divine mercy. The Lord our God will crown His message with success, and give it an abundant entrance into the hearts of men. It is a blessing that such men have been raised up.[17]

The 'liberalism' of which Doddridge was accused by the sectarian ultra-orthodoxy of his day was the very generous and 'large-hearted' disposition that enabled him to rejoice in the labours of those beyond his denominational tradition.

It must be said that there were some just grounds for concern over the activities of the early Methodists. There were many things which maturing thought and experience lamented in retrospect. On August 22, 1748, Whitefield wrote to Doddridge asking him to revise the pages of his *Journal* with a view to a further edition. Doddridge accepted the responsibility, and a truer act of friendship could hardly have been shown. Doddridge, in brotherly love, gave

Whitefield some faithful admonitions regarding the evangelist's irregularities, which brought forth a reply characteristic of Whitefield:

> Alas! Alas! How can I be too severe against myself, who, Peter-like, have cut off so many ears, and by imprudence mixed with my zeal, have dishonoured the cause of Jesus. ... Assure yourself, dear sir, everything I print shall be revised.[18]

James Paterson Gledstone speaks of this friendship between God's servants, when he writes that 'two sentences, in which the devout, tender, and humble spirit of Doddridge expresses itself are, when taken in connection with many similar expressions of Whitefield, a sufficient explanation of the firm union between these distinguished Christians. "I am one of the least of God's children," said Doddridge, "and yet a child; and that is my daily joy. Indeed, I feel my love to Him increase; I struggle forwards towards Him; and look at Him, as it were, sometimes with tears of love, when, in the midst of the hurries of life, I cannot speak to Him otherwise than by an ejaculation."'[19] Doddridge's spiritual vitality, so uncharacteristic of the generality of his dissenting brethren, found him ready acceptance with the men of the revival. Another of the Methodists, the Revd Samuel Walker of Truro, when writing to Darracott, said by way of confession:

> I have not your warm heart. Doddridge was not my tutor. Dear man! I love him more since I have known you.[20]

Doddridge did not meet John Wesley until 1745. Their relationship was always cordial. His *Journal* entry for September 9 reads:

> I left London, and the next morning called on Dr Doddridge, at Northampton. It was about the hour when he was accustomed to expound a portion of Scripture to the young gentlemen under his care. He desired me to take his place.[21]

As well as seeking help in the guidance of his lay preachers' reading, Wesley was to express his debt to Doddridge in the preface to his *Notes on the New Testament*: 'I am indebted for some useful observations to ... the *Family Expositor* of the late pious and learned Dr Doddridge.[22] We may ask, what of John's brother Charles? Did the two hymn writers ever meet? Yes, according to Charles Wesley's *Journal*:

> Tuesday August 15 [1749]. We had the satisfaction of two hours conference at Mr Watkins with that loving, mild, judicious Christian, Dr Doddridge.[23]

Doddridge was not disposed to aggravate the doctrinal differences that, for a while, rendered the relations between Whitefield and the Wesleys unhappy. As we have seen, Mercy drew her husband's attention to the impact of Wesley's *Free Grace* sermon in London but Doddridge did not become personally involved in the controversy. That said, it seems that his relationship with Whitefield was always special. Despite holding an ultra-Calvinist interpretation of Anglican 'moderate Calvinism', evangelistic 'free offer' Whitefield was welcomed by 'Baxterian Calvinist' Doddridge. They enjoyed fellowship in the doctrines of free and sovereign grace. The nature of their friendship, in which Lady Huntingdon also shared, is seen in Whitefield's letter of May 19, 1750 to Doddridge:

> Your kind letter found me happy at our good Lady Huntingdon's, whose path shines brighter and brighter until the perfect day. Gladly shall I call upon you again at Northampton, if the Lord spares my life; and in the meanwhile shall not fail to pray that the work of our common Lord may more and more prosper in your hands. I thank you a thousand times for your kindness to the chief of sinners, and assure you, reverend Sir, that the affection is reciprocal. Good Lady Huntingdon greatly esteems you.[24]

There was something of the fervour of early Methodism in the preaching of Philip Doddridge. Whilst his reputation has not been that of a preacher in the class of effectiveness of Whitefield, a comparison between the two men is not out of place. In his lectures on preaching, Doddridge told his students what true preaching is:

Charles Wesley
(1707 - 88)

Let it be affectionate. Feel all you say. If a tear will fall, do not restrain it, but it should never be forced. 'Nothing is more indecent than a dead preacher, speaking to dead hearers the living truths of the living God' (BAXTER).[25]

Noticing Doddridge's reference to Baxter, we have already seen the nature of Baxter's influence over Doddridge. Whitefield evidently shared this admiration for the great Puritan, judging by one of his letters in which he describes a visit to Kidderminster:

I was greatly refreshed to find what a savour of good Mr Baxter's doctrine, works and discipline remained to this day.[26]

Doddridge therefore shared the Methodist concern for evangelism. Like Whitefield, the doctrine of election did not deaden Doddridge's desire for the salvation for souls. In 1748, Doddridge published another sermon entitled, *Christ's Invitation to Thirsty Souls*, in which we see the passionate heart of a faithful evangelist:

I aim, in my present discourse, not so much in enlightening the understanding in the evidence of a doctrine so universally allowed amongst all professing Christians; as at affecting your heart, and my own, with a sense of what, even while we acknowledge, we are all so prone to forget ... Do you thirst for the pardon of sin? ... Do you thirst for the favour of God? ... Do you thirst for the communications of the Spirit? The Lord Jesus Christ can abundantly relieve you ... Do you thirst for the joys and glories of the heavenly world? The Lord Jesus Christ is able to relieve you. ... I know there is a great deal of difference between the common operations of the Spirit on the minds of those who continue obstinate and impenitent, and those special influences by which he sweetly but powerfully subdues the hearts of those who are chosen in Christ Jesus before the foundation of the world. Yet I am persuaded, that none to whom the Gospel comes are utterly neglected by that sacred agent. ... Behold then the tears of a Redeemer over perishing souls, and judge by them of the compassions of His heart. ... Surely nothing can be more melting, than such tears, falling from such eyes, and in such circumstances. And if our Lord could not give up the impenitent sinners of Jerusalem without weeping over them, surely He will not despise the humble and penitent soul, who is, perhaps with tears, seeking His favour, and flying to his grace as his only refuge. ...

The tears of our blessed Redeemer must needs be convincing and affecting, if the mind be not sunk into an almost incredible stupidity; but his blood is still more so. View him, my brethren, not only in the previous scenes of his abasement, his descent from heaven, and his abode on earth; but view him on mount Calvary, extended on the cross, torn with thorns, wounded with nails, pierced with a spear; and then say, whether there be not a voice in each of these sacred wounds, which loudly proclaims the tenderness of his heart, and demonstrates, beyond all possibility of dispute or suspicion, his readiness to relieve the distressed soul, that cries to him for the blessings of the gospel. He died to purchase them, not for himself, but for us; and can it be thought he will be unwilling to bestow them? We may well conclude that he loved us, since he shed his blood to wash us from our sins (Rev. 1: 5): For greater love hath no man than this, that a man lay down his life for his friends (Jn. 15: 13); but he hath commended his love toward us, hath set it off by this illustrious and surprising circumstance, that while we were strangers and enemies he hath died for us. (Rom. 5: 8).

I hope, through grace, there are some such among you ... who are now thirsting for the blessings of the Gospel. ... To you my friends, I would briefly say ... Go directly, and plead the case with Him ... for that soul will surely be relieved, and God in Christ be glorified and exalted ...[27]

When Whitefield obtained and read a copy of this sermon, he wrote to Doddridge in a letter already referred to:

> ... dear Sir, I must thank you for your sermon. It contains the very life of preaching, I mean sweet invitations to close with Christ. I do not wonder you are dubbed a Methodist on account of it ...[28]

It is interesting to note that although this sermon was published in 1748, it was first preached at Northampton in 1729 (see p. 45), six years before Whitefield's conversion and nine before John Wesley's. Doddridge wrote of the occasion that 'something of a peculiar blessing seemed to attend the discourse, when delivered from the pulpit; and that to such a degree, as I do not know to have been equalled by any other sermon I ever preached'.[29] Here then was Methodism at Northampton, at a time when Oxford Methodism was in its infancy. Thus Professor Alan Everitt has written: 'If any event can be regarded as beginning the Evangelical Movement it is probably the appointment of the Independent Philip Doddridge to Castle Hill Chapel in 1729'.[30]

Furthermore, while Oxford Methodism was still 'legal' (or 'non-evangelical'), Doddridge was preaching a [Baxterian] 'Calvinistic Methodism' similar in character to the evangelistic theology of Whitefield. The sermon style of the two preachers was also sufficiently similar for one of Doddridge's to pass as one of Whitefield's! When a selection of the latter's sermons was published, it included one entitled, *The Care of the Soul*.[31] In fact, it was preached by Philip Doddridge on June 22, 1735 at Maidwell in Northamptonshire![32] If *Christ's Invitation to Thirsty Souls* reveals something of the fervent evangelicalism of Philip Doddridge, the circumstances of its publication tells us a little more of his 'catholicity'. It was published 'chiefly for the benefit of the poor, at the earnest request of a gentleman of the Established Church of England'. The gentleman in question was the Revd James Hervey, Rector of Weston Favell, to whom the sermon is dedicated. The village of Weston Favell is about a mile to the east of Northampton and now within the borough boundary. By virtue of the close proximity of their ministries, Hervey and Doddridge had frequent occasions for fellowship. Hervey had been a member of the Holy Club at Oxford but he was converted somewhat later than his better known fellow-Methodists. After spending some time in Devon, he became Rector of Weston Favell in 1743. Unlike Whitefield and the Wesleys, Hervey's ministry was restricted in the main to his parish. He is the author of *Meditations among the Tombs* and *Theron and Aspasio*, both of which were very popular at one time. These and other works qualified Hervey as a seminal influence in the growth of the 'evangelical party' in the Church of England, associated later with men like John Newton, Charles Simeon and J. C. Ryle. Hervey died at Weston Favell in 1758.[33]

Doddridge was ever anxious to demonstrate the true unity of God's people despite their different denominational traditions. The

THE
CARE of the SOUL

Urged as the

ONE THING NEEDFUL.

A

SERMON

PREACH'D

JUNE 22, 1735.

By P. DODDRIDGE, D.D.

Ὁ βαλόμενος ἀνθρώπε ἐπιμελεῖθαι τῆς ψυχῆς ἐπιμελείθω
τῆς λογικῆς.   Simplic.

The THIRD EDITION.

LONDON:

Printed for RICHARD HETT, at the *Bible* and
Crown in the *Poultry.* 1740.

[Price Four-Pence.]

mutual affection between Doddridge and Whitefield was also witnessed between Doddridge and Hervey. In the dedication to *Christ's Invitation*, Doddridge gives a spirited though courteous defence of his nonconformity, but affirms with equal zeal, the unity in truth and love that he enjoyed with Hervey:

> ... I am persuaded, you will on the whole forgive the desire I had, that all, to whom this little piece may come, should know, what most who are personally acquainted with us both already know, that I most highly esteem you, and most affectionately love you; and that no diversity in our professions and forms could prevent our entering into the strictest bonds of friendship, or make me unwilling most openly to profess it, and to perpetuate the memory of it, while this shall remain.[34]

In 1754, three years after Doddridge's death, Hervey clearly remembered his brother in Christ with esteem and affection. In a letter to a friend he mentions the generosity of another:

> He was so obliging, as to present me with the picture of the late worthy Dr Doddridge. I hope, when I view it, I shall be reminded of the inscription of Sennacherib's statue, 'Whoever looks on me, let him worship God'. Or rather, that it will address me with the Apostle's admonition, 'Be ye not slothful, but followers of them, who through faith and patience inherit the promises'.[35]

With the advent of the Methodist revival, attention became focused on the doctrine and work of the Holy Spirit. Doddridge made plain his view of the Holy Spirit's work in conversion in his *Practical Discourses on Regeneration*.[36] As regards what is known today as the 'Baptism in the Holy Spirit', Doddridge believed a distinction was to be drawn between this and the 'new birth'. Thus in the *Family Expositor*, he comments on the outpouring of the Holy Spirit at Pentecost:

> Thus did the blessed Jesus accomplish what had been foretold concerning him (Matthew 3:11), that he should baptize his disciples with the Holy Ghost and with fire. And surely the sacred flame did not only illuminate their minds with celestial

brightness, but did also cause their whole hearts to glow with love to God and zeal for his gospel. To this purpose, may he still be imparted to us, whether we hold public or private stations in the church; and may our regards to him be ever most dutifully maintained. Especially may he be poured out upon the ministers of it, to direct them how they should speak the wonderful things of God; and may their hearers, under his gracious energy, gladly receive the word *(Improvement on Acts 2:1-21)*.[37]

Doddridge chiefly understood the pentecostal blessing in terms of assurance. Thus he viewed the 'sealing' or 'witness' of the Holy Spirit in Romans 8: 16 as 'some inward impression of God's Spirit upon the believer's mind, assuring them that they are Christians indeed'.[38] For this blessing Doddridge urges the doubting believer to 'Plead hard ... at the throne of grace. Lay hold on God by faith; and say, "Lord, I will not let Thee go till Thou bless me."'[39] However, Doddridge also distinguished between the *baptism* of the Spirit and the extraordinary 'revelatory' *gifts* of the Spirit (tongues, prophecy and word of wisdom). Now that the Canon of Scripture was complete, the latter were not necessary. He was at one with the Reformers, the Puritans, the Methodists and Jonathan Edwards when he said that:

> Many things may be said of the *charismata*, or the extraordinary gifts and powers of the Apostles and primitive (i.e. early) Christians, which were so peculiar to that age, that we have no personal concern in them at all.[35]

As Doddridge was fully concerned to embrace the New Testament teaching on Christian experience, he also responded to the missionary challenge of the 'Great Commission' (Matt. 28: 18-20). It has to be said that missionary enterprise was slow to appear on the agenda of Protestants following the Reformation. Even if Richard Baxter's enthusiastic support for John Eliot's mission to the American Indians was rare in the seventeenth century,[41] Doddridge's similar passion for mission was not widespread in the early eighteenth century. With knowledge of the revival in New England (through reading Jonathan Edwards' *Narrative of Surprising Conversions*) and the success of David Brainerd among the Indians

The EVIL *and* DANGER
of Neglecting the Souls of Men,

plainly and ſeriouſly repreſented

IN A

SERMON

Preach'd at

A MEETING of MINISTERS

At *Kettering* in *Northamptonſhire,*
October 15, 1741.

[Price Six Pence.]

(i)

TO THE

ASSOCIATED

Proteſtant Diſſenting Miniſters,

IN THE

COUNTIES of *Norfolk* and *Suffolk,*

Particularly

THOSE with whom the AUTHOR had an Interview at *Denton, June* the 30th, 1741.

GENTLEMEN,

My Reverend FATHERS and BRETHREN, and much eſteemed FRIENDS,

*T*HE *condeſcending Reſpeƈt, and endeared Affeƈtion, with which you were pleaſed to receive me, in my late Viſit to your Parts, and the very great Satiſfaƈtion which I found in your Company at* Denton, *and elſewhere, have left a very delightful Memorial on my Heart, and have impreſſed thoſe unfeigned Sentiments of Gratitude and Eſteem, which it would be painful to ſuppreſs. Moſt gladly therefore do I take this Method, in a few Words, publickly to avow them : And I ſincerely congratulate the happy* Societies, *reſpeƈtively under your* Care, *who ſtatedly enjoy the Benefit of thoſe valuable Labours,* both serving to quicken Doddridge's zeal, he was to have a prophetic role in world mission besides a pioneering role in revival.

Doddridge outlined his concerns for revival at an assembly of 'The Associated Protestant Dissenting Ministers in the Counties of Norfolk and Suffolk' held at Denton, Norfolk in June 1741. By all accounts, this was an extraordinary occasion. Doddridge's friend Richard Frost of Great Yarmouth wrote:

> A remarkable day indeed, when the presence of God filled our assembly; and not myself only, but many others have with pleasure owned it was one of the best days of our lives. Though the season was hot, the auditory very much crowded, and between four and five hours spent in public worship, none thought the hours tedious and wished for a dismission.[42]

Likewise Doddridge wrote to Mercy:

> We spent Tuesday [June 30] at Denton & it was one of the most delightful Days of my whole life. Seventeen Ministers were there of whom 8 officiated indeed excellently well. We held a Kind of Council afterward concerning the Methods to be taken for the Revival of Religion & I hope I have set them on Work to some good purpose.[43]

One scheme led to another. So, in October 1741, Doddridge preached a remarkable sermon at Kettering in Northamptonshire during another meeting of ministers. It was eventually published with the title *The Evil and Danger of Neglecting the Souls of Men*. John Stoughton, Doddridge's third biographer, is of the opinion that this work is worthy of a place alongside Baxter's *Reformed Pastor*, an 'incomparable treatise' according to Doddridge and so much admired by him.[44] Indeed, both works continue to command the attention of the twenty-first century Church. Time taken in studying them today would be well spent.

When Doddridge published his Kettering sermon in 1742, he dedicated it to his brethren in Norfolk and Suffolk. The dedication included the proposals he advanced at Denton the previous June *plus* supplementary ones agreed at Kettering and among his own Northampton congregation. Concerned with 'the propagation of the kingdom of Christ in the world', it was proposed that 'petitions' be 'put up' to 'the throne of grace' for 'the advancement of the gospel in the world, and for the success of all the faithful servants of Christ, who are engaged in the work of it, especially among the heathen nations'.[45]

Here are suggestions, almost identical to those advanced by William Carey fifty years later, but made twenty years before Carey was born (1761)! It is quite possible that since Carey took Doddridge's *Family Expositor* with him to India, that he might have read and been stimulated by this moving sermon and set of proposals advanced by Doddridge. Is it possible that he discovered a copy in the Castle Hill vestry at the time of his baptism in Northampton in 1783? Dr Ernest Payne seems to think so:

> Had some stray copy of Doddridge's sermon on *The Evil and Danger of Neglecting the Souls of Men* come into Carey's hands? Or had its substance been mediated to him in some way? We do not know. But it is surely no coincidence that it was in Northamptonshire [Carey came from Paulersbury], in the Doddridge country and so nearly in the Doddridge manner, that the first of modern missionary societies [the Particular Baptist Mission] had its birth.[46]

Doddridge had an almost mystical spirituality. He declared that 'Religion is with me an inward thing'.[47] But although he believed the issues of eternity to be infinitely more important that those of time, he was not slow in seeking to meet the temporal needs of men. As with the early Methodists, so Doddridge gave expression to an all-embracing Christianity. Unlike the secularised 'social gospel' mentality of later generations of nonconformists, Doddridge's love to men was a direct consequence of his knowledge of the love of God. He believed that the destinies of men were wrought only in terms of the Gospel, and not without it.

Thus, Doddridge had a Christ-centred philanthropic concern. As Whitefield and the Wesleys visited the prisoners at Oxford, so Doddridge acquainted himself with the felons at Northampton. Nowhere is this more perfectly illustrated than in the 'Connell Affair' mentioned in the previous chapter. When Bryan Connell was found guilty of murdering a man at Weedon, near Northampton.

Compaſſion to the Sɪᴄᴋ recommended and urged,

Iɴ A

S E R M O N

Pʀᴇᴀᴄʜᴇᴅ ᴀᴛ

N O R T H A M P T O N,

Sᴇᴘᴛᴇᴍʙᴇʀ 4, 1743.

In Favour of a Deſign then opening to
erect a Cᴏᴜɴᴛʏ Iɴғɪʀᴍᴀʀʏ there
for the Relief of the Poor *Sick* and
Lame.

Publiſhed at the Requeſt of ſeveral who heard it.

By P. D O D D R I D G E, *D. D.*

Homines ad Deum nullâ Re propius accedunt, quam
Salutem *Hominibus dando.* Cic. pro Lig. *ad fin.*

L O N D O N:

Printed for M. Fᴇɴɴᴇʀ, at the *Turk's Head* in
Gracechurch-ſtreet; and W. Dɪᴄᴇʏ, at *North-*
ampton. Mᴅᴄᴄxʟɪɪɪ.

[Price Six-pence.]

THE

CASE

Of RECEIVING the

SMALL-POX

BY

INOCULATION,

Impartially confidered, and efpecially
in a Religious View.

Written in the Year M.DCC.XXV.

By the late

Rev^d. Mr. DAVID SOME,

of *Harborough:*

And now publifhed from the Original Manufcript,

By P. DODDRIDGE, *D. D.*

*I will afk you one Thing, Is it lawful to fave Life, or to
deftroy it ?* Luke vi. 9.

LONDON:

Printed for JAMES BUCKLAND, *in* Pater-nofter Row; *and*
JAMES WAUGH, *in* Lombard-Street. M.DCC.L.

Doddridge befriended the poor man who pleaded innocence, and Doddridge - after a thorough investigation of the facts - believed that he was not guilty. Now Connell was an Irish Roman Catholic, and Doddridge's concern for him even led many to suggest that the Reformed pastor was 'in heart an Irish papist'! Despite an appeal, Connell was executed on April 3, 1741. When the day came, the poor wretch was led along Sheep Street, Northampton, to the place of execution. He asked permission to stop at Dr Doddridge's door. Doddridge the gracious benefactor came out to the man who promptly fell upon his knees to pray for the Doctor. In his reflections on this case, it is uncertain whether Connell was converted. Doddridge lamented: 'I did not see the success that I had desired, and which I had sought of God with an importunity of prayer which he himself seemed to have put into my heart, and which I have seldom felt on any other such occasion .[48] Whatever else we learn from this incident, it tells us a lot about Doddridge's Christian compassion.

Few inhabitants of modern Northampton realise that the present General Hospital originated as the County Infirmary, founded as a direct result of schemes proposed by Doddridge and his friend, Dr Stonhouse, who was converted under Doddridge's ministry. Doddridge's eloquent compassion is evident in his sermon *Compassion to the Sick recommended and urged* (1743).[49] He was clearly ahead of his time. Support was sadly slow, not least among some of the jealously disposed Anglican clergy. Thus Doddridge lamented:

> The clergy are strangely backward on the occasion & I fear my Sermon has rather alienated [than] conciliated their regard. For among some men even Charity grows odious when recommended by a Dissenter.[50]

Despite such sourness, the project proved successful. The Bishops of Worcester and Oxford congratulated Doddridge who, in turn, was encouraged that the Northampton venture inspired similar institutions in these cities. Doddridge also championed the cause of inoculation against smallpox, in days when religiously minded people had scruples about it. So in 1750 he published *The*

Case of Receiving the Small-Pox by Inoculation, originally written by his colleague David Some of Market Harborough in 1725.[51] If others had doubts, the text on the title page was decisive for Doddridge: 'I will ask you one thing, is it lawful to save life, or to destroy it' (Luke 6: 9). Always concerned for young people, Doddridge was also responsible for founding a charity school in Northampton for the education of twenty boys. Besides money, books, Bibles and catechisms, the boys were also provided with clothes. Doddridge also wished to admit girls to the school but no information exists about such a development.[52]

If Doddridge's Christianity implied a Christian philanthropy, it also implied a Christian political conscience. He never forgot to 'render unto Caesar the things that are Caesar's' in the process of 'rendering unto God the things that are God's' (Matthew 22: 21). If eighteenth-century England experienced revival, it also had a taste of revolution in the 1745 rebellion. Doddridge the scholarly saint was also the public servant. Indeed, he was no pietistic pacifist. Besides dedicating the *Family Expositor* to the Princess of Wales, his loyalty to the House of Hanover is seen in his active involvement in raising a military force in and around Northampton to oppose the ambitious schemes of the Stuart pretender 'Bonnie Prince Charlie'. In fact it was Doddridge who urged the Earl of Halifax to initiate measures to defend the country. He sent printed circulars by special messengers to all the Dissenting ministers in the county. Within a short time, Halifax and Doddridge raised a force of more than eight hundred men including volunteers from Castle Hill church. By October 1745, Northampton became a centre of military activity. Troops were exercised daily and rations, ammunition and other war materials were stockpiled and distributed. That year, the traditional celebrations of November 5 assumed an added importance as bonfires and church bells drew attention to the growing danger. Besides the dignity of a civic service at All Saints, an effigy of the Pretender was burned outside Doddridge's academy. The *Northampton Mercury* reported that 'the Doctor's house was finely illuminated, the candles, by their position, forming these words, KING GEORGE, NO PRETENDER; there were also sky rockets, and other fireworks'.[53]

The Battle of Prestonpans near Edinburgh (September 21, 1745) was the first major military engagement in the Pretender's march south. In this battle the Royal troops were defeated. But when the invader had reached Derby having met little resistance on the way, the knowledge of troops at Northampton was sufficiently menacing for him to entirely abolish his plans and retreat. In the following February, Doddridge preached two important sermons 'on the occasion of the precipitate Flight of the Rebels from Stirling'. The 'substance' of these was published as *Deliverance out of the Hands of our Enemies, urged as a motive to Obedience* (1746).[54] Thus Doddridge's prayers and public labours contributed no small part to the maintenance of national security and to the eventual collapse of the Pretender's hopes at the Battle of Culloden in 1746. Charles Stanford wrote that 'we claim for [Doddridge] the honour of being the first Englishman in a private station who took action, and roused his countrymen to the like, in defending the threatened throne and liberties of our land'.[55] Notwithstanding his concern to defend the liberties of Englishmen, Doddridge was grieved at the carnage of Culloden. Concerned also for the spiritual and moral welfare of the troops, he published at his own expense on the first anniversary of the battle *A Friendly Letter to the Private Soldiers in a Regiment of Foot, one of those engaged in the important and Glorious Battle of Culloden* (1747).[56]

One of Doddridge's closest friends was the famous Scottish cavalry officer Colonel Gardiner who was tragically killed at the Battle of Prestonpans. Doddridge deeply lamented his friend's death and, in 1747, published *Some Remarkable Passages in the Life of the Honourable Colonel James Gardiner*.[57] This work was widely acclaimed, not least on account of the remarkable circumstances of the Colonel's conversion. Not without its critics, the book was read in instalments by some ministers to their congregations at weeknight meetings. It was also translated into Dutch.

Undoubtedly, Doddridge's most enduring literary contribution to the Evangelical Revival, besides the hymns, was his *Rise and Progress of Religion in the Soul* published in 1745.[58] The work went through many editions and was translated into French, German, Dutch, Danish, Welsh, Gaelic, Tamil and Syriac. By 1895, no less than forty-eight English editions had appeared, and an American reprint was published as recently as 1977. It was hailed

The Chriſtian Warrior animated and crowned :

A

SERMON

Occaſioned by the

HEROICK DEATH

Of the Honourable

Col. James Gardiner,

Who was SLAIN in the

BATTLE at *Preſton-Pans,*

September 21. 1745.

Preached at *NORTHAMPTON,*

October 13.

By *P. DODDRIDGE,* D. D.

——— *Ille* Timorum
Maximus *haud urget Lethi Metus :* ———
——— *Ignavum* REDITURÆ *parcere Vitæ.*
LUCAN.

LONDON:

Printed and Sold by J. WAUGH, at the *Turk's Head* in *Gracechurch-Street.* MDCCXLV.

OORSPRONG
EN
VOORTGANG
VAN WAARE
GODSDIENSTIGHEID
IN
'sMENSCHEN ZIELE,

Aangewezen en opgeheldert, in eenige ernftige
en zedelyke Aanfpraaken, gefchikt naar elks
bizonderen aart en omftandigheden:

Met Godvrugtige
OVERDENKINGEN en GEBEDEN.
DOOR
P. DODDRIDGE,
*Doctor in de H. Godgeleerdheid en Gereformeert Predikant
te Northampton.*

UIT HET ENGELS VERTAALT.

Verrykt met een AANPRYZINGS Brief van den Ectw. Heere
WILHELMUS PEIFFERS,
PREDIKANT TE AMSTERDAM.

TE AMSTERDAM,
By van Gerrevink, Wor, Vieroot, Tirion,
Kuyper, Loveringh, Borstius en van Eyl.
MDCCXLVII.

THE
RISE and PROGRESS
O F
RELIGION in the SOUL:

ILLUSTRATED

In a COURSE of SERIOUS and PRACTICAL ADDRESSES,

Suited to PERSONS of every CHARACTER
and CIRCUMSTANCE:

WITH

A Devout MEDITATION or PRAYER added
to each CHAPTER.

By P. DODDRIDGE, *D. D.*

Quâ feret hic Greſſum, Fontes dabit arida Vallis,
Inque cavas Foſſas depluet Agmen Aquæ:
Inſtaurabit Iter Vires; et Numinis Ora
Viſurus Solymæ figet in Æde Pedem.
Johnſt. Pſal. lxxxiv. 5, 6.

Teſtifying——Repentance toward GOD, *and Faith*
toward our Lord Jeſus Chriſt. Acts xx. 21.
Whom we preach, warning every Man, and teaching
every Man in all Wiſdom: that we may preſent every
Man perfect in Chriſt Jeſus. Col. i. 28.

The SIXTH EDITION.

LONDON:
Printed and Sold by J. WAUGH, at the *Turk's Head* in
Lombard Street. M DCC L.

as one of the finest works of its kind ever published and it also marked the end of an era. The *Rise and Progress* can claim to be the last work of its kind, for in its characteristically puritan exposition of Christian experience, it was the final example of that type of 'practical' work inaugurated by Richard Sibbes in his *Bruised Reed* and *Soul's Conflict*, both published in the 1630s. The *Rise and Progress* marks a transition from the literature of the Puritans to the literature of the Evangelicals. In Doddridge, both Puritan and Evangelical, we see the essential one-ness of the two traditions. In the *Rise and Progress* we see the richness of seventeenth-century Puritanism made serviceable to the needs of the eighteenth-century Evangelical. That said, though the language is somewhat dated, twenty-first century readers would derive much spiritual benefit from the book.

It was Dr Isaac Watts who first suggested that Doddridge should write the *Rise and Progress*. The actual plan for the book was also Watts' but owing to ill health, the younger Doddridge was asked to undertake the work.[59] This fact also illustrates Watts' high regard for Doddridge. In the recommendatory letter to David Longueville in Amsterdam (translated and used in Dutch translations of Doddridge's works), Watts wrote:

> Since I am now advanced in age, beyond my seventieth year, if there were any man, to whom Providence would permit me to commit a second part of my life and usefulness in the Church of Christ, Dr Doddridge should be the man.[60]

Naturally, the *Rise and Progress* was dedicated to Dr Watts. The book was an instant success. Even the Laudian Professor of Arabic at Oxford Thomas Hunt and his wife expressed gratitude for it. Dr Hunt's assessment explains the secret of the book's success:

> Your excellent piece on the *Rise and Progress of Religion in the Soul* [is] a performance which cannot fail of doing much good in the world, as it is judiciously contrived to engage the attention and improve the minds of all sorts of readers; being so plain as to be intelligible to the lowest understanding, at the same time that it is so elegant as to gratify the highest.[61]

Jonathan Edwards
(1703 - 58)

Predictably, both Dissenters and Methodists received the work with enthusiasm. Richard Pearsall of Warminster in Wiltshire wrote to Doddridge:

> I thank you, among many, for your late book, *The Rise and Progress of Religion, &*. We think you have in this performance exceeded yourself. May Divine grace set in with it to the salvation of many souls. I have not known any book, published of late years, that obtains so universally among Christians of various denominations and different tastes in some other things.[62]

The work was even viewed as an ideal model for preaching, both with regard to its orthodoxy and its method. Pearsall wrote again to Doddridge, this time to seek his help in obtaining a minister for a nearby cause. Pearsall supplied the following specification:

> The minister that will be suitable must be not only a serious man, but a thorough Calvinist and one that will preach upon the plan that you have laid down in your *Rise and Progress*.[63]

We also find George Whitefield writing to Risdon Darracott, with obvious reference to the *Rise and Progress*:

> I rejoice in the success of the Doctor's books, and pray the Lord earnestly to bless all his labours more and more.[64]

The work enjoyed considerable usefulness in America, receiving a commendation from Jonathan Edwards. Writing to Dr John Erskine in Scotland, Edwards wrote:

> I cannot but rejoice at some things which I have seen, that have been lately published in England, and the reception they have met with in so corrupt a time and nation. Some things of Dr Doddridge (who seems to have his heart truly engaged for the interests of religion), particularly his *Rise and Progress* and *Col. Gardiner s Life*.[65]

In the nineteenth century, we find C. H. Spurgeon adding his eulogy:

> How many souls may be converted by what some are privileged
> to write and print! There is, for instance, Dr Doddridge's *Rise
> and Progress of Religion in the Soul.* Though I decidedly object
> to some things in it, I could wish that everybody had read that
> book, so many have been the conversions it has produced.[66]

Whitefield's prayers were heard in heaven, and Spurgeon's
verdict was correct. There was one particular instance, in which the
influence of Doddridge's pen was to be more far reaching than even
he could have imagined (see his prayer on page 19 of this book). In
the winter of 1784, Isaac Milner and his friend William Wilberforce
were on a continental tour. Just before they left Nice, Wilberforce
happened casually to pick up a small book. It was the *Rise and
Progress of Religion in the Soul.* Asking Milner what the book was
about, Milner replied, "It is one of the best books ever written. Let
us take it with us and read it on our journey."[67] And so, Doddridge's
masterpiece was to be, under God, the means of awakening William
Wilberforce (later Member of Parliament for Hull and chief mover
in the abolition of the slave trade) to his eternal concerns.
Doddridge therefore contributed no small part to the great social
and political reforms of the nineteenth century, for such were the
fruit of the Great Awakening of the eighteenth century.[68]

9

O Sing unto the Lord

The observant worshipper will soon have discovered the hymns of Philip Doddridge. Indeed, for the vast majority of people, the singing of his hymns occasion their first acquaintance with the author. Even by the twenty-first century, very few Christians have never sung 'O God of Bethel' or 'Hark the glad sound'. It is also equally evident, that the popularity of Doddridge's hymns is not restricted to any particular denomination of Christians. They have always had a truly catholic appeal.

Although the hymns of Philip Doddridge constitute the smallest fraction of his immense literary output, they are more commonly known than anything else he ever wrote. When Job Orton published the third edition of his master's hymns in 1766, the final number was three hundred and seventy-five, although only a small proportion of those known are still sung. As one would expect, Congregationalism has provided the largest selection of Doddridge's hymns. At their nineteenth-century peak, the *New Congregational Hymn Book* (1859) contained forty-six examples. In *Congregational Praise* (1951), only fourteen hymns appear, still an improvement on the earlier *Congregational Hymnary* (1922) which contained only eleven. Other denominations have by no means ignored Doddridge's contribution. The Church of England just recognises his talent by including five of his hymns in *Hymns Ancient and Modern* (1950). In the 1970s, Doddridge made a mini-come-back in two evangelical books. The Strict Baptist *Grace Hymns* (1974) included thirteen but *Christian Hymns* (1977) made space for twenty-three. The latest Methodist book *Hymns and Psalms* (1983) has nine, an improvement on the seven of the earlier *Methodist Hymn Book* (1933). In changing times, the very recent *Praise!* (2000) still manages nine rather heavily-modernised examples.

HYMNS

FOUNDED ON

VARIOUS TEXTS

IN THE

HOLY SCRIPTURES.

By the late Reverend
PHILIP DODDRIDGE, D.D.

Publifhed from the AUTHOR's Manufcript
By JOB ORTON.

I efteem Nepos *for his Faith and Diligence, his
Comments on Scripture, and many Hymns,
with which the Brethren are delighted.*
Eufeb. Eccl. Hift. L. 7. C. 24.

SALOP,
Printed by J. EDDOWES and J. COTTON:
And Sold by J. WAUGH and W. FENNER,
at the *Turk's Head* in *Lombard Street*;
and J. BUCKLAND, at the *Buck* in
Pater-nofter Row, LONDON.
M.DCC.LV.

How does Philip Doddridge rate as a hymn writer? There can hardly be any doubt that Charles Wesley occupies first place, closely followed by Isaac Watts. Dr Erik Routley believes that James Montgomery takes the honours for third place, being equally sure that Doddridge is entitled to fourth place. If John Newton and William Cowper come close behind, Dr Routley says of Doddridge:

> In technique, consistency, sound doctrine, and the sense of what is fit for congregational use, he gives place to neither of our friends at Olney. He is less of a poet than Cowper, more of a scholar than Newton, and, we here claim, a better hymn writer than either.[1]

Regarding doctrinal sentiments, it is generally true that hymns do not reveal the minutiae of every theological conviction held by the hymn writer in question. Hymns are not theological documents as such; they are visions in verse. That said, Dr Routley is prepared to say of Doddridge 'that one prime colour runs right through his hymns from beginning to end, "one quality" gives away his theological leanings in every verse as unmistakably as Beethoven gives himself away in scoring a woodwind chord; this is the tone quality, or colour, of Calvinism'.[2] Dr Routley then explains the lack of general appeal of Doddridge's hymns to the modern generation in terms, not only of what is loosely called 'improvement in congregational taste', but a certain tendency away from his 'virile and salty Calvinism'[3] This is probably true where attachment to historic Calvinism has declined.

However, in today's still-rigid Calvinistic circles, the fact that Doddridge wrote hymns at all is a cause for disapproval! Indeed, exclusive-psalmody Presbyterians reject all hymns of 'human composition' in the name of 'Scripture-sufficiency'.[4] They are seemingly unaware of infringing their own idea of 'the regulative principle' by insisting on subscription to the man-made *Westminster Confession of Faith*. So is the Bible not sufficient as our basis of faith? Surely, if confessions of faith are permissible as well as desirable, why not hymns also? If 'scripture-sufficiency' excludes hymns, the same must apply to sermons, prayers and confessions using words not found in the Bible. But this is absurd. What is required is that all expressions of Christian truth and worship should be governed by the content of biblical truth. So, when Doddridge wrote his hymns, he believed he was acting according to the specific directives of Scripture. After all, the Apostle Paul urged the early Christians to praise God with 'hymns and spiritual songs' besides the 'psalms' (see Ephesians 5: 19; Colossians 3: 16). Thus Doddridge paraphrased Paul saying that 'public worship' should include 'the use of David's psalms, and other evangelical hymns' which may be composed 'under the influences of the Spirit'.[5]

Unjustly blaming Calvin (to whom a hymn is attributable[6]) instead of his more rigid successors, Doddridge rejects the idea that Paul's words simply refer to three types of Old Testament psalm. After observing the gift of hymnody in the New Testament (see 1 Corinthians 14: 15, 26), Doddridge adds that if the exclusive psalmody view is granted, 'it would certainly be as reasonable for us, in these later ages, to explode all kind of prayers in public, but liturgies collected from the words of scripture, as all sacred songs in divine worship but literal translations from ... the book of Psalms'. So he concludes that 'Numberless passages of the Old and New Testament are equally capable of furnishing us with sacred anthems'.[7] In short, the exclusive psalmody case is not persuasive. The fact that Mary, Zacharias and Simeon praised God in other words - albeit influenced by the psalms - is sufficient to confirm this. To insist that their 'canticles' are Scripture (see Lk. 1: 46-55; 68-79; 2: 29-32) misses the point. It is Luke's account that made them Scripture not the original utterances.

A brief digression is in order. Consistent with his radical *sola scriptura* stance, Doddridge had something to say on other controversial aspects of worship. Like John Owen and many other Puritans who usually declined to use liturgies, he was not absolutely opposed to them, only their imposition.[8] Regarding the Lord's Prayer, he was happy to use it as a 'directory' but equally as an optional form.[9] Not averse to the use of fixed prayers, he supplied the like at the end of each chapter of the *Rise and Progress*. While he said little about the use of a Christian calendar, he was critical of the traditional Christmas.[10] The Revd George Costard, Fellow of Wadham College, Oxford commented thus on Doddridge's *Family Expositor*: 'As to December being the time of Christ's birth, I think with you that the opinion is without foundation'.[11]

Unlike those who tend to disregard the psalms in favour of other compositions, Doddridge recognised that both have a place in Christian worship. So, out of a total of 375 examples including 43 new metrical versions of psalms, he based his paraphrases on New Testament and other Old Testament passages. While they arguably lack the bold brilliance of Charles Wesley, they are, like his sermons, always expository. Unlike Wesley who could never resist controversial versification when the High Calvinist Toplady was around, Doddridge's hymns are free from the occasional theological dissonance of Wesley's productions. While Wesley and Toplady - who never settled their disputes - produced excellent hymns, the undoubtedly 'Calvinistic' hymns of Doddridge, with their perpetual spiritual fragrance and warmth, are worthy companions to the other hymns of the Evangelical Revival.

The circumstances of composition tell us a good deal about worship on the Lord's Day at Castle Hill, Northampton during the ministry of Philip Doddridge. The hymns were written when the author had completed his sermon preparation, and they were based on the text of the sermon. After the sermon had been preached, the new hymn would be given out, line by line, the singing of which would bring the service to a close. We therefore can deduce the subject-matter of Doddridge's sermons from his hymns. When advising his students on the kinds of subject they should prefer in preaching, Doddridge suggests:

> 1. Those that relate more immediately to Christ. The glories of His person; the riches of His grace; His incarnation and birth; His life, ... His preaching, ... The sufferings and death to which He voluntarily submitted, ... His resurrection, ... His intercession on our behalf, ...

> 2. The constitution of the Covenant of Grace ... The blessings of pardon, grace, and glory, ... The nature of faith, ... of repentance, ... The freedom of God's grace manifested in this covenant; how ratified by the blood of Christ, the Mediator, ...

> 3. The influences and operations of God's Holy Spirit, and our need of them; their use and efficacy in enlightening the mind,

convincing the judgement, renewing and sanctifying the soul; quickening to duty, fortifying against temptation, assisting in prayer, and comforting true Christians, by witnessing their adoption, &c ...

4. The privileges of true Christians, e.g. pardon of sin, renewing, strengthening and confirming grace; adoption, perseverance, through continued Divine influences; God's providential care over them, ordering all things for their advantage; giving them access to His presence, believing views of glory, &C ...[12]

If such subjects as these formed the staple diet of Doddridge's congregation, we can be sure that the edification received through the preached Word was given suitable expression in praise following the sermon. It is perhaps highly significant, that those hymns which continue to enjoy considerable popularity, centre their subject matter on the very subjects Doddridge suggested for preaching.

Before we acquaint ourselves with some examples of Doddridge's hymns, we should pause to consider his technique. Unlike the endless variations of metre employed by Charles Wesley, Doddridge's compositions are, in the main, restricted to the use of common (CM), short (SM) and long (LM) metres. This is not because Doddridge was devoid of imagination but because of the limited range of tunes he was able to utilise. The tradition which Doddridge inherited based its worship exclusively on the metrical psalms, and it was the set of psalm-tunes which Doddridge was restricted to. In the process of 'lining out' the new hymn, it would have been absolutely essential for at least the tune to have been familiar. Although, in all, Doddridge used nine metres, exactly three hundred hymns appear in either common or long metre, one hundred and sixty-one being in common metre. Despite the restrictions that Doddridge laboured under, his compositions soar beyond the mould in which they are cast.

Selected verses from four seldom-sung hymns merit a mention in relation to debates over the author's orthodoxy. (NB: all hymns are numbered as in the original published collection followed by the text to which they relate).[13] Glorying in Christ's deity, Doddridge *first* invites us to worship the *incarnate* Saviour:

(200: Lk. 2: 10-12)

1. Hail, progeny divine!
   Hail, virgin's wondrous Son!
   Who, for that humble shrine,
   Didst quit the Almighty's throne:
   The Infant-Lord
   Our voices sing,
   And be the king
   Of grace ador'd.

Second, Doddridge moves us to worship the *crucified* Saviour. This large-scale example - a rare use of the obsolete '50th' metre - comes from a hymn entitled 'God's Love to the World in sending Christ for its Redemption':

(220: Jn. 3: 16)

3. God's only son with peerless glories bright,
   His Father's fairest image and delight,
   Justice and grace the victim have decreed,
   To wear our flesh, and in that flesh to bleed.
   Prostrate in dust, ye sinners, all adore him,
   And tremble, while your hearts rejoice before him.

Third, Doddridge calls us to worship the *risen* Saviour:

(218: Lk. 24: 34)

5. All-hail, triumphant Lord,
   Who sav'st us with thy blood!
   Wide be thy name ador'd,
   Thou rising, reigning God!
   With thee we rise,
   With thee we reign,
   And empires gain
   Beyond the skies.

Fourth, Doddridge - in another rare use of the '50th' metre - calls us to worship the Church's *ascended Head*:

(299: *Col. 2: 10*)

4. We sing the blood, that ransom'd us from hell;
    We sing the graces, that in Jesus dwell;
    Led by his Spirit, guarded by his hand,
    Our hopes anticipate the [heav'nly] land
    Still his incarnate Deity admiring,
    And with heaven's [angel hosts] in praise conspiring.

On a less ambitious scale, there can be no finer tribute to Doddridge's method and purpose than the hymn 'Hark the glad sound'. Some regard this as his finest. It relates 'immediately to Christ' and does more than any similar composition to set forth 'the glories of His person' and the 'riches of His grace'. Let us have the hymn in its original form:

(203: *Lk. 4: 18-19*)

Hark the glad sound! the Saviour comes,
    The Saviour promis'd long;
Let every heart prepare a throne,
    And every voice a song.

2. On him the Spirit largely pourd,
        Exerts its sacred fire;
    Wisdom and might, and zeal and love
        His holy breast inspire.

3. He comes the prisoners to release,
        In Satan's bondage held;
    The gates of brass before him burst,
        The iron fetters yield.

4. He comes from thickest films of vice
        To clear the mental ray,
    And on the eye-balls of the blind
        To pour celestial day.

5. He comes the broken heart to bind,
        The bleeding soul to cure,
    And with the treasures of his grace
        To enrich the humble poor.

6. His silver trumpets publish loud
    The jubilee of the Lord;
    Our debts are all remitted now,
      Our heritage restor'd.

7. Our glad hosannas, Prince of Peace,
    Thy welcome shall proclaim;
    And heaven's eternal arches ring
      With thy beloved name.

This hymn, along with another, was the favourite of Colonel Gardiner, Doddridge's close friend who was slain at the Battle of Prestonpans. Let Doddridge introduce the other hymn for us:

There is one hymn more, I shall beg leave to add, plain as it is, which Colonel Gardiner has been heard to mention with particular regard, as expressing the inmost sentiments of his soul; and they were undoubtedly so, in the last rational moments of his expiring life. It is called, Christ precious to the believer; and was composed to be sung after a sermon on 1 Peter 2: 7:[14]

(335: *1 Pet. 2: 7*)

Jesus! I love thy charming name,
    'Tis music to mine ear;
    Fain would I sound it out so loud,
      That earth and heaven should hear.

2. Yes, thou art precious to my soul,
    My transport, and my trust;
    Jewels to thee are gaudy toys,
      And gold is sordid dust.

3. All my capacious powers can wish
    In thee doth richly meet:
    Nor to mine eyes is light so dear,
      Nor friendship half so sweet.

4. Thy grace still dwells upon my heart,
    And sheds its fragrance there;
    The noblest balm of all its wounds,

The cordial of its care.

5. I'll speak the honours of thy name
   With my last labouring breath;
   Then speechless clasp thee in mine arms,
   The antidote of death.

This fine hymn is perhaps a little too quaint for some modern congregations, and it has not appeared in hymnbooks for some decades. However, at one time it was greatly loved. It was not only sung by Anglo-Saxon believers, as one very interesting incident would seem to suggest. In March 1792, The President and Congress of the United States invited a deputation of Indians to be their guests at Philadelphia. In the course of their journey, the party of fifty chiefs and warriors marched into Nazareth, Pennsylvania, accompanied by a missionary named Kirkland. Indians had not been seen in the town for many years, and so their presence excited considerable interest. The local minister invited the visitors to the church, and hymns were sung in English, which some of the Indians understood. Let the record complete the story:

> After a short pause, a select company of them rose, and joined their minister in singing hymns in the same strain in the Indian language, among which was that beautiful hymn of Dr Doddridge, "Jesus! I love Thy charming name."[15]

How thrilled Doddridge would have been to know of this little incident, especially since he was so deeply concerned that people everywhere should hear the everlasting Gospel of the grace of God. Doddridge was a true evangelist at heart, a fact that may serve to introduce another little known hymn, which also has connections with Colonel Gardiner.

We have already observed the quickening effect that Whitefield's first visit to Northampton (in May 1739) had upon Doddridge. Doddridge was preaching at Leicester the following month from the words, 'I beheld the transgressors, and was grieved, because they kept not Thy law' (Psalm 119: 158). In a moving and eloquent sermon, he gave expression to his great longing for the salvation of souls. After the sermon, the congregation united to sing the following hymn:

(64: *Ps. 119: 136, 158*)

Arise, my tenderest thoughts, arise,
    To torrents melt my streaming eyes!
And thou, my heart, with anguish feel
    Those evils which thou can'st not heal!

2. See human nature sunk in shame!
        See scandals pour'd on Jesus' name!
    The Father wounded through the Son!
        The world abus'd, the soul undone!

3. See the short course of vain delight
        Closing in everlasting night!
    In flames that no abatement know,
        The briny tears forever flow.

4. My God, I feel the mournful scene;
        My bowels yearn o'er dying men:
    And fain my pity would reclaim,
        And snatch the fire-brands from the flame.

5. But feeble my compassion proves,
        And can but weep where most it loves:
    Thine own all-saving arm employ,
        And turn these drops of grief to joy!

Little did Doddridge know that Colonel Gardiner was in the congregation; up until this time, the two men were entire strangers to each other. As soon as the service was over, Doddridge retired to the vestry, rapidly followed by the good Colonel. The soldier threw his arms around the preacher in an unrestrained expression of affection. Colonel Gardiner, who had been remarkably converted in 1719, told Doddridge how much he had profited from his writings; a friendship commenced between the two men which only death was to terminate. It was later learned by Doddridge that the hymn quoted above was a perfect description of his friend's sad state before his glorious conversion some twenty years before.[16]

When James Montgomery said, "Blessed is the man that can take

Manuscript page of her husband's hymns
attributed to Mercy Doddridge

the words of this hymn and make them his own from similar experience,"[17] he was speaking of the ever-popular 'O happy day, that fixed my choice'. The hymn takes its inspiration from the Old Testament, not the New as one might expect. Doddridge has in mind the Reformation which took place in the reign of King Asa, when all idolatrous practices were done away with (2 Chronicles 15). After the people entered into a solemn covenant to seek God and purge away the idolatry, we read the words, 'And all Judah rejoiced at the oaths for they had sworn with all their heart, and sought him with their whole desire; and he was found of them: and the Lord gave them rest round about '(v.15).

In his hymn, Doddridge gave an evangelical interpretation of this Old Testament event. We thus see his typical puritan attitude to conversion. The Puritans spoke much of 'closing with Christ', or entering into covenant with Him. The popular modern idea of 'making a decision' was foreign to the puritan Christian. It is impossible to determine whether or not Doddridge was describing his own 'closing' with his Saviour, but it is more than likely that he remembered his own conversion in the writing of the hymn. This much is certain, Doddridge describes what conversion ought to be like. He did not compose the chorus to this magnificent hymn included in some hymnbooks, so we will quote it in its virgin form:

(23: 2 Chr. 15: 15)

O happy day, that fix'd my choice
    On Thee, my Saviour, and my God!
Well may this growing heart rejoice,
    And tell its raptures all abroad.

2. O happy bond, that seals my vows
    To him, who merits all my love!
Let cheerful anthems fill this house,
    While to that sacred shrine I move.

3. 'Tis done; the great transaction's done:
    I am my Lord's, and he is mine:
He drew me, and I followed on,
    Charm'd to confess the voice divine.

4. Now rest my long divided heart,
     Fix'd on this blissful centre rest;
    With ashes who would grudge to part,
     When called on angels bread to feast?

5. High heaven that heard the solemn vow,
     That vow renew'd shall daily hear;
    Till in life's latest hour I bow,
     And bless in death a bond so dear.

Henry James Garland says that if this had been the only hymn that Doddridge wrote, then it would have preserved his influence for all generations. In this verdict, one can most surely concur. However, when this writer interprets the hymn in terms of the day when a man 'decided to receive Christ into his heart',[18] he could be sure that the implication that the believer takes the initiative in his conversion would be firmly rejected by Doddridge. In another hymn, he reveals his head as well as his heart:

(240: *Jn. 15: 16*)

I own, my God, thy sovereign grace,
 And bring the praise to thee;
If thou my chosen portion art,
 Thou first hast chosen me.

Indeed, in verse 3, line 3 of 'O happy day', the theology is simple but clear: 'He drew me, and I followed on'. Doddridge preached, and his people sang, according to his own maxim: preach 'The freedom of God's grace manifested in this covenant'. Such is Doddridge's 'virile and salty Calvinism'.

This may be added by way of additional interest, that, at the suggestion of Prince Albert, 'O happy day' was used at the confirmation service of one of Queen Victoria's children.[19] It also became the confirmation hymn of the American Episcopal Church.

'Grace! 'tis a charming sound' is also associated in some hymnbooks with an added chorus. Although Doddridge the 'Baxterian Calvinist' would doubtless approve of the author's universalist sentiments, he did not write it. Some hymn books include this delightful hymn without realising that three of the verses were added by Augustus Montague Toplady, author of the famous hymn 'Rock of Ages'. It is quite likely that Doddridge would have welcomed the development of his own exposition. We will give the hymn together with Toplady's verses marked thus (*):

(286: *Eph.* 2: 5)

Grace! 'tis a charming sound,
　　Harmonious to my ear;
Heaven with the echo shall resound,
　　And all the earth shall hear.

2.　Grace first contriv'd a way
　　　To save rebellious man,
　　And all the steps that grace display;
　　　Which drew the wondrous plan.

3.　'Twas grace that wrote my name*
　　　In life's eternal book:
　　'Twas grace that gave me to the Lamb,
　　　Who all my sorrows took.

4.　Grace taught my wandering feet
　　　To tread the heavenly road;
　　And new supplies each hour I meet
　　　While pressing on to God.

5.　Grace taught my soul to pray,*
　　　And made my eyes o'erflow;
　　'Tis grace has kept me to this day,
　　　And will not let me go.

6.　Grace all the work shall crown
　　　Through everlasting days;
　　It lays in heaven the topmost stone,
　　　And well deserves the praise.

7.　O let that grace inspire*
　　　My soul with strength divine!
　　May all my powers to Thee aspire,
　　　And all my days be thine.

A characteristic feature of Doddridge's hymns is their ability to lift the worshipper from earth to heaven. As Doddridge saw the Gospel, Christ came to earth to take us back to heaven. The sinners He came to save, He transforms into saints. One is always left with the desire for holiness, heaven and God. For Doddridge, therefore, the atoning work of Christ on the cross, His resurrection, and the Holy Spirit's application to the believer of the benefits of the covenant of grace, are all designed with glory in view. Another favourite hymn embraces all these themes. It shows how Doddridge can concisely and efficiently weave a variety of biblical themes into a dynamic pattern of devotional theology:

(325: *Heb. 13: 20-1*)

Father of peace, and God of love,
    We own thy power to save;
That power, by which our Shepherd rose
    Victorious o'er the grave.

2. We triumph in that Shepherd's name,
    Still watchful for our good;
Who brought the eternal covenant down,
    And sealed it with His blood.

3. So may thy Spirit seal my soul,
    And mould it to Thy will;
That my fond heart no more may stray,
    But keep thy covenant still.

4. Still may we gain superior strength,
    And press with vigour on;
Till full perfection crown our hopes,
    And fix us near thy throne.

Whilst Doddridge panted and longed for holiness, he was never deceived by John Wesley's delusion of 'Christian perfection'. Doddridge taught with the Apostle Paul, that earth could no more tolerate perfection than heaven can tolerate imperfection. Until we come to heaven, we must 'wrestle, fight and pray'. Employing another of Paul's metaphors, Doddridge gives his poetic exposition of the 'Christian race':

(296: *Phil. 3: 12-14*)

Awake, my soul, stretch every nerve,
And press with vigour on;
A heavenly race demands thy zeal,
And an immortal crown

2. A cloud of witnesses around
Hold thee in full survey:
Forget the steps already trod
And onward urge thy way.

3. 'Tis God's all-animating voice
That calls thee from on high;
'Tis his own hand presents the prize
To thine aspiring eye.

4. That prize, with peerless glories bright,
Which shall new lustre boast,
When victor's wreaths and monarch's gems
Shall blend in common dust.

5. Blest Saviour, introduced by thee
Have I my race begun;
And crowned with victory at thy feet
I'll lay my honours down.

Another popular hymn was also inspired by Paul's epistle to the Philippians. Here we see Doddridge taken up with the love of Christ which renders obedience delightful, a life centred on Him a continual joy, and death a comfortable transition to glory. "For me to live is Christ, and to die is gain!" cries Paul. "Amen! Amen!" exclaims Doddridge. If 'Awake my soul' is an example of Doddridge's energetic Puritanism, the following hymn expresses his vibrant Methodism:

(294: *Phil. 1: 22*)

My gracious Lord, I own thy right
To every service I can pay;

And call it my supreme delight
　　To hear thy dictates and obey.

2.　What is my being, but for thee,
　　　Its sure support, its noblest end?
　　Thy ever-smiling face to see,
　　　And serve the cause of such a friend?

3.　I would not breathe for worldly joy,
　　　Or to increase my worldly good;
　　Nor future days, or powers employ
　　　To spread a sounding name abroad.

4.　'Tis to my Saviour I would live;
　　　To Him, who for my ransom died,
　　Nor could untainted Eden give
　　　Such bliss, as blossoms at his side.

5.　His work my hoary age shall bless,
　　　When youthful vigour is no more:
　　And my last hour of life confess
　　　His love hath animating power.

Of all the hymns of Doddridge, probably 'O God of Bethel' is the
best known. It was one of his earliest hymns, being written in 1731.
The manuscript of the original hymn still exists, and is headed
'Jacob's vow', the theme being derived from the patriarch's first
encounter with God. The version of the hymn most commonly sung
is a revision of the original by the Revd John Logan, first published
in his *Poems* (1781). The version that came from Doddridge's quill
is:

(4: *Gen. 28: 20-2*)

O God of Jacob by whose hand
　　thine Israel still is fed,
Who through this weary pilgrimage
　　Hast all our fathers led.

2.　To thee our humble vows we raise,
　　　To thee address our prayer,

And in thy kind and faithful breast
Deposit all our care.

3. If thou, through each perplexing path,
Wilt be our constant guide;
If thou wilt daily bread supply,
And raiment wilt provide;

4. If thou wilt spread thy shield around,
'Til these our wand'rings cease,
And at our Father's loved abode
Our souls arrive in peace:

5. To thee, as to our Covenant-God,
We'll our whole selves resign;
And count, that not our tenth alone,
But all we have is thine.

While it cannot be questioned that Logan's revision is a splendid one, it almost qualifies as a separate hymn. The last three verses of the original are more closely dependent upon one another than Logan's, and a certain degree of individual completeness is required for verses in corporate singing, a facility lacking in the original but present in the revised version.

Whichever author is entitled to a greater share of the honours, 'O God of Bethel' is a justly celebrated piece. It has been sung in times of peace and times of war. For two centuries, it has been used on national days of humiliation, thanksgiving and prayer. His Majesty King Edward VII found the hymn to be a great source of help and it was sung at his funeral. 'O God of Bethel' was the favourite hymn of David Livingstone, who derived unspeakable comfort from its lines during his wanderings through Africa. Fittingly, the hymn was sung for Livingstone's funeral at Westminster Abbey by a vast congregation, which filled the national shrine to its capacity. The eminent William Ewart Gladstone, Prime Minister in the reign of Queen Victoria, was also laid to rest in Westminster Abbey to the strains of 'O God of Bethel'.[20] Surely, 'O God of Bethel' requires no further commendation; it has served God's people well.

Dr Routley called our next example 'another forgotten

treasure'.[21] Here we have Doddridge's Augustan expression of his passionate Puritanism. Indeed, for him, the purity, preservation and triumph of the Church were essential features of the salvation, character and destiny of God's people:

(107: *Isa. 51: 1-2*)

Triumphant Zion, lift thy head
    From dust, and darkness, and the dead,
Though humbled long, awake at length,
    And gird thee with thy Saviour's strength.

2.   Put all thy beauteous garments on,
    And let thy various charms be known;
The world thy glories shall confess,
    Deck'd in the robes of righteousness.

3.   No more shall foes unclean invade,
    And fill thy hallowed walls with dread;
No more shall hell's insulting host
    Their victory, and thy sorrows boast.

4.   God from on high thy groans will hear;
    His hand thy ruins shall repair;
Rear'd and adorn'd by love divine,
    Thy towers and battlements shall shine.

5.   Grace shall dispose my heart and voice
    To share, and echo back her joys;
Nor will her watchful monarch cease
    To guard her in eternal peace.

As a Reformed churchman, Doddridge was thoroughly persuaded of the practice of covenant baptism (believers and their children). His deep life-long concern for children and young people reflect this conviction. Not surprisingly, he wrote a beautiful baptismal hymn for children. In the final verse, Doddridge probably had his daughter 'Tetsy' in mind:

(198: *Mk. 10: 14*)

See Israel's gentle Shepherd stand

With all-engaging charms;
Hark how he calls the tender lambs,
And folds them in his arms!

2. "Permit them to approach," he cries,
   "Nor scorn their humble name;
   "For 'twas to bless such souls as these,
   "The Lord of angels came."

3. We bring them, Lord, in thankful hands,
   And yield them up to thee;
   Joyful, that we ourselves are thine,
   Thine let our offspring be.

4. Ye little flock, with pleasure hear:
   Ye children, seek his face;
   And fly with transport to receive
   The blessings of his grace.

5. If orphans they are left behind,
   Thy guardian-care we trust:
   That care shall heal our bleeding hearts,
   If weeping o'er their dust.

Dr Routley claims that Doddridge was the inventor of hymns which express 'the social implications of the Gospel'.[22] Surprisingly, one looks in vain in the textual index of the 1904 *Methodist Hymn Book* for a hymn on the Good Samaritan. Yet Doddridge produced this concise and challenging gem:

(205: *Lk. 10: 30-7*)

Father of mercies, send thy grace
All-powerful from above,
To form in our obedient souls
The image of thy love.

2. O may our sympathising breasts
   That generous pleasure know
   Kindly to share in others' joy,
   And weep for others' woe!

3. When the most helpless sons of grief
  In low distress are laid,
  Soft be our hearts their pains to feel,
  And swift our hands to aid.

4. So Jesus looked on dying men,
  When thron'd above the skies,
  And, 'midst the embraces of his God,
  He felt compassion rise.

5. On wings of love the Saviour flew
  To raise us from the ground,
  And made the riches of his blood
  A balm for every wound.

Of all the hymns of Philip Doddridge, it is difficult to determine which was his first composition. It is tempting to think that his last might have been the one headed: 'Praising God through the Whole of our Existence'. The entire hymn is a perfect testimony to Doddridge's life and serves to introduce us to our last chapter. The second verse obviously alludes to the stresses and strains of his busy life. As he wrote in a recently discovered letter to George Whitefield, 'the composition of [hymns] often refresh my soul'.[23] It also reminds us of the author's personal motivation as a hymn writer. This great hymn is the portrait of a great soul filled with a great sense of God's goodness, grace and glory. To Doddridge, the first principle of the Christian life is praise; the second principle is also praise, and likewise the third principle. Doddridge was at his happiest when he was praising God. Let him lead us in so noble and exalted a work as together we praise the God of our salvation:

(71: *Ps. 146: 2*)

God of my life, through all its days
  My grateful powers shall sound thy praise;
The song shall wake with opening light,
  And warble to the silent night.

2. When anxious cares would break my rest,
  And griefs would tear my throbbing breast,

Thy tuneful praises rais'd on high
    Shall check the murmur and the sigh.

3. When death o'er nature shall prevail,
    And all its powers of language fail,
Joy through my swimming eyes shall break,
    And mean the thanks I cannot speak.

4. But O! when that last conflict's o'er,
    And I am chain'd to flesh no more,
With what glad accents shall I rise,
    To join the music of the skies!

5. Soon shall I learn th' exalted strains,
    Which echo oe'r the heavenly plains;
And emulate, with joy unknown,
    The glowing seraphs round thy throne.

6. The cheerful tribute will I give,
    Long as a deathless soul can live;
A work so sweet, a theme so high,
    Demands and crowns eternity.

Doddridge

In living, LIVE!

10
An Immortal Crown

The wisdom with which the great Head of the Church pursues His purposes of salvation will be understood only in eternity. Until the completed tapestry of time is revealed the Church militant can but humbly admire God's ways 'through a glass darkly' (1 Cor. 13: 12) and say in faith 'He hath done all things well' (Mk. 7: 37). Thus the wisest human judgements will always prove defective. Accordingly, it is not the length of a man's life that matters when eternity is kept in view. As Doddridge constantly urged, total submission and cheerful obedience to the will of God is all that matters however long we might live. It is therefore with regard to quality of life rather than quantity of years that the life of Philip Doddridge is to be seen. If other men existed longer, he lived more fully; if they lived for pleasure, he lived for God and was happier by far. These are the considerations that should be borne in mind as we survey the last years of Doddridge's 'short, uncertain, earthly life and pilgrimage'.

When Doddridge wrote to Benjamin Fawcett in 1750, he exclaimed at the head of the letter, 'I am this day forty-eight years old; but, O, how unworthy and unprofitable a creature!'[1] With a humility typical of him, Doddridge revealed his self-estimate. We would be somewhat suspicious of his spirituality had he concluded otherwise, but we are entitled to a different conclusion when we remember his achievements.

As his life was drawing to a close, we see Doddridge's labours multiplying not diminishing, and not without considerable drama. During his summer vacation in the summer of 1748, he was in London as a guest of Lady Huntingdon. Never averse to healthy pastimes, Doddridge was enjoying a trip on the Thames when a near-fatal incident occurred. He attributed his 'remarkable deliverance' from death to the merciful providence of God and Mercy: '... your prayers have long contributed to my safety and comfort'.[2]   Such was the impression made that we find him recalling the incident in his *Diary* for New Year's Day 1749:

> I ought to [mention] the wonderful instance of the Divine goodness in preserving me from drowning on Monday, July 25, as I was attempting to pass under Westminster Bridge, when the wind set contrarily, and blew so violently, that we were in danger of being borne violently against the side of the bridge and dashed to pieces.[3]

So bright a light in the Church of Christ was never so close to being extinguished, but 'his hour had not yet come'.

Even on his vacations, Doddridge could not escape work. He did, however, manage to relax a little. The Saturday following the incident on the river, Doddridge wrote to Mercy. Besides relating his happy escape he affectionately reported:

> I can conclude, my dearest, with telling you that I am now come to the conclusion of one of the most pleasant days I shall ever spend without you. After an hour's charming conversation with Lady Huntingdon and Mrs Edwin, I preached in her family by her express desire, and met Colonel Gumley, who is really a second Colonel Gardiner. Such a monument of the power and sovereignty of Divine grace as, truly, I have hardly ever met with, since I was acquainted with his story. After dinner, the ladies entertained us with their voices, and a harpsichord, with which I was highly delighted.[4]

If the airs of Purcell, Handel and possibly Boyce delighted Doddridge, he was ever concerned with harmony of a more sublime kind. Like Baxter before him, Doddridge did not merely lament the sad divisions between the people of God; he actively sought to promote unity whenever he could. Before returning to Northampton, he had an interview with Dr Herring the Archbishop of Canterbury. In the course of the conversation, the matter of church unity was raised.

Since the fires of persecution had died away, there was much discussion among Churchmen and Dissenters alike on the possibility of the two branches of British Protestantism being 'comprehended' in one national church. The thought of a visible unity of all protestant churches was one at which the heart of Doddridge always leapt. Only ten years before (in 1738) he wrote to George Whitefield saying of the Church of England: 'so much do I love her, notwithstanding our dissent'.[5] While his association with the Methodist Anglicans was sufficient to draw criticism upon himself, Doddridge was prepared to go as far as his dissenting conscience would permit. Whilst even moderate dissenting opinion was ready to be absorbed into the state church, Doddridge thought the scheme of comprehension was sacrificing too much. He suggested an alternative to the Archbishop:

> ... when I mentioned to him a sort of medium between the present state, and that of a perfect coalition, which was that of acknowledging our Churches as unschismatical by permitting their clergy to officiate among us, if desired, which he must see had a counterpart of permitting Dissenting ministers occasionally to officiate in churches, it struck him much, as a new and very important thought.[6]

Doddridge was advocating a mutual recognition of ministries, rather than the Comprehension scheme, which called into question the validity of ordination amongst the Dissenters. Doddridge would never have tolerated this. It further appears that Doddridge's views of unity were founded upon the truth of the biblical gospel. 'Unity at any price' was never a slogan with Doddridge. As for the Archbishop of Canterbury Dr Herring, he seems to have been a generally sound and godly man, a prelate with theological convictions. However, he was not alone. If the Anglican bishops would have benefited from an injection of Methodism, they were not wholly devoid of piety. Another feature of Doddridge's untiring labours will serve to illustrate this welcome observation.

On August 20, 1749, Doddridge preached at the famous Salters' Hall. It was one of his most powerful sermons. Ever grieved at the godlessness of his native city, Doddridge faithfully yet tenderly warned the inhabitants of London of the judgements of God. The sermon was *The Guilt and Doom of Capernaum*,[7] based on Christ's words in Matthew 11: 23-4. Pressed by work on the *Family Expositor*, Doddridge had no immediate thoughts of publishing the

The Guilt and Doom of CAPERNAUM, *seri-ously recommended to the Confideration of the Inhabitants of* LONDON:

IN A

SERMON

PREACHED AT

SALTERS-HALL,

Auguft 20, 1749.

PUBLISHED

On Occafion of the late Alarm by the Second Shock of an EARTHQUAKE, *March* 8, 1749-50.

WITH A

PREFACE relating to that Awful Event.

By P. DODDRIDGE, *D. D.*

LONDON:

Printed and Sold by J. WAUGH, at the *Turk's Head* in *Lombard-Street.* M,DCC,L.

sermon although many requested him to do so. But when London was shaken by an earthquake on two separate occasions in February and March 1750, Doddridge rushed the manuscript to his printers. Many feared the end of the world and George Whitefield found himself preaching to enormous congregations at Hyde Park.[8] Doddridge's sermon was warmly and gratefully received, not least by the Bishop of London himself, Dr Sherlock:

> It was with great pleasure and satisfaction that I received and read your very excellent and seasonable sermon, published upon the occasion of the late earthquakes. I pray God it may have a due influence upon the minds of all who read it; and I wish all would read and consider it. Though I am a stranger to your person, yet I am not so to your character and abilities, ... Whatever points of difference there are between us, yet I trust that we are united in a hearty seal for spreading the knowledge of the gospel, and for reforming the lives and manners of the people according to it, ... and there will be little hope of a reformation, till we are humble enough to be willing to know Christ and Him crucified.[9]

Doddridge's interest in these events was scientific as well as pastoral. After another earth tremor was felt in Northamptonshire on September 30, 1750, he submitted a report to the Royal Society with details of time, locations and damage to property.[10]

Continuing with things ecumenical, Doddridge had fraternal relations with such eminent prelates as Dr Secker, Bishop of Oxford, Dr Warburton, Bishop of Gloucester and Dr Maddox, Bishop of Worcester. It would not be difficult to predict that his motives would suffer from misrepresentation. In fact this was the case, for in 1750, rumours were spread in London that Doddridge was about to conform to the Church of England. Since his ecumenical tendencies have been misrepresented and exploited in later generations, it is important to give his own answer (with some important background) to those unfounded speculations.

As early as 1723 Doddridge declared his conviction that 'the Dissenting Interest' was 'the Interest of Jesus Christ'.[11] Three years later, he provided a thoughtful and charitable assessment of the claims of conformity, and his statement is instructive:

> I am now studying the business of conformity ... as indeed I think it necessary to examine into the affair again, before I determine upon being ordained among the Dissenters, which will probably fix me among them for life. On the whole I must say, that as nothing has had a greater tendency to confirm my belief of Christianity, than the most celebrated writings of Jews and Deists, and my adherence to the protestant cause, than the apologies of many of the Roman communion, so the study of the best defences of the Church of England, which I have seen, has added a great deal of weight to my former persuasion, not only of the lawfulness, but expediency of a separation from it. Yet when I see how many plausible arguments may be advanced on the contrary side, I am the less inclined to censure those who yield to their apparent force.[12]

Thus, ordained as a convinced Dissenter in 1730, Doddridge gave his students the following directives regarding Anglican clergy:

> Treat them on all occasions with respect. Do not enter into controversies with them, much less rail against the establishment. ... Protest, if it be necessary, that you are conscientious in your dissent; and appear ready to be informed on any point of the controversy; but having the chief reasons of your nonconformity at hand, do not fail to produce them if you are forced to defend yourselves.[13]

So in 1750, consistent with his earlier statements, Doddridge was not about to betray His Lord:

> Assure those, who may have heard of the report, that though my growing acquaintance with many excellent persons, some of them of great eminence in the establishment, increases those candid, respectful sentiments of that body of Christians, which I had long entertained, yet I am so thoroughly persuaded of the reasonableness of nonconformity, and find many of the terms of ministerial conformity so contrary to the dictates of my conscience in the sight of God, that I never was less inclined to submit to them; and I hope I shall not be willing to buy my liberty or my life at that price. But I think it my duty to do my part towards promoting that mutual peace and goodwill, which

I think more likely than anything else, either to reform the church, or at least to promote true Christianity, both in the establishment and separation; to strengthen the Protestant cause, and defeat the designs of our common enemies. And, conscious that I speak and act from these principles, and that I am approved of God in it, I do not fear the resentments of any narrow-spirited persons. I would not be a knight-errant in the cause of candour itself; nor would I so fear the imputation of mean and unworthy designs, as to be deterred, by the apprehensions of it, from what is in itself right. [14]

Doddridge clearly had certain limits for his ecumenical hopes; he was concerned to 'strengthen the *Protestant* cause', even if the further reformation of the Church of England was expecting a little too much! However charitably he expressed himself, we may surmise that he would remain just as decisive had he lived in the 'post J. C. Ryle' era of 'diluted' Anglican evangelicalism. The recent compromise evident in the pro-Rome sympathies of Dr George Carey, Dr John R. W. Stott, Dr J. I. Packer and others would have left him both unimpressed, unmoved and gravely concerned.

Doddridge saw no inconsistency between his own view of catholicity and his orthodoxy, since his motivation for unity was directed by truth not sentiment. In fact Doddridge strongly argued the case in one of the last sermons published in his lifetime. In January 1750, he preached to an assembly of ministers at Creaton in Northamptonshire from the words of Paul, 'If there be therefore any consolation in Christ, if any comfort of love, if any fellowship of the Spirit, if any bowels and mercies; fulfil ye my joy, that ye be like minded, having the same love, being of one accord, of one mind (Philippians 2: 1-2). In this sermon, the preacher bared his soul. Thus *Christian Candour and Unanimity Stated, Illustrated and Urged* was to be Doddridge's most accurate self-portrait. He demonstrates from the Greek that the Apostle is not pleading for an exact conformity on all points of doctrine as a necessary prerequisite for fellowship (see 3: 15-16). Therefore, since Paul is stressing 'the advancement of vital, practical holiness', we are to temper orthodoxy with charity:

Truth is indeed too sacred a thing ever to be denied on any

consideration: and so far as we are in our own consciences persuaded that any truth is important, neither honour nor charity will allow us to give it up, as a point of mere indifferent speculation. Let us therefore ever be ready, when properly called out to the service, to plead its cause in the name of the God of truth; but let it be in a manner worthy of him, a manner which may not offend him as the God of love. And let us be greatly upon our guard that we do not condemn our brethren, as having forfeited all title to the name of Christians, because their creeds or confessions of faith do not come up to the standard of our own.[15]

When this admirable discourse was published, it was dedicated to the Countess of Huntingdon, both Anglican and Methodist, 'that eminent example of the Christian candour here recommended, and of every other virtue and grace, which can inspire, support, and adorn it'.

Doddridge practised what he preached by seizing every opportunity for evangelical fellowship. Such an opportunity occurred early in May 1750 when Whitefield travelled from London to Ashby Place to visit the sick Lady Huntingdon. On Monday May 7, Doddridge joined Dr Stonhouse, James Hervey of Weston Favell and Thomas Hartley, Rector of Winwick for a 'private interview' with Whitefield 'about six miles from Northampton' (in fact Horton, the seat of the Earl of Halifax). On the following morning, Whitefield preached to Doddridge's students at the Academy before continuing his journey to Ashby Place.[16]

Writing to Doddridge about a month later, Lady Huntingdon was doubtless alluding to Doddridge's sermon:

> Your candour is such a blessedness about you, that I fear it will make you too soon fit for heaven, and leave us mourning followers of your example.[17]

Little did the good Countess realise that in less than eighteen months the earthly labours of Dr Doddridge would be at an end. Towards the end of June, having recovered from her illness, Lady Huntingdon enjoyed the presence of Doddridge who wrote to Mercy:

*Chriſtian Candour and Unanimity
ſtated, illuſtrated and urged.*

IN A

SERMON

PREACHED AT A

MEETING

OF

MINISTERS

AT

CREATON in *Northamptonſhire,
January* 12, 1749-50.

By *P. DODDRIDGE,* D.D.

Publiſhed at the united and earneſt Requeſt of
the MINISTERS that heard it.

LONDON:

Printed and Sold by J. WAUGH, at the *Turk's Head*
in *Lombard-Street.* 1750.

225

Lady Huntingdon
(1707 - 91)

Shall I make a Merit of taking a few minutes from Lady Huntingdons charming Company to tell you that I am well & happy here. ... Her Ladyship is recovered to an astonishing degree. We walked together almost two Hours last Night & she is this Morning as lively as if she had never known an Hours Illness or Fatigue in her life. ... My Lady desires me to add how very sorry she is that you are not here & how glad she shall be to see you & thanks you for *'letting me come'*.[18]

Back at home with Mercy a few days later, humorous Doddridge revealed an interesting detail to Benjamin Fawcett. Indomitable and tireless Lady Huntingdon could certainly talk! 'She walked with me in the garden and park, and almost wearied me'.[19]

If Doddridge's warm-hearted catholicity caused the icy barriers of party spirit to melt, it is a tribute to his noble spirit that he was prepared to embrace bishop and Methodist alike. However, his influence and concern were not restricted to these shores; his catholicity had a geographical as well as theological dimension. Doddridge could never be accused of insularity, being interested in the extension of Christ's kingdom in America and Europe, in the New World, as well as the old. The Revd James Robertson, formerly pupil and assistant to Dr Doddridge, and afterwards a professor in the University of Edinburgh, studied for a while at the University of Leiden in Holland. In December 1749, he wrote to his former tutor:

The Abbot of Sternmetz, in Magdeburg, who is a man of great piety and of considerable character among the Lutherans, proposed some time ago to translate the *Family Expositor* into High Dutch; upon which the Lutheran clergy were alarmed, and dreadfully afraid of your introducing the leaven of Calvinism into the Lutheran churches, which obliged the good Abbot to translate your sermons on the Nature and Efficacy of Grace, as a proof of your moderation in these points; which I believe by this time had the desired effect. [20]

This is an important letter. The sterile continental high Calvinism feared by the Lutherans was one of the influences suffered by John Fletcher of Madeley before he left his native Switzerland to come to

England.[21] It is possible that this eminent man might never have so readily embraced Arminianism if he had tasted Doddridge's warm-hearted, evangelical 'Baxterian Calvinism'.

Doddridge was also cheered by other news from Germany. Writing to Samuel Wood in Norwich in 1750, he reported:

> I believe a college of the Reformed (that is the Calvinists) will be formed at Breslau; which will have a wonderful influence on the state of religion in Silesia, and probably be attended with the greatest effects of anything that has happened in Germany, since that wonderful affair at Halle.[22]

Doddridge's concern for the unity of the Protestant Churches also made him vulnerable. Whenever division was apparent, he was distressed. One of the factors which contributed to the breakdown of his health was the divisive influence of the Moravians in Northampton. Mention has been made of this in an earlier chapter. When several of Doddridge's well established (or so he thought) members were drawn away from his ministry, he suffered deep discouragement. Doddridge confided in a number of his friends over the matter, including Whitefield, Samuel Wood of Norwich, Richard Pearsall of Warminster and Samuel Clark, his old friend at St Albans. Whitefield replied with tender sympathy, describing how his own labours had been similarly disrupted by sectarian strife.[23] Richard Pearsall gave Doddridge the timely reminder of Paul's 'thorn in the flesh', adding the following encouragements:

> Consider, Sir, the Lord has done you more honour than even any man in your day; there is no one whose works have been translated into such various languages, and have had so wide a spread. Methinks, I cannot but apply to you those words, "Thou art a chosen vessel unto me, to bear my name among the Gentiles." Among the Dutch, the French, and Germans! O, Sir, while this honour is so extraordinary, it is a great trial of your humility. I know you will adore, with a profound prostration of soul, and say, that by the grace of God you are what you are; that every part of your furniture, both in head, heart and elocution, comes from on high: go on to do so, and it will be a token for good, that the Lord will do more still by you.[24]

Doddridge was cheered by the kindness of his friends. However, though sanctified to him, the disappointments left their mark.

The chief factor in Doddridge's physical decline was the death of his 'worthy and honoured friend', the Revd Samuel Clark on December 5, 1750. Riding in wintry conditions to preach at the funeral, Doddridge caught a chill from which he never fully recovered. The symptoms hung around him all the following summer. Writing to Samuel Wood from Sudbury in June 1751, Doddridge revealed what were in fact the symptoms of tuberculosis:

> Hardly any disappointment of the kind ever hung heavier upon me than that of not seeing you here ... Go on vigorously with the youth's scheme. It is our sheet anchor ... The frequent returns of my cough alarm my friends, and those in town say I am grown many years older since they saw me last. I leave the event with God.[25]

In August 1751, Doddridge was advised by his physician to visit Bristol and avail himself of the 'hot-wells' there. Before leaving, he preached what proved to be his last sermon to his people from the words, 'For whether we live, we live unto the Lord; and whether we die, we die unto the Lord: whether we live therefore, or die, we are the Lord's' (Romans 14: 8).[26] On arriving at Bristol, Doddridge was greeted by the Bishop of Worcester Dr Maddox. Another Anglican clergyman provided hospitality (despite only slight acquaintance with the sick man) until accommodation could be found nearer the wells. The stay at Bristol did not bring the hoped for recovery, yet the dying man could write to a friend:

> I see, indeed, no hope of recovery, yet my heart rejoiceth in my God, and in my Saviour; and I can call Him under this failure of everything else its strength and everlasting portion... God hath, indeed, been wonderfully good to me; but I am less than the least of His children. Adored be His grace for whatever it hath wrought by me.[27]

On becoming weaker still, Doddridge was advised to take a voyage to Lisbon, where it was hoped the more clement weather might stimulate a recovery. Leaving Bristol for Falmouth on September

17, Doddridge and his wife stayed for a few days at Bath as the guests of Lady Huntingdon. Numerous letters arrived full of anxious enquiries after his health. Faithful John Barker was almost beside himself :

> Stay, Doddridge, Oh, stay, and strengthen our hands, whose shadows grow long. Fifty is but the height of vigour, usefulness, and honour. Do not take leave abruptly. Providence hath not yet directed thee on whom to drop thy mantle. Who shall instruct our youth, fill our vacant churches, animate our associations, and diffuse a spirit of piety, moderation, candour, and charity through our villages and churches, and a spirit of prayer and supplication into our towns and cities, when thou art removed from us? Especially, who shall unfold the sacred oracles, teach us the meaning and use of our Bibles, rescue us from the bondage of systems, party opinions, empty, useless, speculations, and fashionable forms and phrases, and point out the simple, intelligible, consistent religion of our Lord and Saviour? Who shall – but I am silenced by the voice of Him who says, "Shall I not do what I will with my own? – Is it not my prerogative to take and leave, as seemeth me good? – I demand the liberty of disposing of my own servants at my own pleasure. He hath laboured more abundantly. His times are in my hand."[28]

Dr Oliver was convinced that Doddridge would never see his native land again and Doddridge himself did not relish the approaching voyage. But having agreed to go, he confessed in a hoarse whisper:

> The means I am pursuing to save life, so far as I am solely concerned, are to my apprehension worse than death. My profuse night-sweats are very weakening to my material frame; but the most distressing nights to this frail body have been as the beginning of heaven to my soul. God hath, as it were, let heaven down upon me in those nights of weakness and waking. Blessed be His name.[29]

On the morning of the day on which Doddridge, his wife and some friends set out for Falmouth, Lady Huntingdon came into the

Doctor's room, only to find him weeping, with his Bible open before him. He had been reading the words, 'O Daniel, a man greatly beloved' (Daniel 10: 11-12). "You are in tears, sir," said the Countess. "I am weeping, madam," replied the good doctor, "but they are tears of comfort and joy. I can give up my country, my relations, and friends into the hand of God; and as to myself, I can as well go to heaven from Lisbon as from my study at Northampton."[30] After a tiring journey to Falmouth, Doddridge wrote to Risdon Darracott:

> I am, upon the whole, better than could be expected after such a journey. Let us thank God, and take courage. We may yet know many cheerful days. We shall at least know (why do I say *at least*) one joyful one, which shall be *eternal.* ... Oh! When shall we meet in that world, where we shall have nothing to lament, and nothing to fear for ourselves or each other, or any dear to us! Let us think of this as a momentary state, and aspire more ardently after the blessings of that. If I survive my voyage, a line shall tell you how I bear it; if not, all will be well; as good Mr Howe says, I hope I shall embrace the wave which, when I intended Lisbon, would land me in heaven! I am more afraid of doing what is wrong than of dying.[31]

On September 30, accompanied by an anxious Mercy, Doddridge set sail for Lisbon. He enjoyed the voyage, but far more did he enjoy the blessed presence of his Lord. He would say, "Such transporting views of the heavenly world is my Father now indulging me with, no words can express."[32] Mercy afterwards related how the rapture that lighted his face reminded her of his own lines:

> When death o'er nature shall prevail,
> And all the powers of language fail;
> Joy through my swimming eyes shall break,
> And mean the thanks I cannot speak.[33]

Philip and Mercy reached Lisbon on 13 October. The next day he wrote his final letter to Samuel Clark, Jnr. After describing the voyage and the magnificent view of Lisbon from the sea, Doddridge movingly declared:

Falmouth

I bless God, the most undisturbed serenity continues in my mind, and my strength holds proportion to my day. I still hope and trust in God and joyfully acquiesce in all he may do with me. When you see my dear friends of the congregation, inform them of my circumstances, and assure them, that I cheerfully submit myself to God. If I desire life may be restored, it is chiefly, that it may be employed in serving Christ among them; and that I am enabled by faith to look upon death, as an enemy that shall be destroyed; and can cheerfully leave my dear Mrs Doddridge a widow in this strange land, if such be the appointment of our heavenly Father. I hope I have done my duty, and *the Lord do, as seemeth good in his sight.*[34]

A brief recovery gave way to a blessed end. Comforting an apprehensive Mercy, he said:

I am sure my heavenly Father will be with you. – It is a joy to me to think, how many friends and comforts you are returning to. So sure am I that God will be with you and comfort you, that I think my death will be a greater blessing to you, than ever my life hath been.[35]

The sinking man told his courageous wife that he had been renewing his covenant engagements with God, and that he had a cheerful well-grounded hope through Christ of being received to His everlasting mercy.[36] By 3 am of the morning of October 26, 1751, Philip Doddridge was in heaven. Says Charles Stanford, 'Poor Mercy! To her the sun shone with a cruel glory, and the air swept with a mocking freshness now. But she was not left comfortless'.[37] Writing home to their children, Mercy declared:

Oh, my dear children, help me to praise Him! Such supports, such consolations, such comforts has he granted to the meanest of His creatures, that my mind at times is held in perfect astonishment, and is ready to burst into songs of praise, under its most exquisite distress. ... I mourn the best of husbands and of friends, removed from this world of sin and sorrow to the regions of immortal bliss and light. What a glory! What a mercy is it that I am enabled with my thoughts to pursue him there! You have lost the dearest and best of parents, the guide

The CHRISTIAN'S *Triumph over Death.*

A
SERMON

Occafioned by the much-lamented

DEATH

Of the REVEREND

PHILIP DODDRIDGE, D.D.

And MINISTER of the GOSPEL at
NORTHAMPTON.

Who died OCTOBER 26, 1751. in the
Fiftieth Year of his Age.

By *JOB ORTON.*

LONDON:

Printed and Sold by J. WAUGH at the *Turk's-Head* in
Lombard-ftreet, Mr. TOZER at *Exeter*, Mr. HOTHAM
at *York*, Mr. TRAIL and Mr. MILLER at *Edinburgh*, and Mr. BARRY at *Glafgow.*

MDCCLII.

of your youth! ... Our loss is great indeed! Yet let us be thankful that God ever gave us such a friend; that He has continued him so long with us ... And let us remember, that the best respect we can pay to his memory is to endeavour as far as we can to follow his example, to cultivate those amiable qualities that rendered him so justly dear to us, and so greatly esteemed by the world.[38]

George Whitefield was in America when he heard the news of Doddridge's death the following February. His words, in a letter to a friend in Charleston, were the prayer of many, 'Doctor Doddridge I find is gone; Lord Jesus prepare me to follow after!'[39]

No grave is to be seen in England to Dr Doddridge, since his remains were placed in the English cemetery in Lisbon. However, a fine monument was placed in Castle Hill Meeting House which includes the following epitaph by his friend Gilbert West:[40]

To the memory of
PHILIP DODDRIDGE, D. D.
Twenty-one years pastor of this church,
Director of a flourishing academy,
And author of many excellent writings;
By which
His pious, benevolent, and indefatigable zeal
To make men wise, good and happy,
Will far better be made known,
And perpetuated much longer,
Than by this obscure and perishable marble;
The humble monument, not of his praise,
But of their esteem, affection and regret,
Who knew him, lov'd him and lament him;
And who are desirous of recording in this inscription,
Their friendly but faithful testimony
To the many amiable and Christian virtues,
That adorned his more private character;
By which, though dead, he yet speaketh,
And, still present in remembrance,
Forcibly, though silently, admonisheth

His once beloved and ever grateful flock.
He was born [June 26], 1702
And died October 26, 1751

Despite Doddridge's many critics, others had the spiritual perception to discern his true worth. An example worth mentioning is the Revd Samuel Davies, 'one of the greatest divines the American Presbyterian Church has produced'.[41] He was author of the hymn, 'Great God of wonders' and, in his last years, President of New Jersey College (later Princeton University). Like his predecessors Aaron Burr and Jonathan Edwards, Davies delighted in Doddridge's writings. On January 25, 1752, he wrote to Mercy of her late husband:

> Though I never had the happiness of an interview with him, he has made an entire conquest of my heart, in a degree peculiar to himself, that I am often surprised at it, and am at a loss to account for it. I am an admirer of his writings, and both I and my family are everyday instructed by his excellent *Family Expositor*. But it is his spirit and temper that most powerfully charms me. There are two things which for some years have appeared to me as the most amiable accomplishments of human nature, and they are - an ardent zeal for God, and a generous benevolence to all mankind. These, I must own, are my favourite virtues, and these appear to me to have been the very characteristics of the Doctor's spirit which so peculiarly endears his memory to me. I think you also inherit no small share of his spirit, and therefore you have a proportionate share in my affection ... You could not have complimented Mrs Davies with a more acceptable present than Dr Doddridge's hymns, and I shall sometimes circulate the pleasure through our congregation by using them in public worship. ... I know no book in the world of human composition better adapted to good in Virginia than the *Rise and Progress of Religion*. God has already blessed it to sundry.[42]

Two years later, Samuel Davies visited England on a fund-raising tour for the College. His *Diary* records a moving visit to Northampton:

August 11 [1754], Preached in Dr Doddridge's pulpit; and the sight of his monument with a very significant inscription, struck my mind with uncommon energy. The congregation is decreased since the doctor's death, as they can find none to supply his place fully. ... Mrs Doddridge procured me three guineas. Dined with her, and found her conversation animated with good sense and piety. She remembered me as a correspondent of 'the dear deceased', as she calls the doctor, and treated me with uncommon friendship. I was surprised that she could talk of him with so much composure, notwithstanding her flowing affections. She told me she never had a more comfortable season, than when returning from Lisbon, on the boisterous ocean, after the doctor's death.

Davies left Northampton the next day after another remarkable conversation with Mercy:

August 12, Spent an hour with dear Mrs Doddridge, and at her request, parted with prayer, in which I found my heart much enlarged. She made a remark that has often occurred to me since, that 'she rejoiced that the dear deceased was called to the tribunal of his Master with a heart full of such generous schemes for the good of mankind, which he had zeal to project, though not life to execute'. May this be my happy case.[43]

Davies himself was to have an early entrance into heaven, dying in 1761 at the age of only thirty-eight. Whitefield was to end his extraordinary earthly course in 1770 at the age of fifty-six. Charles Wesley laboured on fruitfully until 1788, dying at the age of eighty-one. At the remarkable age of eighty-eight, his brother John died in 1791 having preached the Gospel for forty years after Doddridge's death.

What estimate can be made of Doddridge's life and labours? As with all of God's servants, the true worth of their exploits is recorded above. One hazards the opinion that the traditional human assessment of Doddridge is at greater variance with the divine than one may imagine. Not all will agree with the conclusions of Samuel Davies. A division of opinion will no doubt always exist on the many facets of Doddridge's life and work. In a 'dumbed down' age when truth continues to be discounted and true charity is also in short supply, some will continue to think he was too charitable while others will lament his orthodoxy. This much will not be contested, except by his bitterest critics, that Philip Doddridge was a man after God's own heart. In physical terms, Orton tells us that Doddridge was 'rather above the middle stature, extremely thin and slender',[44] but in spiritual terms he was 'a giant'. The secret of his godliness seems to be, that in him, truth and charity were happily united. If one was to follow him, as he followed Christ, one would not go far astray.

Viewing the work of Doddridge as a whole, his piety was his primary motivation in everything he did. His spirituality is diffused through all his works. Notwithstanding this necessary observation, what are we to make of Doddridge's response to the demands of his age? In academy lectures and meeting house expositions, Doddridge made a contribution that was intellectual without becoming scholastic, spiritual without becoming mystical, warm without being sentimental and practical without being hypocritical. He demonstrated biblical balance and integrity. For him the Word of Truth was the Word of Life and Christian life demanded Christian action.

We must however ask, whether a different Doddridge might have emerged had he not distributed his energies over so wide a field. Did the demands of the academy affect the success of the pastorate? Did the roles of lecturer and preacher demand too much of one man? These and other questions naturally arise from a study of this man's life. Whether or not he had too many irons in the fire must be left to the reader's judgement. As with Whitefield, Doddridge desired to wear out in his Master's service rather than rust away. If he could have chosen his life span, Doddridge would not have desired a life different from the one he had, unless greater usefulness would have resulted. We must not forget that God equips His servants with the gifts and abilities they require for the work they are called to perform. As an intellectual, Doddridge did not perhaps have the metaphysical genius of Jonathan Edwards. As a hymn-writer, he did not have the poetical genius of Charles Wesley. As a preacher, he did not have the oratorical genius of George Whitefield. Yet, having said this, who among those eighteenth-century worthies could be compared with Philip Doddridge for an all-round competence? For sound biblical balance, practical wisdom, orthodox hymnology and consistent preaching, he was probably unsurpassed. If others were greater in their particular spheres, none was more useful overall.

Of all Doddridge's published works, the hymns will continue to honour his memory, cheering God's people until the end of time. The *Lectures* soon became, for the greater part, a museum piece, due to their largely contemporary value. The comprehensive syllabus became too broad for later generations of more pietistic and socially orientated Evangelicals, whilst the theological orthodoxy appeared too conservative for later generations of liberal Nonconformists. If ever the *Rise and Progress* were to be republished, it would be warmly received by those who seek to 'do justly, love mercy and walk humbly with their God' (Micah 6: 8). If the *Family Expositor* was again made available, it would make no less a contribution in meeting the needs of pastors, Bible class leaders, Sunday-school teachers and parents than Matthew Henry's *Commentary* continues to make.

Perhaps one further question remains. What might Doddridge have accomplished had he lived longer? In general terms, he would doubtless have continued as productively as he had lived. His evangelistic publishing plans were truly international. Concerned no less for the spread of the Gospel in the United Kingdom, he contributed to the publication of evangelical literature in Wales. A Welsh translation of the *Rise and Progress* appeared in 1788. Among several publishing proposals mentioned by Kippis was a new translation of the minor prophets. This work was 'nearly completed ... in which [Doddridge] displayed his critical knowledge of the Hebrew language'.[45] His friend Richard Pearsall of Warminster urged him more than once to produce a *Body of Divinity*, 'of a mixed nature, doctrinal and practical ... Do not let the proposal die as soon as read, but think of it. Hereby you might instruct and lead towards heaven, after you are safely lodged there'.[46] When Pearsall first suggested the idea as early as 1741, he thought 'that Dr Doddridge is the finest man to execute it in Great Britain. I believe I should call such a performance, if I lived to see it, the best that I had ever seen'.[47]

Whatever Doddridge thought of the idea, he left no record of it.

DECHREUAD a CHYNNYDD

CREFYDD yn yr ENAID.

A eglurwyd mewn amryw

GYFARCHIADAU

Difrifol ac ymarferol,

wedi eu cymhwyſo

At bob Mâth ac Amgylchiad o Ddynion;

GYDA

DUWIOL FYFYRDOD, neu WEDDI,

Wedi ci 'chwanegu at bob Pennod.

Gan P. DODDRIDGE, D. D.

———

Agyfieithwyd i'r Gymraeg allan o'r unfed ar ddêg
Argraffiad yn Saef'neg, er llês i'r Cymru un Iaith,

Gan JOHN GRIFFITH, Gweinidog yr Efengyl.

———

Gan dyſtiolaethu — yr Edifeirwch ſy tuag at Dduw, a'r Ffydd ſy
tuag at ein Harglwydd Ieſu Griſt. *Aɛtau* xx. 21.

Yr hwn ydym ni yn ei bregethu, gan rybyddio pob Dyn, a dyſgu pob
Dyn ym mhob doethineb, fel y cyflwynom bob Dyn yn berffaith
yn Ghriſt Ieſu. *Col.* i. 28.

———

Yn YMWYTHIG:

Argraffwyd ac ar werth gan J. a W. EDDOWES,
a chan yr Awdwr yn ABERGAFENNY, 1788.

Pris 2s. mewn papur glâs, neu 2s. 6c. wedi ei rwymo.]

However, he showed definite interest in another publishing project in the last year of his life. When Isaac Toms of Hadleigh in Suffolk wrote to Doddridge about the continuing sufferings of the Huguenots, the 'excellent letter' clearly revived a concern which was already close to his heart. Despite worsening ill health, he replied with deep feeling:

> I have read and heard a great deal of the sufferings of our Protestant brethren in France; I have conversed with those who saw their assemblies dissolved, their temples ruined, and their dead torn out of the graves and given to the fowls of the air. I have read the letters of their pastors, and their martyrs; and the incomparable discourses of Superville and Saurin, which so pathetically represent their sufferings; and one of the last was before me when your letter came; and yet, alas! I have in great measure forgotten the afflictions of Joseph [Amos 6: 6]; now and then a transient prayer for them, or the telling of their sad sorrows (with a few tears) to my pupils, children and friends, has been all the fruit of my compassion.[48]

Doddridge agreed with Toms that approaches should be made throughout England, Scotland, Ireland and America to arrange a day of fasting and prayer for their French brethren. Despite being busily engaged finishing his *Family Expositor*, Doddridge promised, 'If God spare my life I will preach, and, if it be thought proper, will publish the discourse'.[49]   Now, one of the chief sources of information about the Huguenots was John Quick's double-folio, the *Synodicon in Gallia Reformata*, published in 1692. The same author had also compiled a series of biographies of fifty pastors, theologians and martyrs of the French Reformed Churches, the *Icones Sacrae Gallicanae*.[50] The manuscript remained unpublished at the time of Quick's death in 1706. Doddridge evidently shared Toms' enthusiasm for publishing Quick's material:

> Quick's *Synodicon* I have. The *Icones* I shall be very glad to see, when you can conveniently spare them, but I think whatever views we may have secretly, with regard to their publication, it will be proper to reserve them in our own breasts till the first grand part of our scheme is brought into full execution, which

may prepare a way for the other.[51]

Sadly, with his death eight months later, nothing came of this project. One may even say – two-and-a-half centuries later – that it remains unfinished business.

Had he lived, Doddridge would undoubtedly have been drawn more deeply into the activities of Whitefield and the Wesleys. His 'Baxterian Calvinist' position ideally placed him to promote harmony between the two evangelists and keep the Methodist movement united. Besides aiding his own evangelistic concerns, Methodism would have reinforced Doddridge's passion for Protestant unity. As we have seen, his ecumenical commitment involved him in practical discussions with Anglican churchmen. Although Doddridge was the pastor of an independent or congregational church, no Dissenter of his day could be less isolationist than he. One may even argue that despite his misgivings about the hierarchical nature of both episcopalian and presbyterian church order, Doddridge never entirely forsook his presbyterian origins. Notwithstanding his rejection of 'authoritative synods', he restored the office of elder at Castle Hill. Furthermore, in his reply to Toms, he desired 'concurrence with our brethren of the [Scottish] establishment, for which, as an Establishment, we have something of a regard'.[52] Without speculating too much beyond the available evidence, it is very possible that Doddridge's increasing contact with the Dutch Reformed Churches in his last decade might have drawn him to an English ecclesiastical model based on the non-hierarchical synodical polity established in the Netherlands. Unlike Presbyterian order, where authority is derived from both Scripture *and* the power of the assembly, Reformed polity bases its power exclusively on the Word of God.[53] This was a principle of paramount importance to Philip Doddridge. Thus, he might have approved of a *via media* between English Independency and Scottish Presbyterianism.

More important than either books or church government, the fragrance of Doddridge's piety would have continued to exert a wonderful influence had he lived. In this respect, Doddridge was a legend in his lifetime. So much so that the physician Thomas Pearce was tempted to leave Somerset:

I am heartily glad there is such a spot of ground in Great Britain as Northampton, so well planted, and with so much love and heaven in it; [but] I must not think of attempting a removal.[54]

Of course, we must be thankful to God for the life span Doddridge was given and the many legacies we possess from his pilgrimage and ministry. Accordingly, the unworthy author of this brief and inadequate portrait of a spiritual giant includes Doddridge among that glorious host, 'of whom the world was not worthy' (Hebrews 11: 38). We best honour his memory by endeavouring to live as he lived. Doddridge, though dead, 'yet speaketh', encouraging us to go on singing:

> Blest Saviour, introduced by thee
>   Have I my race begun;
> And crowned with victory, at thy feet
>   I'll lay my honours down.[55]

It is fitting to conclude with our hero's own epigram on the family motto, 'Dum Vivimus Vivamus' (In living, LIVE!), described by Dr Johnson as one of the finest ever written in the English language.[56] Nothing says more, in so few words, to explain the fragrant faithfulness of this blessed man's life:

> Live while you live, the epicure would say,
> And seize the pleasures of the present day.
> Live while you Live, the sacred preacher cries,
> And give to God each moment as it flies.
> Lord, in my view, let both united be,
> I live in pleasure, when I live to Thee!

A

C O U R S E

OF

L E C T U R E S

On the PRINCIPAL SUBJECTS in

PNEUMATOLOGY, ETHICS,

AND

D I V I N I T Y:

WITH

REFERENCES to the moſt conſiderable AUTHORS on each Subject.

By the late Reverend PHILIP DODDRIDGE, D.D.

The SECOND EDITION, Corrected.

L O N D O N,

Printed by Aſſignment from the Author's Widow,

For J. BUCKLAND, J. F. and C. RIVINGTON, W. CLARKE and R. COLLINS, S. CROWDER, T. LONGMAN, B. LAW, E. JOHNSTON, G. ROBINSON, R. BALDWIN, and W. OTRIDGE.

MDCCLXXVI.

Note: The archaic 'pneumatology' means 'the study of spiritual beings'. Nearest modern equivalent is 'psychology'.

Appendix
Doddridge: Hero or Heretic?
A response to Professor Donald Macleod (and others)

I

Nichol's evaluation (see p. 130) is also cited in a recent discussion of Doddridge by Professor Donald Macleod.[1] However, he is quick to point out that no documentation is given. Macleod then conducts an analysis of Doddridge's views, first on the popular level and second on the academic. Turning to Doddridge's treatment of such key texts as John 1: 1, Acts 20: 28 and Romans 9: 5 in the *Family Expositor*, Macleod is happy to report that Doddridge is 'unashamedly, indeed aggressively, orthodox'.[2] However, a less confident verdict is given on the contents of the *Course of Lectures on the Principal Subjects in Pneumatology, Ethics and Divinity*.

While Macleod acknowledges that 'the arguments for Christ's Deity are clearly stated' in the lectures, he laments an element of ambiguity.[3] This chiefly concerns Doddridge's apparent endorsement of Isaac Watts' speculative theory of the pre-existence of the [created or derived] human soul of Christ. Whatever may be said of the theory, Doddridge did not, like over-conciliatory Watts, advance it as a concession to the Arians. And why? Clearly because he did not agree with Watts that the theory makes sense of the favourite Arian proof text: 'He is the image of the invisible God, the first born of every creature' (Col. 1: 15). In short, in no sense is Paul suggesting that Christ was a 'creature'. Thus Doddridge paraphrases Paul:

> For he is indeed *the* brightest and most express *image of the invisible* and eternal *God*, whom no man hath seen at any time, nor can see; *[and] the First-born of the whole creation*, existing before it, and begotten to inherit it as the great Heir of all. And his nature has a transcendent excellency, infinitely superior to any thing that is made; *for by him were all things created, things in heaven and things on earth*.[4]

Significantly, Doddridge's precise fidelity to Scripture rescues him from the deleterious potential of doubtful speculations. (Indeed, this has been the case with all the great but fallible minds of the Christian Church. Augustine, Luther, Calvin and even Jonathan Edwards have all exhibited theological blemishes. (Happily, this deters – or should deter – Christians from idolising men!) Furthermore, peppered as Doddridge's lectures are with Scripture references and comments, he frequently refers the student to the *Family Expositor* for clarification. In short, where relevant, the *Lectures* should be studied in the light of the *Expositor*. In this respect, as Macleod seems to agree without reservation, Doddridge is impeccably orthodox.[5] While Watts' theory certainly touches on fundamental Christian truth, nonetheless, where the lectures are concerned, nothing that Doddridge argues for interferes with his clear, biblical affirmation of the Deity of Christ. One may confidently say that he had no sympathy for Arian error even though he admits to leaning towards this view in his early years. For those who demand evidence of Doddridge's orthodoxy, the following extracts from the *Family Expositor* should suffice:

> (I AM ALPHA AND OMEGA). That these titles should be repeated so soon, in a connection which demonstrates they are given to Christ, will appear very remarkable & And I cannot forbear recording it, that this text has done more than any other in the Bible, toward preventing us from giving in to that scheme, which would make our Lord Jesus Christ no more than a deified creature *(Note on Revelation 1:11).*[6]

> I am deeply sensible of the sublime and mysterious nature of the doctrine of Christ's deity, as here declared; but it would be quite foreign to my purpose to enter into a large discussion of that great foundation of our faith, it has often been done by much abler hands. It was, however, a matter of conscience with me, on the one hand, thus strongly to declare my belief of it; and, on the other, to leave it as far as I could in the simplicity of scripture expressions *(Note on John 1:1).*[7]

> Justly hath our Redeemer said, blessed is the man that is not offended in me: and we may peculiarly apply the words to that great and glorious doctrine of the deity of Christ, which is here before us. A thousand high and curious thoughts will naturally arise in our corrupt hearts on this view of it; but may divine grace subdue them all to the obedience of an humble faith; so that, with Thomas, we may each of us fall down at his feet, and cry out with sincere and unreserved devotion, My Lord and my God! *(Improvement on John 1:1-14).*[8]

Whatever doubts Macleod and others have expressed regarding Doddridge's lectures, it should be remembered that in their published form they could not reflect all that was said in the lecture room. Questions by the students and elaborations by the tutor would have shed light on any misunderstandings. So, as published, they require careful reading. This certainly applies to Professor Macleod's next point that Doddridge 'gave the impression of being uncommitted on the question' of whether the Holy Spirit is a *person or a power*.[9] Macleod states that Doddridge 'contents himself' with summarising the arguments for and against. But nothing could be further from the truth. Had Macleod read on a little further he would have seen Doddridge's clear conclusion:

> On the whole, forasmuch as the Spirit is plainly spoken of in Scripture under a personal character, it is proper to retain that language in discoursing of him and praying for him, ... [10]

This clearly reflects Article 18 of Doddridge's ordination *Confession of Faith* (1730):

> I believe that the sacred SPIRIT, who is the grand agent in the Redeemer's Kingdom, is a divine person united with the Father and the Son in an adorable and incomprehensible manner; and thus I learn and firmly believe the great doctrine of a TRINITY of persons in the unity of the Godhead, an aweful mystery which, being a matter of pure revelation, I apprehend I should only obscure by attempting fully to explain it.[11]

On so basic a doctrine as the Trinity, Doddridge honestly faced the problems we all have in making conceptual sense of our faith. He was afraid of giving the impression that there are three gods – a misunderstanding which the Athanasian creed might suggest but is careful to avoid – and equally he was at pains to avoid the idea that the names of the three persons are but mere names of one person – the Sabellian heresy. His statement of the Trinity in his Divinity Lectures is, like his Confession, simple and straightforward:

> The Scripture represents the Divine being as appearing in, and manifesting himself by the distinct persons of Father, Son, and Holy Ghost, each of which has his peculiar province in accomplishing the work of our redemption and salvation, and to each of which we owe an unlimited veneration, love and obedience.[12]

Professor Macleod's fourth criticism concerns Doddridge's teaching method, a matter discussed in Chapter 5. Even here, Macleod is rather misleading when he says that Doddridge simply referred his students to the relevant literature on a given question, leaving them to decide for themselves.[13] Our understanding is not helped by Macleod's citation of the notorious Joseph Priestley who (as the professor does admit) actually studied under Doddridge's former assistant, Caleb Ashworth at Daventry. Undoubtedly, Priestley relished the 'free enquiry' encouraged by the course: ' ... we were referred to authors on both sides of every question, and were then required to give an account of them'.[14]   But, is Macleod right to conclude that Doddridge appears indifferent to truth?   The student recollections (italics mine) of Job Orton produce a fuller and rather different impression:

> He never expected nor desired, that they should *blindly* follow his sentiments, but permitted and encouraged them to judge for themselves.   To assist them herein, *he laid before them what he apprehended to be the truth with all perspicuity*, and impartially stated all objections to it.   He never concealed the difficulties which affected any question, but referred them to writers on both sides, without hiding any from their inspection. *He frequently and warmly urged them not take their system of divinity from any man or body of men, but from the Word of God. The Bible was always referred and appealed to upon every point in question* to which it was supposed it could give any light.[15]

As a son of the Reformation, believing with Luther in *sola scriptura* and the right of private judgement, is it too much to claim that Philip Doddridge was a theologian in the Reformed tradition?   Professor Macleod (and others) might contest the claim, if only on the grounds that Doddridge, to preserve his theological freedom, refused to subscribe to the Catholic creeds (Apostles, Nicene and Athanasian) *and* the major confessions of the Reformed tradition.   Indeed, although Doddridge represented the English puritan tradition, one looks in vain in his writings for references to the Presbyterian *Westminster Confession* (1645) or even the Congregational *Savoy Declaration* (1658).   Not that he was entirely opposed to man-made confessions and catechisms or that he disapproved of their essential teachings, but, as has already been noted, at his ordination in 1730 Doddridge summed up his convictions in a 26-article confession.   This was not a mere account of 'personal experience' as Macleod seems to imagine.[16]   As a credal statement, it certainly reflected many of the convictions of the 16th, 17th and even earlier centuries. While he refused an invitation from a London church since subscription to the *Westminster Shorter Catechism* was required,[17] he was happy to recommend its use to his students in their pastorates.[18]

What then was Doddridge's concern?   In view of the divisions between the different varieties of Protestant churchmanship – Anglican, Presbyterian, Independent and Baptist (in which much basic agreement could be demonstrated), Doddridge believed that *sola scriptura* had to be the only *obligatory* basis of faith and unity. Since all believed in the inspiration and authority of the Bible, so Doddridge makes this moving appeal in his *Dissertation on the Inspiration of the New Testament*:

> O that the powerful charm of this blessed book might prevail to draw all that do sincerely regard it, into this centre of unity! That, dropping those unscriptural forms, which have so lamentably divided the church, we might more generally content ourselves with the simplicity of divine truths as they are here taught, and agree to put the mildest and kindest interpretation we can, upon the language and sentiments of each other.[19]

In his academy lectures, Doddridge rejects *obligatory* subscription to human standards for five reasons. *First*, Scripture provides no instance of such a requirement; *second*, such could never be superior to the Scriptures themselves; *third*, such standards have generally led to division rather than unity; *fourth*, such potential for disunity would deter men of 'tender conscience'; *fifth*, men of little integrity might, in the name of a spurious peace, subscribe to things they really doubt by 'putting the most unnatural sense on the words'.[20]

After admitting that Doddridge's case is both 'plausible' and 'honest', Professor Macleod argues that it 'represents an attempt to escape from history'.[21] But this verdict is simply wrong. Doddridge's point is that so much church history is *bad* history and should be assessed critically. If sound affirmations created 'good history' according to the criterion of Scripture, then all that matters is subscribing to Scripture in the first place. Indeed, Christians are arguably obliged *only* to submit to Scripture. As for the orthodoxy Macleod feels is threatened without the Nicene Creed, Doddridge's writings endorse all that is biblical in the creed's exclusion of Arian heterodoxy. His dismissal of Arianism is on the basis of Scripture rather than the formal say-so of Nicaea. If this radical appeal to *sola scriptura* is indeed 'honest' in Macleod's view, what may be said of the 'confessional' outlook? Does it really possess *biblical* integrity?

Professor Macleod also criticises Doddridge's use of a 'personal' confession at his ordination as being 'excessively individualistic'.[22] Thus he objects: why did he not use 'one of the great ecumenical creeds or one of great Protestant confessions?' Doddridge's answer – evidently missed by Macleod – is found in his lectures: 'Great care ought to be taken, that we subscribe nothing that we do not firmly believe'.[23] Yes, he had studied the Fathers, the Reformers and the Puritans, and the world-wide theological community down the ages, but – apart from the dubious principle of obligatory subscription to man-made creeds – Doddridge evidently found ideas and terminology in the historic symbols that he could not honestly accept. Indeed, does Professor Macleod 'firmly believe' *every* word of the *Westminster Confession*? I very much doubt it!

An important ingredient in Doddridge's approach is his opposition to the scholasticism of the patristic, medieval *and* post-Reformation periods – even among the Reformed. In his lectures on the Trinity, he rounds off the discussion by a telling and striking quotation:

> Dr Jeremiah Taylor says, "that he who goes about to speak of the mystery of the trinity, and does it by words and names of man's invention, talking of essences and existences, hypostases and personalities, priorities in co-equalities, &c, and unity in pluralities, may amuse himself and build a tabernacle in his head, and talk something he knows not what; but the good man, that feels the power of the Father, and to whom the Son is become wisdom, sanctification and redemption, in whose heart the love of the Spirit of God is shed abroad, this man, though he understands nothing of what is unintelligible, yet he alone truly understands the Christian doctrine of the Trinity."[24]

Thus Macleod also accuses Doddridge of resorting to a 'simplistic biblicism'.[25] What a strange criticism for a Reformed theologian to make of a faithful and radical biblicist! Did not Luther effectively face the same criticism in his day? Macleod continues: 'There is nothing whatever in the Reformation slogan, *sola scriptura*, to preclude the use of creeds and confessions in the church'.[26] But this is not the issue. Doddridge is opposed to *obligatory* not voluntary subscription, as his own Northampton confession proves. Neither was he being inconsistent in using non-biblical terms like *Trinity* and various traditional scholastic concepts like *substance* and *person* (political and philosophical!) in his lectures. The *chief issue* – reflected in his life-long policy – is clearly stated in his confession (italics mine):

> ... This I offer not as a complete abstract of the Christian revelation in all its branches, but as such an account of my own belief as the occasion requires and present convenience would admit. I have nothing further to add but that, though *I have used some human phrases which seemed to me properly to express the sense of Scripture, yet I would by no means offer any of them as a standard by which opinions are to be tried, nor quarrel with any who may not be thoroughly satisfied with them*, for it is one very important article of my faith that I am bound in duty affectionately to esteem and embrace all who practically comply with the design of the revelation and love of our Lord Jesus Christ in

sincerity, how much soever they may differ from myself in their language or their conceptions about any speculative points.[27]

Doddridge's position is clear. While he never denied that the Anglican, Westminster, Savoy and Baptist divines sincerely sought to draft their confessions 'in submission to Scripture', he obviously could not agree that they were successful in every respect. Since 'great care ought to be taken, that we subscribe nothing that we do not firmly believe', Doddridge had no honest alternative to the policy he adopted for himself and recommended to his students. The sad fact that some abused Scripture in the interests of Unitarianism is no reason to adopt a 'Bible *plus* Creed' subscriptionism. Indeed, it is always the *plus* factor that creates problems, whether the theology is Roman or Anglican – or even Reformed!

Macleod further criticises what he calls Doddridge's 'appeal to the sufficiency of Scripture' on the grounds that the New Testament writers never faced the issues raised by 4th century Arianism.[28] Does Macleod realise what he is pleading for? Isn't he suspiciously close to the Roman Catholic view that the Bible requires the magisterial pronouncements of dogmatic tradition to safeguard its true meaning? To say that Doddridge merely resorts to 'the mechanical citation of biblical texts' to settle the true meaning of John 1: 1 and Colossians 1: 15 in favour of Christ's deity, is to impugn the adequacy of the Holy Spirit's revelatory influence. A reading of *The Family Expositor* easily proves that Doddridge was perfectly capable of rescuing these texts from Arian exegesis without resorting to the protection of Nicene or Athanasian orthodoxy. He clearly had a higher view of Scripture – its inspiration, authority *and* sufficiency – than Professor Macleod has. In the face of heresy, Doddridge clearly believed the Bible could stand on its own feet!

Dr Carl Trueman's explicit and implicit references to Doddridge[29] *vis-à-vis* John Owen are relevant at this point. Regarding the latter's Trinitarian scholasticism, Trueman states that 'it would be inaccurate to interpret the Protestant notion of *sola scriptura* in such a way as to regard it as a sufficient safeguard in and of itself to safeguard the church against heresy in the seventeenth-century context. In fact, Owen's defence of orthodox Christology in the face of the radically biblicist attacks of the Socinians clearly depends upon setting the notion of *sola scriptura* and scriptural exegesis within the ongoing catholic theological tradition'.[30] This is a clear denial of the sufficiency of Scripture, as one reviewer of Trueman's *The Claims of Truth* was quick to point out.[31] As such, the consequences are serious. If Trinitarian believers cannot refute Arians and Socinians by appealing to the Bible only, then their claim to champion the biblical Gospel is open to question.

Trueman traces the rise of eighteenth-century 'Enlightenment' heterodoxy (the kind common in Doddridge's day) to a repudiation of Owen's type of 'scholastic Protestantism'.[32] Of course, this was the great difference between Owen's and Doddridge's eras, occasioned by the rise of John Locke's empiricism and the scientific movement. But Trueman sees necessary connections between scholasticism and orthodoxy on one hand, and between Enlightenment thought and heterodoxy on the other. This is all highly questionable if only because Doddridge, though a son of the Enlightenment and an admirer of Locke,[33] tenaciously held to a truly biblical Christology and soteriology without any help from Owen's type of scholasticism. Enlightenment thought was not necessarily opposed to biblical orthodoxy. Doddridge and his evangelical friends did not adopt the reductionist agenda of Enlightenment liberals who tended to throw the baby out with the bathwater. That said, unlike Owen's era, Doddridge's was marked by an appeal to *data* rather than *dogma*. Whereas the 'over-orthodox' elements in Owen's theology – a kind of medieval hangover – were d*ogma-driven*, Doddridge's biblical theology was *data-driven*. In short, an incipient rationalism was at work in Owen's thought (as Richard Muller would doubtless agree[34]). To be sure, not the kind of liberal rationalism of the eighteenth century but a rationalism all the same. By Trueman's own admission, Owen's theology was impossible on a purely *sola scriptura* basis. For Doddridge, the textual data of Holy Scripture was sufficient and decisive in the conflict with the *three* heterodoxies of Arianism, Arminianism *and* High Calvinism.

So, a case may still be made that much of Owen's ultra-orthodoxy is due to the influence of Aristotelian scholastic methodology and not simply to his Trinitarianism, as Trueman maintains.[35] But why, in Trueman's view, does a Trinitarian soteriology necessarily commit one to Owen's type of exclusive particularism? Calvin was no less Trinitarian when he anticipated the kind of 'double-aspect' soteriology embraced later by Amyraut, Baxter, Doddridge and others. Neither does this 'proto-Amyraldian' Trinitarianism drive a wedge between the intentions of the Father and the Son, as Roger Nicole and other critics repeatedly state.[36] It is a caricature to argue that it ends up with a disjunction between the universal intent of the Son and the particular intent of the Father. True, it teaches that the efficacy of an otherwise universal atonement is guaranteed by the Holy Spirit's work. However, Calvin – like his 'authentic disciples' – evidently taught that the persons of the Trinity concur in redeeming activity, *each in a dualistic way*: The Father reaches out to all while only grasping the elect; the Son redeems all sufficiently but only the elect effectually; the elect alone are regenerated by the Holy Spirit but others are still subject to His influence.[37] This soteriological scenario is no less

Trinitarian than Owen's but arguably more biblical as Doddridge evidently thought.[38]

A final criticism of Dr Trueman is in order. The title of his work, *The Claims of Truth* is unfortunate, since his interest is not, by his own admission, 'to discover whether Owen was right or wrong'.[39] Indeed, in view of his concern to validate Owen's approach, the book should have been called *The Claims of Scholasticism*. Of course, he attempts to dismiss my critique of Owen's Aristotelianised soteriology. But, besides his failure to grasp the details of my philosophical case against Owen, his aggressive 'boxing' style is as ineffective as it is inappropriate. In short, as 'referee' Dr Richard Muller virtually implied in an e-mail 'decision' to a friend of mine, I am 'still on my feet'! Without ever denying the scholastic element in Baxter's work,[40] I focused on Owen's scholasticism because, unlike Baxter's much less defective view, it had a detrimental influence on his treatment of the nature and extent of the atonement. It is undeniable that for Owen, his 'method' influenced the 'content' of his theology.

II

Despite his various misgivings, Professor Macleod is certainly justified in rescuing Doddridge's Trinitarian theology from unjust aspersion. However, his description of him as a 'Calvinist' is more generous than accurate if he means a theologian in the mould of Dr John Owen and the Westminster (or Savoy) divines. This is a point requiring detailed examination. For in failing to quote Doddridge *fully* in the context of his development, Macleod misrepresents him. It was an immature and undecided Doddridge who wrote to his brother-in-law about his Kibworth tutor, John Jennings (italics mine):

> He does not entirely accord with the system of any particular body of men; but is sometimes a Calvinist, sometimes a Remonstrant [Arminian], sometimes a Baxterian, and sometimes a Socinian, as truth and evidence determine him. *He always inculcates it upon our attention, that the Scriptures are the only standard of orthodoxy*, and encourages the utmost freedom of enquiry.[41]

The date should be noted. Doddridge wrote this in February 1723. What really impressed 'early Doddridge' was the appeal not to man-made systems (however acceptable) but to the Bible 'as the only standard of orthodoxy'. Like his Unitarian authority (who actually deleted it), Macleod fails to quote this key sentence[42]. In short, Doddridge is far from being inept. Five months before, in a letter to Samuel Clark, he made the same point with greater force and precision:

> Mr Jennings encourages the greatest freedom of enquiry, and always inculcates it as a law, that the Scriptures are the only genuine standard of faith.[43]

This leads us to the next important question: in what theological direction did Doddridge proceed? As we saw in Chapter 7, he became a 'Baxterian Calvinist', a label which requires careful clarification.

What then did 'Baxterian Calvinist' mean in Doddridge's day? First, we must be clear what 'Calvinism' meant to his generation. This was in reality an exaggerated, distorted and unbalanced version of the 'free grace' theology taught by Calvin and other theologians of the Reformation. Distinguishing between God's secret and revealed wills (Deut. 29: 29), Calvin urged believers to focus their faith on the latter. He consequently advised against a speculative preoccupation with the divine decrees. Notwithstanding his commitment to the doctrines of predestination and election *(secret will)*, Calvin taught the free offer of the Gospel and a universal atonement *(revealed will)*. In the face of such a paradox, reason must give way to faith. He urged people to turn to Christ and view election as a basis of assurance *after believing*. Under the influence of Calvin's successor Theodore Beza, the character of Reformed theology began to change into something significantly different from Calvin's Bible-based, Christ-centred emphasis. Driven by the desire for tighter systematisation, predestination was given greater prominence and the atonement was taught as strictly limited to the elect. Thus Aristotelian rationalism began to influence the form and content of dogma.[44] Reacting more to Beza's teaching than to Calvin's, Jakob Hermanszoon or Arminius led a protest in the Netherlands. His equally rationalistic five-point reaction produced the famous so-called 'five-point' or TULIP Reformed response at the Synod of Dordt (1618-9). Under the continuing influence of scholastic methodology, Calvin's balanced Biblicism – faithfully reflected in the Canons of Dordt – was replaced by the high orthodoxy of the Westminster Confession which gave greater priority to the divine decrees and maintained a rigid doctrine of limited atonement.[45]

Richard Baxter contested these 'over-orthodox' developments in England, and similar debates had occurred slightly earlier in France where Moïse Amyraut argued for a return to the more biblical views of Calvin. The 'High Calvinism' Doddridge faced in the eighteenth century exhibited further development during his lifetime. While many 'High Calvinist' Puritans had preached a 'free offer gospel', including a distinction between 'common' and 'special grace' and the duty of all to repent and believe, a simplistic logic led others to renounce these teachings. Thus in the even more extreme outlook of the 'Hyper Calvinists', election and limited atonement excluded the 'free offer' and 'duty faith'. All grace was 'special' and 'irresistible', and justification was 'eternal' rather than at the moment of believing. Among Doddridge's contemporaries, Dr John Gill was the chief exponent of these ideas. Another and more famous contemporary, John Wesley perpetuated the Arminian teaching, more as a continuing reaction to 'High Calvinism' than to Calvin's original emphasis. As we shall see, partly through Baxter's influence, Doddridge's theology was, in important respects, a return to Calvin's balanced biblicism.[46]

Dr Richard Muller concedes that Calvin's successors were more scholastic in method than the reformer. He even admits they were 'more rationalistic'.[47] However, he is careful to point out that Calvin, notwithstanding his strongly-expressed aversion to scholasticism in general, was not totally opposed to such modes of thought.[48] But despite Muller's attempts to argue continuity between Calvin and his successors, he fails to close the gap on the question of the extent of the atonement. He acknowledges that Calvin distinguished between the universalist and particular aspects of Christ's work, insisting that the reformer employs a distinction between what is 'unlimited' in 'fullness' and what is 'limited' in 'actuality'[49] (incidentally, the very kind of distinction affirmed by Amyraut but denied by many of the Reformed scholastics). While Muller agrees that Calvin's use of 'satisfaction' and 'expiation' connotes 'unlimited atonement', he argues that the reformer uses 'reconciliation' and 'redemption' in respect of 'limited atonement'.[50] There is confusion here. Calvin clearly uses *all* these terms to express 'benefits' available to all but only 'actually' enjoyed by the elect. Surprisingly, Muller fails to document his claims. The simple fact is that Calvin clearly used 'reconciliation' and 'redemption' in a universal sense, as a few brief specimens will show:

> When the Father calls Him the Beloved ... He declares that He is the Mediator in whom He reconciles the world to Himself *(Comment on Matthew 17:5).*[51]

> For [by Christ s death] we know that by the expiation of sins the world has been reconciled to God *(Comment on John 17:1).*[52]

> Moreover, we offer up our prayers unto Thee, O most Gracious God and most merciful Father, for all men in general ... as Thou art pleased to be acknowledged the Saviour of the whole human race by the redemption accomplished by Jesus Christ *(Forms of Prayer for the Church).*[53]

The draught appointed to Christ was to suffer the death of the cross for the reconciliation of the world *(Comment on John 18:11).*[54]

We have been reconciled to God by the death of Christ, Paul holds, because His was an expiatory sacrifice by which the world was reconciled to God *(Comment on Romans 5: 6-10).*[55]

God was in Christ and ... by this intervention He was reconciling the world to Himself. ... [Paul] says again that a commission to offer this reconciliation to us has been given to ministers of the Gospel ... He says that as He once suffered, so now every day He offers the fruit of His sufferings to us through the Gospel which He has given to the world as a sure and certain record of His completed work of reconciliation *(Comment on 2 Corinthians 5:19).*[56]

Whereas it is said that the Son of God was crucified, we must not only think that the same was done for the redemption of the world: but also every of us must on his own behalf join himself to our Lord Jesus Christ, and conclude, It is for me that he hath suffered. ... But when we once know that the thing was done for the redemption of the whole world, pertaineth to every of us severally: it behoveth every of us to say also on his own behalf, The Son of God hath loved me so dearly, that he hath given himself to death for me *(Sermons on Galatians).*[57]

Furthermore, regarding Muller's insistence that a 'hypothetical' dimension to the atonement is 'superfluous',[58] such a view is obviously not shared by Calvin who clearly taught that the benefits of Christ's death are available to all *if* only they believe:

To bear the sins means to free those who have sinned from their guilt by his satisfaction. He says many meaning all, as in Rom. 5:15. It is of course certain that not all enjoy the fruits of Christ's death, but this happens because their unbelief hinders them *(Comment on Hebrews 9:27).*[59]

If Muller fails, at the outset, convincingly to demonstrate Calvin's affinity with later Reformed orthodoxy, his thesis that 'the master' was part of its development is as doubtful as the scholastic cause is flawed from a truly *sola scriptura* standpoint.

This brings us to the 'Baxterian' element in Doddridge's thought. His hero Richard Baxter believed that the Arminian and High Calvinist views represented an unhappy theological polarisation. He believed that both sides – in different respects – undermined effective evangelism. Thus he argued for a 'middle way' which became known as 'moderate Calvinism'. In many ways, 'authentic Calvinism' is a better and more accurate expression since Baxter's view was more a moderation of *High* Calvinism than Calvin's original teaching. Thus Alexander Gordon wrote (correctly in this instance):

> Baxter's Calvinism differed from that of the Westminster divines, simply by the purity of its adhesion to the original type, unaffected by the Arminian reaction. His Calvinism, like that of the framers of some of the Anglican formularies, admitted, nay insisted, that our Lord, by His death, had redeemed all mankind.[60]

In view of his awareness of the reformer's teaching on the extent of the atonement and other matters, it is not surprising to find Baxter writing thus of Calvin:

> I know no man, since the Apostles' days, whom I value and honour more than Calvin, and whose judgement in all things, one with another, I more esteem and come nearer to.[61]

While Baxter expressed a high regard for the divines of both Dordt and Westminster, he was perfectly happy to endorse the Synod of Dordt's formulation on the atonement:

> In the article of the extent of redemption, wherein I am most suspected and accused, I do subscribe to the Synod of Dordt, without any exception, limitation, or exposition, of any word, as doubtful and obscure.[62]

Baxter's reference to the Synod of Dordt would appear a surprising concession to those who subscribe to 'TULIP'. But they are generally unaware that Dordt is much more moderate than Westminster, as Articles 3, 6 and 8 of the second Canon clearly demonstrate:

> The death of the Son of God is the only and most perfect sacrifice and satisfaction for sin; and is of infinite worth and value, abundantly sufficient to expiate the sins of the whole world. ... That, however, many who have been called by the gospel neither repent nor believe in Christ but perish in unbelief does not happen because of any defect or insufficiency in the sacrifice of Christ offered on the cross, but through their own fault. ... [This] was the most free counsel of God the Father, that the life-giving and saving efficacy of the most precious death of His Son should extend to all the elect.[63]

Unlike the Westminster Confession, the Dordt statement includes a universal dimension to the atonement. Furthermore, unlike the popular perception of the 'five points of Calvinism', neither the terms 'limited' nor 'particular' are used. Thus 'TULIP' is questionable as a mnemonic for Dordt theology! In addition, like Baxter, the French Reformed theologian Moïse Amyraut utilised the language of Dordt Calvinism for his very similar and much maligned view on the atonement:

> Jesus Christ died for all men sufficiently, but for the elect only effectually: and that consequentially his intention was to die for all men in respect of the sufficiency of his satisfaction, but for the elect only in respect of its quickening and saving virtue and efficacy; which is to say, that Christ's will was that the sacrifice of his cross should be of an infinite price and value, and most abundantly sufficient to expiate the sins of the whole world; yet nevertheless the efficacy of his death appertains only unto the elect; ... for this was the most free counsel and gracious purpose both of God the Father, in giving his Son for the salvation of mankind, and of the Lord Jesus Christ, in suffering the pains of death, that the efficacy thereof should particularly belong unto all the elect, and to them only.[64]

This then, was Doddridge's 'Baxterian Calvinism'. So Professor Macleod is incorrect to distinguish Doddridge from Amyraut and Baxter.[65] But let Doddridge speak for himself. Yes, like Calvin, Baxter and Amyraut, he taught divine predestination. Unlike his famous American contemporary Jonathan Edwards, Doddridge avoiding reinforcing his view of divine sovereignty with the doubtful philosophical doctrine of deterministic necessity.[66] Thus, in his lectures, Doddridge prefers to speak of the 'certainty' rather than the 'necessity' of God's sovereign purpose,[67] a distinction reflected in his exegesis. Accordingly, he wrote in the *Family Expositor*:

> ... let us go back with unutterable pleasure to the gracious purpose which he was pleased to form in his own compassionate breast, when he chose us in Christ before the foundation of the world, when he predestinated us through him to the adoption of children. Let us acknowledge the freedom of his grace in it, that we are thus predestinated according to the purpose of him who, with proper regard to the nature of his intelligent and free creatures, worketh all things agreeably to the good pleasure of his will, and maketh us accepted in the beloved, that we may be to the praise of the glory of his grace (*Improvement on Ephesians 1:1-14*).[68]

There's no denying that salvation was the gracious work of a sovereign God. In Doddridge's *Lectures* we read:

From hence it will further appear, that the reason of God's predestinating some to everlasting life, was not fetched from a foresight of their faith and obedience, considered as independent upon any communication of grace from him, but that it is to be referred into his sovereign mercy and free grace; which is also the language of many other scriptures. Titus 3:4,5: Ephesians 2: 8, 9.[69]

As a concomitant to the natural unbelief of the human heart, Doddridge – with Calvin and Baxter – resolves the difference between the believer and unbeliever in terms of common and special grace. In *Christ's Invitation to Thirsty Souls* he says:

I know, there is a great deal of difference between the common operations of the Spirit on the minds of those who continue obstinate and impenitent, and those special influences by which he sweetly but powerfully subdues the hearts of those, who are chosen in Christ Jesus before the foundation of the world. Yet I am persuaded, that none to whom the Gospel comes are utterly neglected by that sacred agent.[70]

So, as a theological tutor, Doddridge was aware of the danger of pushing logic too far; it must be kept under a tight rein. Like Baxter before him, Doddridge resisted the temptation to deduce from election that Christ only died for the elect. There were too many 'alls' in Scripture. So, in his *Lectures*, Doddridge says:

It is plain ... that there is a sense, in which Christ may be said to have died for all, i.e. as he has procured an offer of pardon to all, provided they sincerely embrace the Gospel. Cf. John 3: 16, 6: 50, 51, Romans 5: 18, 8: 32, 1 Corinthians 8: 11, 2 Corinthians 5: 14, 15, 19, 1 Timothy 2: 4, 6, Hebrews 2: 9, 1 John 2: 2.[71]

This direct appeal to Scripture mirrors Baxter's biblical case for his own position:

When God saith so expressly that Christ died for all [2 Cor. 5: 14-15], and tasted death for every man [Heb. 2: 9], and is the ransom for all [1 Tim. 2: 6], and the propitiation for the sins of the whole world [1 Jn. 2: 2], it beseems every Christian rather to explain in what sense Christ died for all, than flatly to deny it.[72]

Like Baxter and Amyraut, Doddridge cited John Calvin's views on the extent of the atonement. The following additional extracts surely justify their appeal:

True it is that the effect of [Christ's] death comes not to the whole world. Nevertheless, forasmuch as it is not in us to discern between the righteous and the sinners that go to destruction, but that Jesus Christ has suffered his death and passion as well for them as for us, therefore it behoves us to labour to bring every man to salvation, that the grace of our Lord Jesus Christ may be available to them *(Sermons on Job [later interpolation deleted]).*[73]

Yet I approve of the ordinary reading, that he alone bore the punishment of many, because on him was laid the guilt of the whole world. It is evident from other passages, and especially from the fifth chapter of the Epistle to the Romans, that 'many' sometimes denotes 'all' *(Comment on Isaiah 53:12).*[74]

Paul makes grace common to all men, not because it in fact extends to all, but because it is offered to all. Although Christ suffered for the sins of the world, and is offered by the goodness of God without distinction to all men, yet not all receive him *(Comment on Romans 5:18).*[75]

God commends to us the salvation of all men without exception, even as Christ suffered for the sins of the whole world *(Comment on Galatians 5:12).*[76]

Christ is in a general view the Redeemer of the world, yet his death and passion are of no advantage to any but such as receive that which St Paul shows here. And so we see that when we once know the benefits brought to us by Christ, and which he daily offers us by his gospel, we must also be joined to him by faith *(Sermons on Ephesians).*[77]

This is His wondrous love towards the human race, that He desires all men to be saved, and is prepared to bring even the perishing to safety ... It could be asked here, if God does not want any to perish, why do so many in fact perish? My reply is that no mention is made here of the secret decree of God by which the wicked are doomed to their own ruin, but only of His loving-kindness as it is made known to us in the Gospel. There God stretches out His hand to all alike, but He only grasps those (in such a way as to lead to Himself) whom He has chosen before the foundation of the world *(Comment on 2 Peter 3:9).*[78]

As we can see, Calvin was careful to maintain that the efficacy of the atonement was guaranteed by election, and this was where Doddridge's 'Baxterian Calvinism' differed from the universalist view of the Arminians. Accordingly, he says in his *Lectures*:

... there (is) a sense, in which Christ might be said to die for all; as all men partake of some benefit by his death, and such provision is made for their salvation, as lays the blame of their ruin, if they miscarry, entirely upon themselves: but it was in a very peculiar and much nobler sense, that he died for the elect, intending evidently to secure for them, and only for them, the everlasting blessings of his Gospel & John 10: 15, 16, 26; 17: 2, 9, 16.[79]

Thus it is possible to see why Doddridge agreed with Calvin and Baxter rather than Beza and Owen. The doctrine of limited atonement was an instance of logic going beyond Scripture. Accordingly, Baxter called Owen the 'over-orthodox doctor'[80] because of his controversial treatise *The Death of Death*. One of the weaknesses of Owen's argument is the way he particularises universal texts like 1 Timothy 2: 6 in the interests of maintaining limited atonement.[81] Thus 'all' becomes 'some'! Doddridge has no time for such textual tampering. In the *Family Expositor*, he says:

> *(Will have all men to be saved)* It is far from being my design, in any of these notes, to enter deep into controversy, but I must confess I have never been satisfied with that interpretation which explains all men here merely as signifying some of all sorts and ranks of men; since I fear it might also be said, on the principles of those who are fondest of this gloss that he also wills all men to be condemned. On the other hand, if many are not saved, it is certain the words must be taken with some limitation, which the following clause, he wills their coming to the knowledge of the truth, must also prove. The meaning therefore seems to be, that God has made sufficient provision for the salvation of all, and that it is to be considered as the general declaration of his will, that all who know the truth themselves, should publish it to all around them, so far as their influence can extend *(Note on 1 Timothy 2:4)*.[82]

Neither does Doddridge agree with Owen's [world] = [world of the elect] exegesis of John 3: 16.[83] He simply writes of 'the world of mankind', also paraphrasing John 1: 29 to mean that Christ's 'great atoning sacrifice ... expiates and takes away the sin of the whole world, and is set forth to be a propitiation, not only for the Jews ... but for the Gentiles too'.[84] Even stronger is his paraphrase of John 6: 51. According to Doddridge, Christ intends 'That the bread which I will give ... is my own flesh, which I will give as an atoning sacrifice for the forfeited life of the whole world of Jews and Gentiles, of which every true [chosen] believer shall partake'.[85]

Although Doddridge never uses the scholastic formula 'sufficient for all, efficient for the elect', the idea is clearly discernible in his statements. Like Calvin, whose rare use of the formula is more than matched by an uninhibited and unqualified use of the New Testament's universal language, Doddridge is obviously concerned to avoid Owen's type of scholastic particularism.

In view of the differences between Doddridge's theology and Westminster orthodoxy, the most charitable critic would have to deny that Doddridge was orthodox according to strict Westminster criteria. However, a Continental dimension presents an alternative picture, with significant implications for the issue of subscription. The excellent and illuminating studies of Professor J van den Berg and Dr Geoffrey Nuttall reveal the fascinating influence Philip Doddridge had in the Netherlands.[86] As well as the *Rise and Progress* (English, 1745; Dutch, 1747), several of his works were translated into Dutch including the *Sermons on Regeneration and Salvation by Grace* (English, 1741; Dutch, 1748). After Doddridge's death, the *Family Expositor* (English, 1739-56; Dutch, 1765-83) and the *Course of Lectures* (English, 1763; Dutch, 1771) increased his popularity but also aroused controversy.

In the face of a traditionally critical and rather cold Dutch Reformed orthodoxy, Doddridge's writings had reinforced a growing concern for greater spiritual warmth and openness. As in England, Doddridge was severely criticised by some in the Netherlands. But among his many friends and admirers, the Groningen lawyer Henry Goodricke defended Doddridge against charges of Arianism, Socinianism and Arminianism. In addition, whatever discrepancies exist between Doddridge's theology and the Westminster standards, Goodricke said with justification that Doddridge's teachings did *not* conflict with the Dutch Reformed 'Three Forms of Unity' *(Belgic Confession, Heidelberg Catechism and Canons of Dordt).*[87] It was deemed appropriate therefore for Doddridge to be described on the title pages of the Dutch translations of his works as 'Gereformeert Predikant te Northampton'. In 1745, when Isaac Watts wrote to David Longueville, minister of the English Reformed Church in Amsterdam, he described Doddridge as 'a hearty believer of the great articles and important principles of the Reformed Church'.[88] Watts' recommendation was prefixed to Dutch translations of Doddridge's works. Furthermore, Longueville translated and distributed two of Doddridge's Addresses to Dutch Protestants, written at a time of national emergency when the country was threatened by a French invasion. Translated direct from Doddridge's MS, they were never published in English. Significantly, they were well received as Longueville made clear to Doddridge in 1748: 'Your loving and faithful address to us here has met with uncommon acceptance, and has been warmly recommended from the pulpit by several of the Dutch ministers'.[89]

So, if today's British High Calvinists consider Doddridge to be 'not quite Reformed', his Dutch friends had no doubts! Evidence for this evaluation has already been cited from the *Canons of Dordt*. More may be seen in the *Heidelberg Catechism's* answer to Q. 37 which states that 'Christ bore in body and soul the wrath of God against the sin of the whole human race'. In short, significant differences exist between the *Three Forms of Unity* and the Westminster standards. Regrettably, these differences are smothered by the dubious and misleading matchings of the various confessions in *Reformed Confessions Harmonized* by Joel R Beeke and Sinclair B. Ferguson (Eds).[90]

Not surprisingly, many catechism commentators have been quick to distance the *Heidelberg Catechism* (A. 37) from an Arminian understanding.[91] However, in so doing, they have reflected not the views of the catechism's authors, Ursinus and Olevianus (surely the best guides as to its meaning) but a later and 'higher' orthodoxy of the Westminster type. Notwithstanding the Heidelberg divines' commitment to election and predestination, they nonetheless – like Calvin, Baxter *and* Doddridge – maintained a universal dimension to the atonement. Dr Zacharias Ursinus (1534-83) affirmed that as Christ 'died for all, in respect to the sufficiency of his ransom; and for the faithful alone in respect of the efficacy of the same, so also he willed to die for all in general, as touching the sufficiency of his merit ... But he willed to die for the elect alone as touching the efficacy of his death'.[92] Consistent with his colleague, Caspar Olevianus (1536-87) declared that Christ 'was being tried before God, laden with your sin and my sin and that of the whole world'.[93] What are these statements but Amyraldianism before Amyraut (1596-1664)? Ursinus' successor at Heidelberg, David Pareus (1548-1622) was too old to attend the Synod of Dordt. However, his views on the atonement were heard *in absentia*. Significantly, the words of the *Heidelberg Catechism* are woven into his statement:

> The cause and matter of the passion of Christ was the sense and sustaining of the anger of God excited against the sin, not of some men, but of the whole human race; whence it arises, that the whole of sin and of the wrath of God against it was endured by Christ, but the whole of reconciliation was not obtained or restored to all.[94]

Not only does this shed further light on the significant differences between Reformation Calvinism and Puritan High Calvinism. It also would have solved part of Doddridge's problem over confessional subscription. Since he said that 'Great care ought to be taken, that we subscribe nothing that we do not firmly believe',[95] the *Three Forms of Unity* did not present the problems posed for him by the confessional standards of English Puritanism. This observation applies even to another issue in which Doddridge must be *distinguished* from Richard Baxter – the doctrine of justification.

III

Besides his 'Amyraldian' views, Baxter is well known for his 'deviant' views on justification. He rejected the imputation of Christ's righteousness (active and passive) to the believer, arguing instead (from Romans 4: 22) that personal faith itself is imputed as the sinner's righteousness before God. Furthermore, faced by the apparent contradiction between Paul and James (see Romans 3: 28; James 2: 24), Baxter insisted on a two-fold justification by faith *and* works.[96] Despite the many valuable – and often biblical – insights of Baxter's life-long campaign against antinomianism, it may be said that he fell victim to over-reaction. An element of 'muddle' is present in his endless writings. For instance, with his frustrating use of almost intangible distinctions, he concedes that 'Christ's righteousness' is the meritorious cause of ours' yet he insists that 'our faith now is instead of our innocency'.[97] Doddridge was being fair when he gave this assessment of Baxter: 'He is inaccurate because he had no regular education, and always wrote in haste, as in views of eternity; but generally judicious, nervous, spiritual and evangelical; though often charged with the contrary'.[98]

Always able to get to the heart of the matter, Doddridge effectively eliminated the muddle in Baxter's thought. With obvious reference to Baxter's theory of imputation, Doddridge says: 'It must be flagrantly absurd to talk of resting upon an act [i.e. 'faith'], whereby we do indeed receive and rest upon another'.[99] In short, the believer trusts in Christ not in faith itself – a distinction Baxter would not actually quarrel with!! Making better sense of Paul's point in Romans 4: 22, Doddridge resorts in his *Lectures* to a statement by the Dutch divine Herman Witsius: 'Faith is set down to our account in the book of God, as an evidence that we are in the number of those, who by the righteousness of Christ, according to the tenor of the gospel, are to be justified'.[100] The sense of these words is also reflected in Doddridge's sermon *Salvation by Grace* where he explains 'the righteousness of Christ' as 'his active and passive obedience'.[101] In this respect, his theology accords with both the *Three Forms of Unity* and the Westminster (and more especially Savoy) standards. However, this is not the entire picture. When this particular issue was later discussed in Doddridge's *Lectures*, one wonders whether Baxter's counter-arguments had some weight with him, viz. that specific textual support is wanting for the standard view. (Indeed, Baxter denies that 'Christ's righteousness imputed' is a 'Scripture phrase'.[102] He even complained that John Owen was responsible for the explicit 'passive and active' changes to the *Westminster Confession* (XI. I) in the *Savoy Declaration*.[103]

So, when Doddridge discusses in his *Lectures* whether we are justified by Christ's death alone or by a combination of his active and passive obedience, he considers this to be 'a controversy of much less importance than it has generally been represented'.[104] Here the tone is very different from Owen's if still significantly different from Baxter's. Without discussing Baxter's view that the imputation of Christ's active obedience makes his death unnecessary (since one accounted holy is no more in need of pardon than Christ is),[105] Doddridge is clearly sympathetic to the 'passive' view (also denied by Baxter!) when he concludes that 'Scripture does in many places ascribe our acceptance to this'.[106] Significantly, when he paraphrases the decisive Pauline statement 'justified by his blood' (Rom. 5: 9), Doddridge is under no temptation to amend it to 'justified by his death and life'. He evidently rejects Owen's view which logically implies that Paul's concept is only half right if the puritan position is correct. So Doddridge simply says: '... we conclude that much more being now justified by the efficacy of his most precious blood, we shall be saved from wrath by him .[107]

If a degree of hesitation is evident in Doddridge's view of imputation, where does that leave him in relation to the various confessions? This much is certain, his appeal to Witsius makes sound and acceptable sense of the meaning of imputation *vis-à-vis* Baxter's baffling verbal gyrations. The only remaining question is: what precisely is the righteousness which is imputed? While there's no room for manoeuvre within the standard editions of the *Three Forms of Unity* and the Puritan confessions, Doddridge's exegetical instincts were previously shared by the earliest editions of the *Belgic Confession* and the *Heidelberg Catechism*, both of which were subsequently altered.[108] Both Ursinus and Olevianus (authors of the *HC*) taught the imputation of Christ's passive obedience only – as Calvin arguably, and Piscator certainly, did.[109] Ursinus stated that the sinner's 'evangelical justification' before God is 'the imputation and application of that righteousness which Christ wrought out for us by his death upon the cross'.[110] Posing the question 'What is that thing or gift, then, that is credited to us for righteousness?' Olevianus answers thus: 'The obedience of the suffering and death of our Lord Jesus Christ, or the sacrifice of Christ on the cross. ... This obedience of the death of Christ is freely granted and credited to us, so that from now on it is our own and our righteousness before God'.[111] According to his son, David Pareus loyally defended this view: 'Pareus ... would by no means permit that any should depart from the Catechism of his professor Ursinus, as some divines, I know not who, departed from it, who added no fewer than three kinds of imputations, to that which was laid down by Ursinus, as the matter of our justification before God, viz. the imputation of the death of Jesus Christ, the imputation of his actual righteousness, and habitual holiness'.[112]

Baxter's crusade against antinomianism has been a focus of heated debate. In his concern to stress that the Gospel includes obligations and duties as well as blessings and privileges, his 'New Law' language was easily misunderstood.[113] While Doddridge shared Baxter's concerns about holiness, he was careful to avoid the idea of 'neonomian' legalism. After acknowledging that 'the gospel' ... includes commands, and even threatenings as well as promises, he wisely concludes:

> If law signifies, as it generally does, the discovery of the will of a superior, teaching what he requires of those under this government, with the intimation of his intention of dispensing rewards and punishments, as this rule of their conduct is observed or neglected; in this latitude of expression, it is plain ... that the gospel, taken for the declaration made to men by Christ, is a law, as in scripture it is sometimes called: James. 1: 25; Rom. 4: 15; 5: 13; 8: 2. But if law be taken in the greatest rigour of expression, for such a discovery of the will of God and our duty, as contains in it no intimation of our obtaining the divine favour, otherwise than by a perfect and universal conformity to it, in that sense the gospel is not a law.[114]

Lastly, on the question of the Paul-James antinomy, Doddridge simply and lucidly avoided Baxter's unhappy double talk. He paraphrases Romans 3: 28 by saying that a man 'is justified by a true, lively, and effectual faith in the gospel, without the works of the law'.[115] This is supported by the following note:

> By thus guarding the assertion, we sufficiently see how very consistent it is with that of St James ... who only in effect asserts, that no faith can suffice to our justification which is not in fact productive of obedience; and when the matter is thus stated, there is no appearance of contradiction.[116]

Doddridge's note on James 2: 23-4 (where the key verse Genesis 15: 6 is quoted) completes the picture:

> This very text St Paul quotes [in] Romans 4: 3; to prove that Abraham was justified by faith; which plainly shews, that the faith by which St Paul says he was justified, was such a faith as includes good works in it, as a certain principle of them; and consequently, establishes what was said above for reconciling these two apostles in the easiest manner.[117]

In short, as Doddridge wrote to the Roman Catholic felon Bryan Connell, justification is by a trusting, loving and obedient faith in 'the mercy of God, through the blood and intercession of our Lord Jesus Christ alone'.[118] After all is said and done, this is all that Baxter was attempting to articulate![119]

Thus we have explained what Doddridge (with some qualification) means by 'Baxterian Calvinist'. This is not to imply that he was more partial to Baxter's scholastic discussion of theology (chiefly in his controversial works) than he was to Owen's. No, he clearly disapproved of this medieval *and* seventeenth-century baggage. In a letter, he actually considered Baxter's *Methodus Theologiae* to be 'unintelligible'[120] – at least to his correspondent. But believing that Baxter expressed the best 'head and heart'[121] synthesis of Christian truth and experience, Doddridge's debt to him was chiefly in the realm of 'practical divinity'.[122] That said, and contrary to Professor Macleod's misleading discussion, Doddridge was undoubtedly a 'Baxterian Calvinist'.

IV

To see Doddridge's convictions on the extent and efficacy of the atonement in a wider historico-theological context, four letters of mine (published in the *English Churchman* in the summer of 2000) are offered for concluding clarification:

(1) ANGLICANISM, AMYRAUT AND AUTHENTIC CALVINISM

(EC 16 June 2000)

Sir, – In an otherwise valuable sermon (parts of which I thank him for), the Revd Edward J. Malcolm has supplied some highly flawed information ('The Death of Christ', *The Journal*, May 2000, pp. 23-8). I refer to his dubious assessment of Amyraldianism. Concerned to reaffirm John Calvin's authentic teaching in the face of ultra-orthodox 'high' Calvinism, the French Reformed theologian, Moïse Amyraut (1596-1664) also distanced himself from semi-Pelagian Arminianism. His concern was to avoid unbiblical extremism. Had his teaching been as compatible with Rome's as is suggested, the Edict of Nantes (1598) might possibly have stood. It was revoked by Louis XIV (in 1685) precisely because of the continuing incompatibilities between the Reformed Churches and Rome! The internal Reformed debates over the extent of the atonement had nothing to do with it (for further information, see my book *Calvinus: Authentic Calvinism, A Clarification* and the Norwich Reformed Church website: www.geocities.com/nrchurch).

As for the Huguenot refugees who settled in this country, those who agreed with Amyraut simply reinforced the original sixteenth-century 'Anglican Calvinism' of the Prayer Book and the Thirty-nine Articles (see Arts. 2, 15 and 31). Notwithstanding clear teaching on predestination (see Art. 17), the doctrine of limited atonement is as alien to Reformation Anglicanism as it is to the teaching of Amyraut and Calvin. In the seventeenth century, scholastic influences in Reformed theology affected this country as well as France. Thus the 'over-orthodox' distorted Calvinism of Dr John Owen and many (but not all) of the Westminster divines was rejected by Richard Baxter and others. In the eighteenth and nineteenth centuries, the balanced biblicism of Calvin, the other Reformers, Amyraut and Baxter was maintained by the Nonconformists Matthew Henry, Isaac Watts and Philip Doddridge, and the Anglicans John Newton, Charles Simeon and Bishop Ryle. While I regret Ryle's espousal of episcopacy, his authentic Calvinism is unquestionably on target! According to this view of the New Testament, while ultimately only the elect *effectually* partake of salvation, the universally designed and sufficient atonement of Christ makes the gospel available to the whole world. This is true Christianity and true Calvinism!

Yours faithfully, etc.

(2) ANGLICANISM, AMYRAUT AND THE ATONEMENT

(EC 14 July 2000)

Sir, – Dr George Ella asks me, "Which Anglican reformer did not believe in limited atonement?" Apart from John Bradford who clearly did, several may be listed. Archbishop Thomas Cranmer stated that Christ 'by His own oblation ... satisfied His Father for all men's sins and reconciled mankind unto His grace and favour'. Bishop John Hooper affirmed that Christ died 'for the love of us poor and miserable sinners, whose place he occupied upon the cross, as a pledge, or one that represented the person of all the sinners that ever were, be now, or shall be unto the world's end'. Bishop Nicholas Ridley declared that the sacrifice of Christ 'was, is, and shall be forever the propitiation for the sins of the whole world'. Bishop Hugh Latimer preached that 'Christ shed as much blood for Judas, as he did for Peter: Peter believed it, and therefore he was saved; Judas would not believe, and therefore he was condemned'. Even Bradford admitted that 'Christ's death is sufficient for all, but effectual for the elect only'. The Elizabethan Anglicans were no different in their understanding. Bishop John Jewel wrote that, on the cross, Christ declared "It is finished" to signify 'that the price and ransom was now full paid for the sin of all mankind'. Elsewhere, he made clear that 'The death of Christ is available for the redemption of all the world'. Richard Hooker stated an identical view when he said that Christ's 'precious and propitiatory sacrifice' was 'offered for the sins of all the world' (all source details withheld to save space).

As for Amyraut's supposed semi-Pelagian denial of the Canons of Dordt, Dr Ella is simply misinformed. He specifically affirmed the teaching of Dordt at the National Synod of Alençon (1637), his orthodoxy being further verified in his *Defensio doctrinae J. Calvini* (1641). As for the canons themselves, they are more moderate than many realise. Indeed, the word 'limited' nowhere appears, thus making the mnemonic TULIP rather doubtful! The 'death of the Son of God is ... abundantly sufficient to expiate the sins of the whole world ... many perish in unbelief [not] because of any defect or insufficiency in the sacrifice of Christ ... but through their own fault. ... the saving efficacy of the most precious death of [God's] Son ... extend[s] to all the elect' *(Second Canon, Arts. 3, 6, 8)*.

The Revd Edward Malcolm's further contribution is amusing. He admits Articles XV and XXXI are universalist because the compilers 'are merely quoting Scripture'. He then charges with having a 'preconception' those who take them in their natural sense! If he thinks this is an Arminian view, the Anglican Clement Barksdale objected in 1653 that 'You are mistaken when you think the doctrine of Universal Redemption Arminianism. It was the doctrine of the Church of England before Arminius was born. We learn it out of the old Church Catechism: 'I believe in Jesus Christ, who hath redeemed me and all mankind'. And the Church hath learned it out of the plain scripture, where Christ is the Lamb of God that taketh away the sins of the world'. Richard Baxter surely hit the nail on the head when he wrote, 'When God saith so expressly that Christ died for all [2 Cor. 5:14-15], and tasted death for every man [Heb. 2:9], and is the ransom for all [1 Tim. 2:6], and the propitiation for the sins of the whole world [1 Jn. 2:2], it beseems every Christian rather to explain in what sense Christ died for all, than flatly to deny it'. As for Mr Malcolm's citation of Calvin's isolated apparent support for limited atonement, his partial quotation ignores the fact that the reformer is discussing the implications of the Lutheran theory of consubstantiation rather than the extent of the atonement.

Before the Revd Peter Howe gets too excited by Carl Trueman's *The Claims of Truth*, he should know that the author – apart from resorting to the kind of triviality mentioned – misunderstands and misrepresents my case against Dr John Owen's scholastic high Calvinism (as my forthcoming reply will make clear). Dr Trueman actually admits that Owen did not rely on the *sola scriptura* principle in his theological polemics, a point which rightly disturbed Ewan Wilson (see his *EC* review, June 4, 1999). Owen's Aristotelian rationalism ruins his exegesis of John 3:16. He tampers with the text in a manner Calvin would anathematise. As for C. H. Spurgeon's sermon *Particular Redemption*, the same doubtful exegesis emerges. On the other hand, Bishop Ryle – rightly described by Spurgeon as 'the best man in the Church of England' – handled Scripture with greater integrity. Having little sympathy for Arminianism, Ryle was equally aware of the threat posed by high Calvinism. Commenting on John 1:29, he wrote that 'Christ's death is profitable to none but to the elect who believe on His name. ... But ... I dare not say that no atonement has been made, in any sense, except for the elect. ... When I read that the wicked who are lost, "deny the Lord that bought them," (2 Pet. 2:1) and that "God was in Christ, reconciling the world unto himself," (2 Cor. 5:19), I dare not confine the intention of redemption to the saints alone. Christ is for every man'. Commenting on John 3:16 and appealing to Davenant, Calvin and others, he concludes: 'Those who confine God's love exclusively to the elect appear to me to take a narrow and contracted view of God's character and attributes. ... I have long come to the conclusion that men may be more systematic in their statements than the Bible, and may be led into grave error by idolatrous veneration of a system' (*Expository Thoughts on John's Gospel*, Vol. 1). In short, all that Christ is and did was for all mankind conditionally though for the elect effectually. Mr Howe will be pleased to know that this truly biblical Calvinism motivates Norwich Reformed Church to reach out to the people of the city every Saturday through its all-weather, all-seasons, city-centre evangelistic bookstall.

Yours faithfully, etc.

(3) THE EXTENT OF THE ATONEMENT: WESTMINSTER OR THE BIBLE?

(EC 25 August 2000)

Sir, – In response to Ewan Wilson's recycling of traditional anti-Amyraldian prejudice and Andrew Price's appeal to Westminster orthodoxy, it must be said that the *WCF's* limited atonement teaching goes beyond the Bible, John Calvin, the Thirty-nine Articles and the Synod of Dordt (for all subsequent references, see my *Atonement and Justification*).

However, Dr William Twisse, the first prolocutor (or chairman) of the Westminster Assembly, took a broader and more biblical view when he said: 'I am ready to profess ... that every one who hears the gospel, (without distinction between elect or reprobate) is bound to believe that Christ died for him, so far as to procure both the pardon of his sins and the salvation of his soul, in case he believes and repent'. During the debates, Edmund Calamy resisted ultra-orthodox scholastic pressure when he declared: 'I am far from universal redemption in the Arminian sense; but that that I hold is in the sense of our divines (e.g. Bishop Davenant) in the Synod of Dordt, that Christ did pay a price for all ... that Jesus Christ did not only die sufficiently for all, but God did intend, in giving Christ, and Christ in giving himself, did intend to put all men in a state of salvation in case they do believe'.

While the moderating stance of Twisse, Calamy and others (later embraced by Richard Baxter) failed to halt extremist tendencies, it is clear that successive 'sound' Presbyterians including Matthew Henry did not feel comfortable with strict Westminster orthodoxy. Several of their statements reflect Calvin's biblical balance rather than the ultra-restrictive language of the *WCF*. When Thomas Boston published the Scottish edition of *The Marrow of Modern Divinity* (1726), he was clearly happy to endorse the words (of John Preston): 'Go and tell everyman without exception that here is good news for him, Christ is dead for him'. In his own book *A View of the Covenant of Grace* (1734), Boston himself stated, '... the extent of the administration [of the covenant] is not founded on election, but on the sufficiency of Christ's obedience and death for the salvation of all'.

In the nineteenth century, several noted Presbyterian theologians clearly preferred Calvin's more flexible language to the rigidities of the *WCF*. The first moderator of the Free Church of Scotland, Thomas Chalmers asked: 'If Christ died only for the elect, and not for all', then ministers 'are puzzled to understand how they should proceed with the calls and invitations of the gospel. ... Now for the specific end of conversion, the available scripture is not that Christ laid down His life for the sheep, but that Christ is set forth a propitiation for the sins of the world. It is not because I know myself to be one of the sheep, or one of the elect, but because I know myself to be one of the world, that I take to myself the calls and promises of the New Testament'. Shortly before his death in 1847, Dr Chalmers virtually endorsed Richard Baxter's view (see Dr Hanna's *Memoirs*).

In the USA, despite his formal rejection of Amyraldianism, even Princeton Presbyterian Charles Hodge could admit that 'there is a sense ... in which Christ did die for all men. His death had the effect of justifying the offer of salvation to everyman; and of course was designed to have that effect. He therefore died sufficiently for all'. The Southern Presbyterian R. L. Dabney was very similar to Hodge. He even criticised William Cunningham for taking a narrow view of the atonement's design. Dabney also distanced himself from John Owen's particularism: 'I have already stated one ground for rejecting that interpretation of John 3:16, which makes 'the world' which God so loved, the elect world. ... Christ's mission to make expiation for sin is a manifestation of unspeakable benevolence to the whole world'.

It is good to see men prepared to be governed by the infallible Word of God rather than the otherwise valuable but fallible confessions of men. May we all do likewise!

Yours faithfully, etc.

(4) PARTICULAR REDEMPTION

(EC 22 September 2000)

Sir, – J. F. Burrows' appeal to Christ's own statements on the subject of redemption will find favour with all true Bible-believing Christians. But why is he so selective? His citations all have to do with the applied efficacy of the atonement. In all I have written, this is not in dispute. The only question concerns the implied provision of the atonement in universal gospel preaching (Mk. 16:15). In this respect, our Redeemer is equally clear: 'For the bread of God is he which cometh down from heaven, and giveth life unto the world. ... the bread that I will give is my flesh, which I will give for the life of the world' (Jn. 6: 33, 51). Clearly, the provision is universal notwithstanding its application to the elect (unless one adopts the exegetical fallacy of equating 'the world' with 'the elect'). Thus the gospel sun is to shine on all even if the eyes of many remain closed.

As for John 10:11-15, this is generally misread. The Lord Jesus is not saying that the provision of His death is only available to 'the sheep' but that His care for them is superior to the cowardly hireling's. The latter flees from the wolf but the good Shepherd yields His life for them. In short, Christ is stressing the *quality* (rather than the *objects*) of His care, i.e. He will give HIS LIFE for the sheep.

Compared with Mr Burrows' exegesis, John Calvin provides a more balanced biblical view: 'Paul makes grace common to all men ... because it is offered to all. Although Christ suffered for the sins of the world, and is offered by the goodness of God without distinction to all men, yet not all receive him' (*Comment on Romans 5:18*); 'This is [God's] wondrous love towards the human race, that He desires all men to be saved, and is prepared to bring even the perishing to safety. ... It could be asked here, if God does not want any to perish, why do so many in fact perish? My reply is that no mention is made here of the secret decree of God by which the wicked are doomed to their own ruin, but only of His loving-kindness as it is made known to us in the Gospel. There God stretches out His hand to all alike, but He only grasps those (in such a way as to lead to Himself) whom He has chosen before the foundation of the world' *(Comment on 2 Peter 3:9)*.

Yours faithfully, etc.

V

LLOYD-JONES AND THE ATONEMENT

The Revd Iain H. Murray has given his account of Dr D. Martyn Lloyd-Jones' views on the extent of the atonement with reference to Dr J. I. Packer and Dr R. T. Kendall (see *D. Martyn Lloyd-Jones: The Fight of Faith 1939-1981*, pp. 231, 721-6). However, more may be said. *First,* Dr Lloyd-Jones' *Evangelistic Sermons at Aberavon* (Banner of Truth Trust, 1983) reveal a very different view of the subject compared with his later limited atonement position. Two examples may be cited:

> But look at [Christ's] death for a moment and consider it as an expiation for the sin of the whole world. What are we told about it? Well, those sufferings were enough, according to John, for all. Listen! 'He is the propitiation for our sins; and not for ours only, but also for the sins of the whole world' (1 Jn. 2: 2). The whole world! ... The sins of the whole world he had borne upon Himself (pp. 87-8).

> [If] ever you feel utterly helpless and hopeless, then turn back to Him, the Christ of the cross, with His arms outstretched, who still says: 'Look unto me and be saved, all ye ends of the earth'. It is there that the whole of humanity is focused. He is the representative of the whole of mankind. He died for all (p. 278).

Second, whatever Dr Lloyd-Jones might have said in private conversations or at conferences, limited atonement never appeared in his sermons. During his doctoral research, Kendall had a number of discussions with Dr Lloyd-Jones on John Calvin's position. Conducting his own examination of the reformer's commentaries, Dr Lloyd-Jones was obviously surprised to discover how frequently universalist Calvin's statements were. During a fortnight period, Dr Lloyd-Jones repeatedly telephoned Kendall and, in excited tones said, "I've found another one!" During one discussion, he said to Kendall with regard to limited atonement, "I never preached it, you know ... only once on Romans 5: 15 and I was in great difficulty when I did so." Being present, Mrs Lloyd-Jones then added, "I have never believed it and I never will!" (Dr Kendall related these facts to me when we met in London in July 1989 to discuss my thesis *Atonement and Justification* (published by OUP the following year). They were confirmed by telephone on November 27, 2001 and are published with Dr Kendall s approval).

These things being so, what applies to the Amyraldian Ryle (whose *Expository Thoughts* are published by the Banner of Truth Trust together with John Owen's *Death of Death*) applies also to the Lloyd-Jones sermons cited above. While Doddridge would be generally comfortable with Lloyd-Jones' position, Owen would doubtless be highly critical of it!

VI

DODDRIDGE AND THOSE WHO NEVER HEAR THE GOSPEL

'It has been much disputed, whether it be possible that the Heathens should be saved. Some have absolutely denied it, upon the authority of the texts mentioned ... which universally require faith in Christ; but to this it is answered, that they can only regard such to whom the gospel comes, and are capable of understanding the contents of it. The truth seems to be this, that none of the Heathens will be condemned for not believing the gospel, but they are liable to condemnation for the breach of God's natural law: nevertheless, if there be any of them in whom there is a prevailing love to the divine being, and care in the practice of virtue [see Acts 10: 1], there seems reason to believe, that *for the sake of Christ*, though to them unknown, they may be accepted by God: and so much the rather, as the ancient Jews, and even the apostles of Christ, during the time of our Saviour's abode on earth, seem to have had but little notion of those doctrines, which those who deny the salvability of the Heathens are most apt to imagine fundamental. Compare Rom. 2: 10 [-16], 26; Acts 10: 34-5; Matt. 8: 11-12 to which may be added 1 Jn. 2: 2 which Mr. R. supposes intentionally decisive on this question, as to the *application of Christ's merits* to all virtuous men, who may not have opportunities of hearing his name. Some also add John 1: 29' (*PD.* v. 226-7, italics mine).

Note: According to Peter, Cornelius was in a state of 'acceptance by God' (Acts 10: 34) *before* hearing of Christ. This is *not* the same as saying 'provided people of any religion are sincere they will be saved by the merit of their virtue'. Christ alone is the mediator of all who are saved. Some will discover in heaven that it was through Him alone they were saved.

References

Abbreviations:

PD   *The Works of the Revd P. Doddridge, DD*, ed. E. Williams and E. Parsons (10 vols.; 1802-5)

JH   *The Correspondence and Diary of Philip Doddridge, DD*, ed. J. D. Humphreys (5 vols.; 1829-31)

CC   *Calendar of the Correspondence of Philip Doddridge, DD* (1702-1751), ed. G. F. Nuttall (1979)

AL   *Philip Doddridge: Additional Letters:* a supplement to Calendar of the Correspondence of Philip Doddridge, ed. G. F. Nuttall (2001)

NB: When complete or partially quoted extracts from the *Correspondence (JH)* appear in the *Calendar (CC)*, two references will be given, e.g. *JH.* i. 43; *CC.* 8. Otherwise, the *Calendar* reference (letter not page) will appear in brackets simply to identify the letter in the *Calendar*, e.g. *JH.* i. 105; (*CC.* 20). A single *Calendar* reference indicates a source other than the *Correspondence*.

Chapter One: The Formation of Character.

1. *PD.* i. 225.
2. *The Sword and Trowel* (1881), 546.
3. *PD.* iii. 86.
4. J. Orton, *Memoirs of the Life, Character and Writings of the late Rev. P. Doddridge, DD of Northampton* in *PD.* i. 16.
5. Ibid. 16.
6. A. Kippis, *The Life of Dr Doddridge in The Family Expositor* (1799), i. p. v.
7. J. Orton, *Memoirs* in *PD.* i. 17.
8. *PD.* i. 598.

9. J. Orton, *Memoirs* in *PD*. i. 18.
10. *PD*. ii. 156.
11. J. Orton, *Memoirs* in *PD*. i. 19.
12. Ibid. 21.
13. Ibid. 21.
14. See Irene Parker, *Dissenting Academies in England: their rise and progress and their place among the educational systems of the country* (1914);
    H. McLachlan, *English Education under the Test Acts* (1931).
15. *JH*. i. 254; *CC*. 69
16. *JH*. i. 33; (*CC*. 1).
17. *JH*. i. 97.
18. *JH*. i. 198; (*CC*. 53). cf. *JH*. i. 155; *CC*. 35.
19. *JH*. i. 84; *CC*. 46.
20. See A. C. Clifford, *Sons of Calvin: Three Huguenot Pastors* (1999), 9-24.
21. *JH*. i. 150; *CC*. 34.

Chapter Two: The Road to Northampton.

1. J. Orton, *Memoirs* in *PD*. i. 26.
2. *JH*. i. 405; (*CC*. 130).
3. *JH*. i. 141; *CC*. 31.
4. *JH*. i. 398; (*CC*. 129).
5. *JH*. i. 443; *CC*. 144.
6. *JH*. i.166; *CC*. 49.
7. *JH*. i. 383; (*CC*. 109).
8. *JH*. i. 44; *CC*. 8.
9. *JH*. i. 460; *CC*. 155.
10. *JH*. i. 470; (*CC*. 159).
11. *JH*. i. 255; *CC*. 71.
12. *JH*. i. 286; *CC*. 84.
13. *JH*. i.317; (*CC*. 96).
14. *JH*. ii. 270; *CC*. 254.
15. *JH*. ii. 62; *CC*. 187.
16. *PD*. i. 31.
17. See J. Macleod, *Scottish Theology* (1974), 151-2.
18. *JH*. ii. 308; *CC*. 264.
19. *PD*. ii. 80.
20. *JH*. ii. 516; (*CC*. 333).
21. C. Stanford, *Philip Doddridge* (1880), 41.
22. *CC*. p. xxxv.

Chapter Three: The Spirit of the Age.

1. *The Letters and Speeches of Oliver Cromwell,*
   ed. T. Carlyle (1888), iv. 209.
2. *The Letters and Works of Lady Mary Wortley Montagu,*
   ed. W. Moy Thomas (1861), i. 351.
3. *The Spectator,* 1st August, 1712, No. 446.
4. F. Jeffrey, *Essays* (1853), 656.
5. *A History of England in the Eighteenth Century*
   (1878), i. 479, 481.
6. *An Enquiry into the Late Increase in Robbers* (1751), 19.
7. *The Early History of Charles James Fox* (1894), 83.
8. A. Skevington Wood, *The Burning Heart* (1967), 11.
9. *Poems,* eds. J. Butt and others (1939-62): 'Essay on Man',
   iii. 305-10 and ii.1-2. I am indebted to J. Downey,
   The Eighteenth Century Pulpit (1969) for these references.
10. *The Works of George Berkeley,* ed. A. A. Luce and
    T. E.Jessop (1953), vii. 211.
11. *The Works of Thomas Secker,* ed. B. Porteus and G. Stinton
    (1811), v. 292.
12. *Fifteen Sermons, preached at the Rolls Chapel; to which is added a
    Charge to the Clergy of Durham,* ed. R. Cattermole (1836), 279.
13. *Worship and Theology in England from Watts and Wesley to
    Maurice (1690-1850)* (1961), 56.
14. *A History of English Thought in the Eighteenth Century* (1876), ii. 347.
15. Crabbe, 'The Borough', letter iv, *Poetical Works,*
    eds. A. J. and S. M. Carlyle (1914), 125.
16. *JH.* iv. 358; CC. 1009.
17. *JH.* iii. 474; (CC. 614).
18. *Encyclopedia of Christianity* (1964), i. 549.
19. *The Complete Works of the Revd Andrew fuller* (1831), i. p. x.
20. See *JH.* iii. 186; CC. 442 and D. Fountain, 'From Puritanism
    to Methodism: 2. Decay and Prosperity 1662-1737' in
    Evangelical Times (June 2001) 27.
21. See A. Skevington Wood, *The Burning Heart* (1967), 59.
22. See J. Lawson and H. Silver, *A Social History of Education in
    England* (1973), 170ff.
23. J. H. Plumb, *England in the Eighteenth Century 1714-1815*
    (1950), 31.
24. See A. P. Davis, *Isaac Watts* (1948), 58ff.
25. Ibid. 103ff.
26. T. Wright, *The Life of Isaac Watts* (1914), 92.

27. *JH*. iii. 487; CC. 623. See Wesley, *Works* (1840), vii. 356.
28. T. Wright, *The Life of Isaac Watts* (1914), 94.
29. See A. P. Davis, *Isaac Watts* (1948), 58.
30. See M. R. Watts, *The Dissenters* (1978), 266.
31. T. Wright, *The Life of Isaac Watts* (1914), 117.
32. Ibid. 119.
33. See D. Fountain, *Isaac Watts Remembered* (1974), 65.
34. T. Wright, *The Life of Isaac Watts* (1914), 139.
35. Ibid. 139.
36. R. Tudur Jones, *Congregationalism in England* (1962), 138.
37. J. H. Taylor, *Philip Doddridge* (1961), 3.

Chapter Four: Dearest Dear of all Dears.

1. *JH*. i. 175-77; CC. 42.
2. CC. p. xii.
3. *JH*. iii. 46; (CC. 346).
4. Ibid. 46-7; (CC. 346).
5. Ibid. 53; (CC. 348).
6. Ibid. 62; CC. 355.
7. *PD*. i. 97.
8. CC. 828.
9. See *JH*. iv. 102; CC. 768.
10. Ibid. 103.
11. CC. p. xv.
12. *JH*. iv. 49; CC. 692.
13. *JH*. iv. 118; CC. 792.
14. CC. p. xxxv.
15. CC. 771.
16. CC. 779.
17. *JH*. iv. 108; CC. 781.
18. CC. 782.
19. A. Kippis, *The Life of Dr Doddridge in The Family Expositor* (1799), i. p. xlix.
20. CC. 1646.
21. *JH*. iii. 93; CC. 366.
22. Ibid. 95; (CC. 368).
23. Ibid. 96.
24. *PD*. iii. 304.
25. J. Stoughton, *Philip Doddridge* (1852), 96.
26. See *PD*. iii. 302.

27. *JH.* v. 365.
28. Ibid. 365.
29. Ibid, 362.
30. Ibid, 366.
31. *JH.* iii. 490, 96; CC. 625, 630.
32. *JH.* iii. 489; CC. 624.
33. CC. 634.
34. *JH.* iv. 107; CC. 778.
35. CC. 997.
36. Ibid. 1647.
37. See the Doddridge pedigree in M. Deacon, *Philip Doddridge of Northampton* (1980), App. II, 176-7.
38. See *JH.* v. 195; CC. 1717.
39. *PD* i. 217.
40. Ibid. 226.
41. *The Confessions of S. Augustine* (1886), 1. Penguin Classics edition (1961), 21.
42. *The Institutes of the Christian Religion*, tr. H. Beveridge (1962 facs.), Book I, chapter 1, 37.
43. Hymn 294. 2, 'My gracious Lord, I own thy right' in *Hymns founded on various texts in the Holy Scriptures*, PD. iii. 595.
44. See *PD.* ii. p. vff.
45. See ibid. 77ff.
46. See ibid. iv. 225ff.
47. See ibid. ii. 207ff.
48. See ibid. i. 591ff.
49. *PD.* i. 476.
50. Ibid. 598.
51. *PD.* iv. 230.

Chapter Five: The School of Christ.

1. *A History of Northampton Castle Hill Church* (1896), 21.
2. See F. Heer, *The Medieval World* (1963), 252; also H. Rashdall, *The Universities of Europe in the Middle Ages*, Revised ed. F. M. Powicke and A. B. Emden (1936), iii. 86-9.
3. *JH.* iii. 85-6; CC. 378.
4. Ibid. 102; CC. 375.
5. Ibid.
6. M. Deacon, *Philip Doddridge of Northampton* (1980), 101.
7. C. A. Davis, *Sword and Trowel* (1881), 546.

8. J. Stalker, *John Knox* (1904), 48; E. Stickelberger, *Calvin* (1959), 142.

9. *JH*. iii. 115; *CC*. 382.

10. See D. Macleod, *Jesus is Lord: Christology Yesterday and Today* (2000), 97-8.

11. A. Kippis, *The Life of Dr Doddridge* in *The Family Expositor* (1799), i. p. lxxi-ii.

12. Ibid. p. lviii.

13. See R. Milton, *The Facts of Life: Shattering the Myths of Darwinism* (1992); J. Blanchard, *Does God Believe in Atheists?* (2000), 78ff.

14. See *PD*. iv. 279 - v. 420.

15. Ibid. iv. 297.

16. Ibid. 282.

17. *The Doctrine of the Knowledge of God* (1952), 15.

18. See *Philosophical Transactions*, xliv. 2 (1747), 596; xlv (1748), 502-4; xlvi (1749-50), 712-21.

19. See *JH*. v. 28-9; (*CC*. 1292).

20. See *Gentleman s Magazine*, xvi (1746), 475-77 for transcripts of papers on 'The Doctrine of Pendulums' and 'The Laws of Communication of Motion as well in elastic as in non-elastic Bodies'.

21. A. Kippis, op. cit. p. l.

22. *Extracts from the Diary of Joseph Williams*, ed. B. Hanbury (1815), 348.

23. *The Monthly Repository* (1824), xix. 85.

24. M. H. Wilkin, *Joseph Kinghorn of Norwich* (1855), 336.

25. *JH*. iv. 492; *CC*. 1166.

26. *JH*. iv. 387; *CC*. 1133.

27. *PD*. i. 495.

28. *JH*. iv. 303; (*CC*. 944).

29. J. Orton, *Memoirs* in *PD*. i. 68.

30. A. Kippis, op. cit. p. lx.

31. Ibid. p. lxvii.

32. Ibid. p. clxxviii.

33. *CC*. 629.

34. *CC*. 902.

35. *CC*. 1231.

36. *CC*. 1651.

37. *JH*. i. 451; (*CC*. 153).

38. 'Improvement' on Eph. 4: 17-30 in *The Family Expositor*, *PD*. ix. 372.

39. *The Rise and Progress of Religion in the Soul*,

19. 17 (6) in *PD*. i. 362.
40. A. Kippis, op. cit. p. clx.
41. C. Brown, *Philosophy and the Christian Faith* (1969), 80-1.
42. *PD*. i. 74.
43. Ibid. iv. 298.
44. *JH*. iv. 293; (*CC*. 934).
45. See G. F. Nuttall, *Richard Baxter and Philip Doddridge: A Study in a Tradition* (1951), 26, n. 49.
46. Ibid. 19.
47. Ibid. 20.
48. T. Coleman, *Memorials of the Independent Churches in Northamptonshire* (1853), 270-2.
49. *A History of Northampton Castle Hill Church* (1896), 63.
50. See M. Deacon, op. cit. 180.
51. Ibid. 191-8.
52. *CC*. 1595.
53. *A History of Northampton Castle Hill Church* (1896), 73.
54. These were Hendrik Beman of Rotterdam, Pieter Abraham de Hondt of The Hague and Pierre Rocquette also of Rotterdam. See *CC*. 1513.
55. H. McLachlan, *English Education under the Test Acts* (1931), 143.
56. Irene Parker, *Dissenting Academies in England: their rise and progress and their place among the educational systems of the country* (1914), 101.
57. See *JH*. iii. 275; *CC*. 469 (n. 1).
58. See *JH*. iv. 305; *CC*. 947 and 961.
59. *JH*. iv. 285; (*CC*. 927).

Chapter Six: Pastor and People.

1. *The Christian Ministry* (Banner of Truth reprint, 1958), 42.
2. *The Diary* in *JH*. v. 400.
3. *JH*. iii. 8.
4. Ibid. 9.
5. J. Orton, *Memoirs ... of Dr Philip Doddridge* in *PD*. i. 51.
6. A. Kippis, *Life of Dr Doddridge* in *The Family Expostor* (1799), i. p. xliii.
7. J. Stoughton, *Philip Doddridge* (1851), 80.
8. *JH*. v. 278.
9. Ibid. 401.

10. Ibid. 466.
11. See M. R. Watts, *The Dissenters* (1978), 31ff.; M. Deacon, *Philip Doddridge of Northampton* (1980), 15, 48.
12. See A. H. Drysdale, *History of the Presbyterians in England* (1889), 448ff; R. Thomas, 'Parties in Conformity' in *The English Presbyterians*, eds. C. G. Bolam et al (1968), 93ff.
13. T. Arnold and J. J. Cooper, *The History of the Church of Doddridge* (1895), 57.
14. *JH*. i. 304; CC. 91.
15. *PD*. v. 500.
16. T. Arnold and J. J. Cooper, op. cit. 112-4.
17. Ibid. 111.
18. *The Diary* in *JH*. v. 303-5.
19. M. Deacon, op. cit. 80.
20. T. Coleman, *Memorials of the Independent Churches in Northamptonshire* (1853), 24; CC. 1239.
21. *JH*. v. 452.
22. *JH*. v. 58; CC. 1327.
23. CC. 1472.
24. *JH*. v. 114-5; CC. 1458.
25. *JH*. iv. 91-2; CC. 755.
26. See *JH*. i. 427; CC. 149.
27. *JH*. v. 172-3; CC. 1630.
28. G. Smith, *The Life of William Carey* (1909), 186.

Chapter Seven: Truth and Charity.

1. Wilhelmus Peiffers in J. Orton, *Memoirs ... of Dr Philip Doddridge* in *PD*. i. 89.
2. A. Kippis, *Life of Dr Doddridge* in *The Family Expostor* (1799), i. p. clxii.
3. R. Thomas, 'Doddridge and Liberalism in Religion' in *Philip Doddridge 1702-51 His contribution to English Religion*, ed. G. F. Nuttall (1951), 134.
4. *JH*. v. 63.
5. *Christian Candour and Unanimity* in *PD*. iii. 267.
6. *Directions for Ministerial Conduct* in *PD*. iii. 199.
7. See T. Myers (tr) in J. Calvin, *Commentaries on Ezekiel* (Calvin Translation Society, 1849), i. p. xxii.
8. *PD*. iv. 168.
9. Ibid. 193.

10. *Rise and Progress of Religion in the Soul*, 26. 2 in *PD*. i. 422.
11. *Directions for Ministerial Conduct* in *PD*. iii. 206-7.
12. T. H. Darlow, *William Robertson Nichol* (1925), 362.
13. See J. Waddington, *Congregational History* (1876), 284-7.
14. *PD*. x. 90.
15. *The Sword and Trowel* (1887), 166-7.
16. *JH*. iii. 293; *CC*. 480.
17. *JH*. iv. 136; (*CC*. 714).
18. Orton, op. cit. in *PD*. i. 151.
19. *The Temper and Conduct of the Primitive Ministers of the Gospel*, *PD*. iii. 184.
20. M. Deacon, op. cit. 124.
21. Orton, op. cit. in *PD*. i. 153.
22. *JH*. v. 174; *CC*. 1633.
23. The Norwich-born Unitarian James Martineau (of Huguenot stock) was possibly an example of a 'border line evangelical'. He pleaded for spiritual warmth in his *Hymns for the Christian Church and Home* (1840). The book included 'more than fifty hymns by the Wesleys, and others by Anglicans and evangelicals, by German pietists and by metaphysical poets of the seventeenth century' (H. L. Short, 'Presbyterians under a New Name' in *The English Presbyterians*, eds. C. G. Bolam et al (1968), 258).
24. *PD*. vi. 503.
25. A. Kippis, op. cit. p. xxii.
26. *History of the Dissenters* (1810), iii. 483.
27. *JH*. i. 68; (*CC*. 13).
28. *JH*. i. 44: *CC*. 8.
29. *JH*. i. 368; (*CC*. 120).
30. *JH*. i. 378; (*CC*. 122).
31. *JH*. i. 426; *CC*. 149.
32. *JH*. i. 460; *CC*. 155.
33. *JH*. i. 439; *CC*. 150.
34. *JH*. ii. 235; *CC*. 242.
35. 'Improvement' on 1 Cor. 1: 10-16 in *The Family Expositor*, *PD*. viii. 564.
36. *PD*. v. 536; *CC*. 1402.
37. *PD*. ii. 553.
38. Ibid. 566.
39. Ibid. 567.
40. Ibid. 495.
41. Ibid. 396.
42. *The Diary* in *JH*. v. 289.

43. *PD*. vi. 125.
44. *PD*. x. 346.
45. *PD*. ii. 217.
46. *Sermons on Regeneration, PD*. ii. 530. 'Whoever you are' is capitalised in some editions.
47. *PD*. v. 263.
48. Orton, op. cit. in *PD*. i. 152.
49. Ibid.
50. *JH*. iii. 163; CC. 416.
51. J. Brine, *The Certain Efficacy of the Death of Christ* (1743), 258-60.
52. *Lectures* in *PD*. v. 264-5.
53. J. Goring, 'The Break-up of the Old Dissent' in *The English Presbyterians*, eds. C. G. Bolam et al (1968), 187.
54. A. Kippis, op. cit. p. clv-vi.
55. Orton, op. cit. in *PD*. i. 89.
56. Ibid.
57. *Commenting and Commentaries* (1969 rep), 4.
58. Ibid. 14.
59. Ibid. 9.
60. *Lectures on Preaching and ... the Ministerial Office* in *PD*. v. 429.
61. Ibid. 429-32.
62. Ibid. 435.
63. Ibid. 474.
64. Ibid. 475.
65. Ibid. 438-9.
66. *JH*. iii. 438; CC. 600 and 1218.
67. *The Whole Works of ... Robert Leighton, DD* (1828), i. 104.
68. Orton, op. cit. in *PD*. i. 159-60.
69. *JH*. iv. 503; (CC. 1170).
70. *PD*. iii. 119.
71. Ibid. 123-4.
72. Ibid. 132.
73. *Sermons against Popery* (? n.d.), 52 cited by Orton, *PD*. i. 123.
74. *The Family Expositor, PD*. ix. 551.
75. Ibid. 554.
76. Ibid. vii. 296.
77. Ibid. vi. 135.
78. Ibid. ix. 596.
79. See Deacon, op. cit. 115-6.
80. *JH*. iii. 556-8; (CC. 667).
81. See Deacon, op. cit. 170, n. 59; E. A. Payne, 'Doddridge and the Missionary Enterprise' in *Philip Doddridge 1702-51*

His Contribution to English Religion (1951), 99.
82. See Lecture ccii, 'Of the Mode of Baptism', *PD.* v. 323-5.

Chapter Eight: The Great Awakening.

1. *Hymns Founded on Various Texts in the Holy Scriptures,* Hymn 297.6, *PD.* iii. 530.
2. *PD.* iv. 213.
3. Ibid. 213.
4. Ibid. 211.
5. *Journal* (1960), 58.
6. *AL.* 527A.
7. *AL.* 527B.
8. *Journal* (1960), 273.
9. *JH.* v. 400-1.
10. Ibid. 587. Humphreys incorrectly assumes the 'clergyman' to be John Wesley, who was still in Georgia at this time.
11. *Journal* (1960), 85-6.
12. *JH.* iv. 269.
13. Ibid. 283.
14. Ibid. 289.
15. *Works* (1771), ii. 41.
16. *JH.* iv. 293; *CC.* 934.
17. Helen C. Knight, *Lady Huntingdon and Her Friends* (1853), 34.
18. *Works* (1771), ii. 214-6; *CC.* 1428.
19. J. P. Gledstone, *George Whitefield, MA, Field Preacher* (1901), 216-7 and J. Orton, *Memoirs ... of Dr Philip Doddridge* in *PD.* i. 183.
20. C. Stanford, *Philip Doddridge* (1880), 105.
21. *The Journal of the Revd John Wesley, AM*, ed. N. Curnock (1909-16), iii. 206.
22. *Explanatory Notes on the New Testament* (1755 ed.), p. v.
23. *The Journal of Charles Wesley*, ed. T. Jackson, ii. 64; also in John Wesley, *Journal*, ed. Curnock, iii. 425n.
24. *Works* (1771), ii. 350; *CC.*1611.
25. *PD.* v. 461.
26. *Works* (1771), ii. 47.
27. *PD.* ii. 593-606.
28. *Works* (1771), ii. 214-6; *CC.* 1428.
29. *PD.* ii. 589.
30. *The Pattern of Rural Dissent: the nineteenth century* (1972), 16.
31. See Revd George Whitefield, *The Care of the Soul Urged as the One*

Thing Needful (Inheritance Publications, 1972) republished from *Sermons on Important Subjects by the Revd George Whitefield, AM* (1833).

32. See *PD*. iii. 283ff.
33. See M. Deacon, *Philip Doddridge of Northampton* (1980), 161, n.53.
34. *PD*. ii. 587.
35. J. Hervey, *Works* (1797), v. 369.
36. See *PD*. ii. 369ff.
37. *PD*. vii. 514.
38. Doddridge, *The Witness of the Spirit in Sermons* (1826), ii. 381.
39. Ibid. iii. 15.
40. Doddridge's reply to *Christianity not founded on Argument*, Letter III (1743) in *PD*. i. 554. Notwithstanding his cessationist position, Doddridge was intrigued by the mystic Mary Wills of Pitsford. Her prophecies about his daughter's death and his own plus the invasion of 'Bonnie Prince Charlie' were seemingly accurate. See M. Deacon, op. cit. 58, 116, 125.
41. See *The Autobiography of Richard Baxter*, ed. J. M. Lloyd-Thomas (1931), pp. xxvii, 96, 117.
42. C. Stanford, *Philip Doddridge* (1880), 97 (Frost's Funeral Sermon for Doddridge, *The Stars in Christ's Right Hand*, 1752); CC. 1749.
43. *JH*. iv. 38; CC. 686.
44. See Banner of Truth edition (1974).
45. *PD*. iii. 232.
46. 'Doddridge and the Missionary Enterprise' in *Philip Doddridge 1702-51: His Contribution to English Religion*, ed. G. F. Nuttall (1951), 100.
47. Orton, op. cit. 156.
48. 'Some Memorandums of Poor Connell's Affair' in *The Diary, JH*. v. 425.
49. See *PD*. iii. 91ff. See M. Deacon, op. cit. 121ff.
50. *JH*. iv. 307; CC. 946.
51. See M. Deacon, op. cit. 119f.
52. Ibid. 103.
53. Ibid. 126.
54. See *PD*. iii. 147.
55. C. Stanford, op. cit. 150; M. Deacon, op. cit. 128.
56. See *PD*. iv. 145; M. Deacon, op. cit. 128.
57. See *PD*. iv. 5ff; M. Deacon, op. cit. 124ff.
58. See A. Gibson, 'Philip Doddridge's "The Rise and Progress of Religion in the soul"', *Increasing in the Knowledge of God* (Puritan and Reformed Studies Conference, 1961), 3-12.
59. See Doddridge's dedication to Watts, *PD*. i. 211; CC. 1023.

60. *JH.* iv. 517; (CC. 1213).
61. *JH.* iv. 426; (CC. 1083).
62. *JH.* iv. 450; CC. 1117.
63. CC. 1117 (Omitted by Humphreys).
64. *Works* (1771), ii. 346.
65. J. Edwards, *Works* (1834, 1974 rep), i. p. cxxiii.
66. *The Early Years* (1962), 392.
67. R. I. and S. Wilberforce, *The Life of William Wilberforce* (1838), i. 76.
68. See J. Wesley Bready, *England Before and After Wesley: The Evangelical Revival and Social Reform* (1939).

Chapter Nine: O Sing unto the Lord.

1. 'The Hymns of Philip Doddridge' in *Philip Doddridge 1702-51: His Contribution to English Religion*, ed. G. F. Nuttall (1951), 47.
2. Ibid. 49.
3. Ibid. 68.
4. See M. Bushell, *The Songs of Zion* (1980), *passim.*
5. *The Family Expositor*, PD. ix. 487.
6. See A. C. Clifford, 'The Westminster Directory of Public Worship' in *The Reformation of Worship* (Westminster Conference Report, 1989), 75, n. 70. Also *Christian Hymns* (1977), 124.
7. Paraphrase of Col. 3: 16, *PD.* ix. 487, n. 'e'.
8. See Lecture cxciv, 'Of the Lord s Prayer ... Liturgies' in *PD.* v. 295f.
9. Ibid. 294.
10. See *The Family Expositor* on Lk. 2: 1-21, *PD.* vi. 65, n. 'i'.
11. *JH.* iii. 411; (CC. 582).
12. *Lectures on Preaching*, PD. v. 444-5. Notwithstanding Doddridge's Trinitarian and Calvinistic convictions, he warned his students against arid technical expositions of the Trinity, the hypostatic union and the 'highest points of Calvinism' (imputation of Adam's sin, reprobation, irresistible grace). 'Hints' on such doctrines rather than 'whole discourses upon them' are 'better'. Preachers must avoid 'puzzling' their hearers. Otherwise they will feed the people 'with roots instead of fruits'. What Doddridge says of the 'evidences of Christianity' applies to these other subjects too. Such things are better said 'from the press than from the pulpit' (Ibid. 440-1). Unlike many today, Doddridge was careful *not* to suppress the reality of God's wrath. However, he urged preachers to avoid 'subjects of great terror – as very strong representations of the

wrath of God, or of the nature, degree and duration of the torments
of hell. – Warn faithfully, but let it be rather in particular parts of
sermons, than in distinct discourses. – Always take care to avoid
representing God as a tyrant' (Ibid. 442).

13. See *Hymns Founded on Various Texts in the Holy Scriptures*, PD.
iii. 430ff.

14. *Some Remarkable Passages in the Life of the Honourable Colonel
James Gardiner* in PD. iv. 94.

15. J. Rippon, *The Baptist Annual Register*, iv. 381, cited in E. A.
Payne, 'Doddridge and the Missionary Enterprise'
in *Philip Doddridge 1702-51: His Contribution to English Religion*,
ed. G. F. Nuttall (1951), 100f.

16. *Life of Gardiner, PD.* iv. 67f.

17. *The Christian Psalmist* (1825), p. xxv.

18. H. J. Garland, *The Life and Hymns of Dr Philip Doddridge* (1951), 44.

19. J. Telford, *The Methodist Hymn-Book Illustrated* (1909), 387.
See also W. J. Limmer Sheppard, *Great Hymns and Their Stories*
(1950 ed), 168.

20. Telford, op. cit. 104.

21. E. Routley, 'The Hymns of Philip Doddridge', op. cit. 66.

22. Ibid. 75.

23. *AL.* 527B.

Chapter Ten: An Immortal Crown.

1. *JH.* v. 171; (CC. 1630).
2. *JH.* v. 73; (CC. 1373).
3. *The Diary* in *JH.* v. 479-80.
4. *JH.* v. 74; (CC. 1373).
5. *AL.* 527A.
6. *JH.* v. 75-6; CC. 1377.
7. See *PD.* iii. 71ff.
8. See J. P. Gledstone, *George Whitefield, MA, Field-Preacher*
(1901), 273.
9. *JH.* v. 153; CC. 1591.
10. See Doddridge's letter of October 17 in Royal Society *Philosophical
Transactions*, xlvi (1749-50). 712. (CC. 1666).
11. *JH.* i. 278; CC. 81.
12. *JH.* ii. 81; CC. 197.
13. *Lectures on Preaching* in PD. v. 500.
14. *PD.* i. 117-8.

15. *PD.* iii. 267.
16. *CC.* 1611; A. Dallimore, *George Whitefield* (1980), ii. 285.
17. *JH.* v. 161; *CC.* 1620.
18. *CC.* 1627. See also Faith Cook, *Selina Countess of Huntingdon* (2001), 133-4.
19. *JH.* v. 171; *CC.* 1630.
20. *JH.* v. 145; *CC.* 1557.
21. See D. R. Smith, 'John Fletcher: An Arminian Upholder of Holiness' in *The Manifold Grace of God* (Puritan and Reformed Studies Conference Report, 1968), 63-4.
22. *PD.* v. 544; *CC.* 1679.
23. G. Whitefield, *Works* (1771), ii. 214; *CC.* 1428.
24. *JH.* v. 107; *CC.* 1448.
25. *JH.* v. 205; *CC.* 1747.
26. J. Orton, *Memoirs ... of Dr Philip Doddridge* in *PD.* i. 185.
27. Ibid. 191; *JH.* v. 215.
28. *JH.* v. 208; *CC.* 1769.
29. Helen C. Knight, *Lady Huntingdon and Her Friends* (1853), 92-3.
30. A. M. Toplady, *Works* (1825), iv. 141; Faith Cook, op. cit. 140.
31. *JH.* v. 232-3; *CC.* 1798.
32. Orton, op. cit. 197; *JH.* v. 234.
33. Ibid.; See 'God of my life, through all its days', Hymn 71. 3 in *Hymns Founded on Various Texts in the Holy Scriptures, PD.* iii. 472.
34. Orton, op. cit. 198; *JH.* v. 235; *CC.* 1801.
35. Orton, op. cit. 199; *JH.* v. 237.
36. Orton, op. cit. 200; *JH.* v. 237.
37. C. Stanford, *Philip Doddridge* (1880), 191.
38. Orton, op. cit. 202; *JH.* v. 239-241.
39. G. Whitefield, *Works* (1771), ii. 429.
40. Orton, op. cit. 201; *JH.* v. 239. The actual Castle Hill memorial gives Doddridge an incorrect date of birth - January 26 instead of June 26 (see M. Deacon, *Philip Doddridge of Northampton* (1980), Illustration 48, opp. 149). Doddridge was thus 49 not 50 as indicated by Orton and Humphreys.
41. C. A. Briggs, *American Protestantism* (1885), 296; *CC.* 1663.
42. J. Waddington, *Congregational History* 1700-1800 (1876), 441-2.
43. J. R. Boyd, *Memoir of the Life, Character, and Writings of Philip Doddridge, DD* (1860), 477-8.
44. Orton, op. cit. 204. Kippis adds 'with a stoop in his shoulders' (see M. Deacon, op. cit. 135.
45. A. Kippis, *Life of Dr Doddridge in The Family Expostor* (1799), i. p. clii.

46. *JH*. iv. 450; *CC*. 1117

47. *JH*. iii. 537-8; *CC*. 726. Humphreys draws attention to the *Sermons* (4 vols; 1826) as a fulfilment of this suggestion.

48. *JH*. v. 187; *CC*. 1696.

49. Ibid. 188-9.

50. See *CC*. 1696; A. C. Clifford, *Sons of Calvin: Three Huguenot Pastors* (1999), 29.

51. *JH*. v. 189.

52. Ibid. 188.

53. See Article 31 of the Church Order of Dordt and S. Greijdanus, 'Scriptural Principles Concerning Broader Assemblies' in *Bound Yet Free*, ed. J. de Jong (1995), 30.

54. *JH*. iii. 275; *CC*. 473.

55. 'Awake, my soul, stretch every nerve', Hymn 296. 5 in *Hymns Founded on Various Texts in the Holy Scriptures*, *PD*. iii. 597.

56. *Works*, i. 107; M. Deacon, op. cit. 144; *Boswell s Life of Johnson*, ed. G. B. Hill and L. F. Powell (1934-50), v. 271.

Appendix: Doddridge: Hero or Heretic?

1. See 'God or god? Arianism, Ancient and Modern' in *The Evangelical Quarterly*, 68.2 (1996), 121-38, more recently published in D. Macleod, *Jesus is Lord: Christology Yesterday and Today* (2000), 87-105.

2. *Jesus is Lord*, 96.

3. Ibid. 97.

4. *PD*. ix. 466.

5. *Jesus is Lord*, 96.

6. *PD*. x. 431.

7. *PD*. vi. 24.

8. Ibid. 29.

9. *Jesus is Lord*, 97.

10. *PD*. v. 186.

11. See J. Waddington, *Congregational History* (1876), 284-7.

12. *PD*. v. 187.

13. *Jesus is Lord*, 97.

14. Cited in R. Thomas, 'Doddridge and Liberalism in Religion', *Philip Doddridge 1702-51: His Contribution to English Religion*, ed. G. F. Nuttall (1951), 132.

15. J. Orton, *Memoirs ... of Dr Philip Doddridge* in *PD*. i. 68.

16. *Jesus is Lord*, 100.
17. *JH*. i. 335; *CC*. 108.
18. See *Lectures on Preaching* in *PD*. v. 480-1.
19. *PD*. iv. 193. See 'early' Calvin's appeal to the Bible *vis-à-vis* creeds in W. Nijenhuis, 'Calvin's Attitude towards the Symbols of the Early Church' in *Ecclesia Reformata: Studies on the Reformation* (1972), 73-96.
20. *PD*. v. 230-1.
21. *Jesus is Lord*, 99.
22. Ibid. 100.
23. *Lecture lxx*, 'Of Oaths, ... and Subscriptions to Articles of Religion', *PD*. iv. 456.
24. *Lecture clxiii*, 'Opinions of the Moderns on the Trinity', *PD*. v. 193. For a critical assessment of Doddridge here, see R. Strivens, 'Philip Doddridge and Theological Education' (Westminster Conference Report, 2001), 18 (pre-pub. MS). Clearly Doddridge refuses to sit in judgement on the *speculative* personal phraseology of others. While he allows latitude here, his main concern is that his students should conform to *biblical* terminology and thought patterns. In the final analysis, a radical *sola scriptura* faith and experience of the triune God is what ultimately matters.
25. *Jesus is Lord*, 100.
26. Ibid. 101-1.
27. J. Waddington, op. cit. 287.
28. *Jesus is Lord*, 101.
29. C. R. Trueman, *The Claims of Truth* (1998), 27, n. 57 (cont), 93.
30. Ibid. 164, n. 41.
31. E. Wilson, *English Churchman* (June 4 & 11, 1999), 6.
32. *The Claims of Truth*, 93.
33. See A. C. Clifford, 'Orthodoxy and the Enlightenment: Theology and Philosophy in the thought of Philip Doddridge, DD (1702-51)' (MLitt, University of Newcastle upon Tyne, 1977), 76ff.
34. R. A. Muller, *Christ and the Decree* (1988), 12.
35. *The Claims of Truth*, 129-48.
36. See A. C. Clifford, *Calvinus: Authentic Calvinism, A Clarification* (1996), 68, 74. Hereafter *Calvinus*.
37. See Calvin's 'dualistic' *Comments* on 2 Pet. 3: 9 (The Father's activity); Rom. 5: 18, Heb. 9: 27 (The Son's activity); Heb. 6: 4-5 (The Holy Spirit's activity).
38. See 'Christ's Invitation to Thirsty Souls', *PD*. ii. 600 (quoted in Chapter 7 above, ref. 27).
39. *The Claims of Truth*, p. ix.

40. See A. C. Clifford, *Atonement and Justification* (1990), 23, 106-7, n. 9, 143 in response to C. R. Trueman, 'Campanella's Impact on Richard Baxter' in *Protestant Scholasticism: Essays in Reassessment*, ed. C. R Trueman and R. S. Clark (1999), 185, n. 13. Whatever Trueman says about the so-called 'root fallacy' of linguistic usage (182, n. 3), it cannot be denied that the means-end terminology of Aristotle's *Nicomachean Ethics* suited and influenced Owen's single-end teleology of the atonement.

41. *JH.* i. 198; (CC. 53).

42. *Jesus is Lord*, 102; R. Thomas, 'Doddridge and Liberalism in Religion', *Philip Doddridge 1702-51: His Contribution to English Religion*, ed. G. F. Nuttall (1951), 132.

43. *JH.* i. 155; CC. 35.

44. See B. G. Armstrong, *Calvinism and the Amyraut Heresy: Protestant Scholasticism and Humanism in Seventeenth Century France* (1969), 3-70.

45. See A. C. Clifford, Atonement and Justification, 69ff.

46. See G. F. Nuttall, *Richard Baxter and Philip Doddridge: A Study in a Tradition* (1951) and *PD.* v. 214, ref. 'c' (to Calvin).

47. *Christ and the Decree*, 12.

48. See R. A. Muller, 'Calvin and the "Calvinists": Assessing Continuities and Discontinuities between the Reformation and Orthodoxy', *Calvin Theological Journal* 31 (1996), 125-60.

49. *Christ and the Decree*, 34.

50. Ibid.

51. See A. C. Clifford, *Calvinus*, #25, 46.

52. Ibid. #50, 50.

53. Ibid. #52, 51.

54. Ibid. #53, 51.

55. Ibid. #57, 52.

56. Ibid. #61, 52-3.

57. Ibid. #66, 54.

58. *Christ and the Decree*, 35.

59. *Calvinus*, #77, 57.

60. *Journal of the Presbyterian Historical Society of England*, I. 2 (1915), 35.

61. See A. C. Clifford, *Atonement and Justification*, 28.

62. Ibid. 27.

63. See *Book of Praise: Anglo-Genevan Psalter* (1984), 545-7.

64. J. Quick, *Synodicon in Gallia Reformata* (1692), ii. 354.

65. *Jesus is Lord*, 102.

66. 'But in a few of Edwards' later works ... certain individual aspects of [his] thought appear and in connection with his concern to employ 'reason' or philosophy to buttress biblical truths. A theory of necessity or determinism is introduced to support the truth of divine sovereignty... (I. H. Murray, *Jonathan Edwards: A New Biography* (1987), 451).

67. Contrary to R. L. Greenall's at best highly ambiguous statement that he 'rejected the grim doctrine of predestination' *(Philip Doddridge, Nonconformity and Northampton* (1981), p. iii), Doddridge believed in predestination no less than Edwards. However, his careful discussion of it avoids the pitfall of a 'mechanistic' determinism. While predestination is 'certain' according to God's sovereign purpose, Doddridge states that 'the *certainty* of an event does not imply *necessity*; ... and consequently, that there may be a foundation for certain foresight, where the event itself is contingent; or in other words, the thing will not be because God *foresees* it, but God *foresees* it because it will certainly be' (*Lecture xli*, 'Of Contingency and Scientia Media', *PD*. iv. 386); '... an event may be allowed *contingent*, though it will *certainly* happen; divine *predestination* ... does not imply the *necessary* salvation or condemnation of any' (*Lecture clxxxiv*, 'Of Predestination and Personal Election', *PD*. v. 257). In short, human beings are not 'automatons' even though God remains sovereign in divine-human interaction.

68. Ibid. ix. 328.

69. Ibid. v. 259.

70. Ibid. ii. 600.

71. Ibid. v. 214.

72. R. Baxter, *The Universal Redemption of Mankind*, ed. J. Read (1694), 286.

73. A. C. Clifford, *Calvinus*, #12, 43.

74. Ibid. #17, 44.

75. Ibid. #58, 52.

76. Ibid. #65, 54.

77. Ibid. #67, 54.

78. Ibid. #83, 58.

79. *PD*. v. 263.

80. R. Baxter, *Reliquiae Baxterianae*, ed. M. Sylvester (1696), ii. 55, para. 199. Cited in G. F. Nuttall, *Richard Baxter and Philip Doddridge* (1951), 10.

81. *The Death of Death in the Death of Christ* in *Works* (1850-5), x. 344.

82. *PD.* ix. 581.
83. *The Death of Death,* op. cit. 321.
84. *PD.* vi. 122.
85. Ibid. 432.
86. See *Philip Doddridge (1702-1751) and the Netherlands* (1987).
87. Ibid. 63.
88. *JH.* iv. 517; (CC. 1213).
89. *JH.* v. 45; CC. 1316.
90. J. R. Beeke and S. B. Ferguson, op. cit. The universalist statement of Dordt correlates with that of the *Heidelberg Catechism* (Q. 37) under 'Justification' (p. 98) but not under 'The States of Christ' (pp. 74-6). While a universalist *Helvetic Confession* statement is quoted on p. 74, why is another placed on p. 68 rather than at p. 74-6? Significantly, since no universalist equivalent exists in the *Westminster Confession,* the WCF column on p. 77 is blank. Clearly, no harmonization is possible on this basic point.
91. See H. Hoeksema, *The Triple Knowledge* (1976), i. 641-2; G. I. Williamson, *The Heidelberg Catechism: A Study Guide* (1993), 70. While G. W. Bethune partially appeals to Ursinus' actual views in *Guilt, Grace and Gratitude* (Banner of Truth edition, 2001), i. 359-60, he omits key statements of the Heidelberg professor. The reader is thus denied the full force of Ursinus' actual teaching.
92. Z. Ursinus, *The Commentary on the Heidelberg Catechism,* ed. G. W. Williard (1985), 223.
93. C. Olevianus, *A Firm Foundation: An Aid to Interpreting the Heidelberg Catechism* (tr. & ed. L. D. Bierma (1995), 65.
94. Cited in J. Davenant, *A Dissertation on the Death of Christ,* tr. J. Allport in *An Exposition of ... Colossians* (1832), ii. 356.
95. *Lecture lxx,* 'Of Oaths, ... and Subscriptions to Articles of Religion', *PD.* iv. 456.
96. See A. C. Clifford, *Atonement and Justification,* 194.
97. Ibid. 191f; R. Baxter, *Catholick Theologie* (1675), I. ii. 63-4, 82, 66.
98. *Lectures on Preaching, PD.* v. 431.
99. *Salvation by Grace, PD.* ii. 561.
100. *PD.* v. 224.
101. *PD.* ii. 562.
102. R. Baxter, *An End of Doctrinal Controversies* (1691), 259.
103. R. Baxter, *Catholick Communion Defended* (1684), II. 8.
104. *PD.* v. 215-6.
105. R. Baxter, *Catholick Theologie,* II. 59.
106. *PD.* v. 216.
107. *PD.* viii. 426.

108. See *Reformed Confessions of the Sixteenth Century*, ed.
A. Cochrane (1966),187; P. Y. de Jong, *The Church's Witness to the World* (1980), 135-6.

109. See A. C. Clifford, *Atonement and Justification*, 190.

110. Z. Ursinus, *The Commentary on the Heidelberg Catechism*, 326.

111. C. Olevianus, *A Firm Foundation*, 111-2.

112. See P. Bayle, *The Dictionary Historical and Critical* (1737), iv. 474.

113. See A. C. Clifford, *Atonement and Justification*, 192ff.

114. *PD*. v. 223.

115. *PD*. viii. 414.

116. Ibid. n. 'h'.

117. *PD*. x. 228, n. 'd'.

118. *JH*. iii. 557; (CC. 667).

119. 'Faith is no justifying act: but faith is in its essence the acceptance of an offered God, Christ, Spirit, for life ... freely given us by God our Redeemer by a Covenant of Grace, merited for us, by the Obedience and Satisfaction given us by Christ our Saviour' (*Catholick Theologie*, II. 82, 70).

120. *JH*. i. 397; (CC. 129).

121. See G. F. Nuttall, *Richard Baxter and Philip Doddridge*, 13ff.

122. See *JH*. i. 368; 378, 380; (CC. 120, 122, 123).

(right)
A page from
a student's
notebook

A
SYSTEM
of
LOGICK,
RULES on Behaviour
and
SHORT HAND;
drawn up at
NORTHAMPTON
By P. DODDRIDGE, DD
VOL. IV.

J.H. Sculp.   T.B. Script.

Bibliography

Primary sources:

The Works of the Revd P. Doddridge, DD, ed. E. Williams and
    E. Parsons, 10 vols (Leeds, 1802-5).
Sermons on Various Subjects, ed. J. D. Humphreys, 4 vols
    (London, 1826)
The Correspondence and Diary of Philip Doddridge, DD, ed.
    J. D. Humphreys, 5 vols (London, 1829-31).
Calendar of the Correspondence of Philip Doddridge, DD (1702-1751),
    ed. G. F. Nuttall (London, 1979).
Philip Doddridge: Additional Letters: a supplement to Calendar of the
    Correspondence of Philip Doddridge, ed. G. F. Nuttall
    (London, 2001).

Biographies of Doddridge:

Boyd, J. R., *Memoir of the Life, Character and Writings of Philip*
    Doddridge, DD (New York, 1860).
Deacon, M., *Philip Doddridge of Northampton 1702-51*
    (Northampton, 1980).
Kippis, A., *The Life of Dr Doddridge in The Family Expositor* (London,
    1799), Vol. 1 (from *Biographia Britannica* (1778-96), ed. Kippis).
Orton, J., *Memoirs of the Life, Character and Writings of the Late Rev.*
    P. Doddridge, DD of Northampton (London, 1766); also in *Works*,
    ed. Williams and Parsons (Leeds, 1802-5), Vol. 1.
Stanford, C., *Philip Doddridge, DD* (London, 1880).
Stoughton, J., *Philip Doddridge: his life and labours* (London, 1851).
Taylor, J. H., *Philip Doddridge* (London, 1961). (Booklet)

Other selected sources:

Armstrong, B. G., *Calvinism and the Amyraut Heresy: Protestant*
    Scholasticism and Humanism in Seventeenth Century France
    (Madison, 1969).

Arnold, T. and Cooper, J. J., *The History of the Church of Doddridge* (Kettering and Wellingborough, 1895).

Baxter, R., *An End of Doctrinal Controversies* (London, 1691).
— — — *Reliquiae Baxterianae*, ed. M. Sylvester (London, 1696).
— — — *Richard Baxter's Catholick Theologie* (London, 1675).
— — — *The Autobiography of Richard Baxter*, ed. J. M. Lloyd-Thomas (London, 1931).
— — — *The Universal Redemption of Mankind*, ed. J. Read (London, 1694).
Bayle, P., *The Dictionary Historical and Critical* (London, 1737), Vol. 4.
Beeke, J. R. and Ferguson, S. B. (eds.), *Reformed Confessions Harmonized* (Grand Rapids, 1999).
Berg, J. van den and Nuttall, G. F., *Philip Doddridge (1702-1751) and the Netherlands* (Leiden, 1987).
Bogue, D. and Bennett, J., *History of the Dissenters*, 3 vols (London, 1810).
Bolam, C. G. et al, *The English Presbyterians: From Elizabethan Puritanism to Modern Unitarianism* (London, 1968).
Bready, J. Wesley, *England Before and After Wesley: The Evangelical Revival and Social Reform* (London, 1939).
Brine, J., *The Certain Efficacy of the Death of Christ* (London, 1743).

Calvin, J., *Calvin's Commentaries*, ed. D. W. and T. F. Torrance, 12 vols (Edinburgh, 1959-72). For other relevant extracts, see Clifford, A. C., *Calvinus* (below).
— — — *The Institutes of the Christian Religion*, tr. H. Beveridge (London, 1962 facs.).
Clifford, A. C., *Atonement and Justification: English Evangelical Theology 1640 - 1790 - An Evaluation* (Oxford, 1990).
— — — *Calvinus: Authentic Calvinism, A Clarification* (Norwich, 1996).
— — — *Sons of Calvin: Three Huguenot Pastors* (Norwich, 1999).
— — — 'Orthodoxy and the Enlightenment: Theology and Philosophy in the thought of Philip Doddridge, DD (1702-51)' (Unpublished MLitt thesis, University of Newcastle upon Tyne, 1977).
Cochrane, A. (ed.), *Reformed Confessions of the Sixteenth Century* (London, 1966).
Coleman, T., *Memorials of the Independent Churches in Northamptonshire* (London, 1853).
Cook, F., *Selina Countess of Huntingdon* (Edinburgh, 2001).

Dallimore, A. A., *George Whitefield* (Edinburgh, 1980), Vol. 2.

Davenant, J., *A Dissertation on the Death of Christ*, tr. J. Allport in *An Exposition of ... Colossians* (London, 1832).

Davis, A. P., *Isaac Watts* (London, 1948).

Drysdale, A. H., *History of the Presbyterians in England* (London, 1889).

Everitt, A., *The Pattern of Rural Dissent: the nineteenth century* (Leicester, 1972).

Fountain, D., *Isaac Watts Remembered* (Worthing, 1974).

Garland, H. J., *The Life and Hymns of Dr Philip Doddridge* (London, 1951).

Gledstone, J. P., *George Whitefield, MA, Field Preacher* (London, 1901).

Greenall, R. L. (ed.), *Philip Doddridge, Nonconformity and Northampton* (Leicester, 1981).

Greijdanus, S., 'Scriptural Principles Concerning Broader Assemblies' in *Bound Yet Free*, ed. J. De Jong (Winnipeg, 1995).

Harris, F. W. P., 'The life and work of Philip Doddridge' (Unpublished BLitt thesis, University of Oxford, 1950).

Jones, R. Tudur, *Congregationalism in England* (London, 1962).

Jong, P. Y. de, *The Church's Witness to the World* (Ontario, 1980).

Knight, H. C., *Lady Huntingdon and Her Friends* (rep. Grand Rapids, 1979).

Leighton, R., *The Whole Works of ... Robert Leighton, DD* (London, 1828).

Macleod, D., *Jesus is Lord: Christology Yesterday and Today* (Fearn, Ross-shire, 2000).

Macleod, J., *Scottish Theology* (Edinburgh, 1974).

McLachlan, H., *English Education under the Test Acts* (Manchester, 1931).

Muller, R. A., *Christ and the Decree* (Grand Rapids, 1988).

Nijenhuis, W., 'Calvin's Attitude towards the Symbols of the Early Church' in *Ecclesia Reformata: Studies on the Reformation* (Leiden, 1972).

Nuttall, G. F. (ed.), *Philip Doddridge 1702-51: His contribution to*

English Religion (London, 1951).

——— and Berg, J. van den, *Philip Doddridge (1702-1751) and the Netherlands* (Leiden, 1987).

——— *Richard Baxter and Philip Doddridge: A Study in a Tradition* (London, 1951).

Olevianus, C., *A Firm Foundation: An Aid to Interpreting the Heidelberg Catechism*, tr. & ed. L. D. Bierma (Grand Rapids, 1995).

Owen, J., *The Death of Death in the Death of Christ* in *The Works of John Owen, DD*, ed. W. H. Goold (1850-5), Vol. 10.

Parker, I., *Dissenting Academies in England: their rise and progress and their place among the educational systems of the country* (Cambridge, 1914).

Plumb, J. H., *England in the Eighteenth Century 1714-1815* (London, 1950).

Quick, J., *Synodicon in Gallia Reformata*, 2 vols (London, 1692).

Routley, E., 'The Hymns of Philip Doddridge' in *Philip Doddridge 1702-51: His Contribution to English Religion*, ed. G. F. Nuttall (London, 1951).

Spurgeon, C. H., *Commenting and Commentaries* (rep. London, 1969).

Stephen, Sir L., *A History of English Thought in the Eighteenth Century* (London, 1876).

Strivens, R., 'Philip Doddridge and Theological Education' (Westminster Conference Report, 2001).

Taylor, J. (ed.), *A History of Northampton Castle Hill Church* (Northampton, 1896).

Trueman, C. R., *The Claims of Truth: John Owen s Trinitarian Theology* (Carlisle, 1998).

Ursinus, Z., *The Commentary on the Heidelberg Catechism*, ed. G. W. Williard (facs. Phillipsburg, NJ, 1985).

Waddington, J., *Congregational History* (London, 1876).

Watts, M. R., *The Dissenters* (Oxford, 1978).

Wesley, C., *The Journal of Charles Wesley*, ed. T. Jackson, 2 vols (London, 1849).

Wesley, J., *The Journal of the Revd John Wesley, AM*, ed. N. Curnock

(London, 1909-16).

— — — *Explanatory Notes on the New Testament* (London, 1755).

— — — *Works of the Revd John Wesley*, ed. T. Jackson, 14 vols (London, 1840-2).

Whitefield, G., *George Whitefield's Journals* (London, 1960).

Wright, T., *The Life of Isaac Watts* (London, 1914).

Note: The sceptical philosopher David Hume (1711-76) had a damaging influence on Christian theology. Dr William Warburton drew Doddridge's attention to Hume's attack on miracles in 1750 (see *JH.* v. 167). Had Doddridge lived longer, he doubtless would have engaged him as he did Dodwell. For a critical assessment of Hume using hints suggested by Doddridge, see my thesis (pp. 86-95).

Index of Persons

(numbers in bold indicate portrait)

Ferguson, Sir J., 104
Fielding H., 48
Flavel, J., 51, 147
Fletcher, J., 227, 289
Foster, J., 132
Fountain, D., 277-8
Franke, A. H., 29
Freeman, K., 63
Frost, R., 179, 286
Fuller, A., 52, 277

Gardiner, J., 120, 163, 185-6, 191, 201, 202-3, 288
Garland, H. J., 206, 288
Gaussen, L., 128
George II, King, 19, 84
Gibson, A., 286
Gill, J., 13, 144, 146, 255
Gladstone, W. E., 211
Gledstone, J. P., 168, 285, 288
Goodricke, H., 262
Goodwin, T., 36, 52, 136, 147
Gordon, A., 130-1, 257
Goring, J., 284
Gough, S., 157
Greenall, R. L., 293
Greijdanus, S., 290
Griffith, J., 240
Guyse, J., 14, 39

Halifax, Earl of, 83, 104, 133, 184, 224
Hall, J., 147
Handel, G. F., 218
Hankins, E., 68
Hanna, W., 271
Hanoverians (Kings George I-II), 48, 58, 81
Hartley, T., 224
Haworth, S., 116
Haydn, J., 11
Heer, F., 279

Henry III, King, 79-81
Henry, M., 23, **25**, 26, 51, 120, 147, 239, 268, 271
Henry, P., 51, 107
Herring, T., 150, 218
Hervey, J., 173, 175, 224, 286
Hodge, C., 271-2
Hoeksema, H., 294
Hondt, P. A. de, 281
Hooker, R., 269
Hooper, J., 268
Horneck, A., 53
Houghton, Sir H., 104
Howe, J., 107, 147, 231
Howe, P., 269-70
Hume, D., 301
Hummel, J. N., 12
Humphreys, J., 72
Humphreys, J. D., 285, 287, 289-90
Hunt, J., 112-4
Hunt, T., 189
Huntingdon, Lady, 167, 169, 217, 224, **226**, 230-1, 285, 289

Ignatius, 83
Ingham, B., 163

Jacobites, 57, 184
James I, King, 22
Jeffrey, Lord, 48
Jennings, D., 85
Jennings, J. Snr, 28, 29, 31, 33, 34, 86, 253-4
Jennings, J. Jnr, 127, 129-30
Jennings, Mrs., 33
Jewel, J., 269
Johnson, S., 49, 243, 290
Jones, R. Tudur, 10, 14, 61, 278
Jones, S., 28
Jong, P. Y. de, 294

Index of Places

Index of Subjects

By the same Author

ATONEMENT AND JUSTIFICATION: ENGLISH EVANGELICAL
THEOLOGY 1640-1790 - AN EVALUATION

xvi + 268 pp. Clarendon Press, Oxford, 1990. £36.99
ISBN 0-19-826195-0

A striking thesis ... a work of major importance for understanding
the history of English-speaking Protestantism. ... It has breadth, for
it covers a century and a half, and it has depth, for it deals with the
central issues of the faith. And it is convincing. It will be difficult
for any future commentator to claim that a continuous tradition of
orthodox Calvinism can be marked off from Arminianising
divergences. ... The theological map has been redrawn.

D. W. BEBBINGTON, *Journal of the United Reformed Church History Society*

Dr Clifford's well documented and carefully argued thesis will serve
to stimulate further and no doubt passionate debate, endorsing as it
does many of the conclusions reached by Dr R. T. Kendall's *Calvin
and English Calvinism to 1649*.

A. SKEVINGTON WOOD, *Evangelical Quarterly*

Dr Clifford in *Atonement and Justification*, following Dr Kendall,
who experienced a rough ride amongst traditional Calvinists, takes
us down the same road. (He too will provoke a forceful reaction,
although he writes fairly and is an irenic spirit.) He has done his
homework very thoroughly and his argument is well documented.
... He has made a very worthy and significant contribution
demanding at least some new thinking.

PETER COOK, *European Christian Bookstore Journal*

A lucid and intelligent book. ... the quality of [Dr Clifford's]
reasoning precludes any curt dismissal of his ideas. ... It is to be

hoped that [his] arguments and conclusions will be treated with the seriousness they so evidently merit.

ALISTER MCGRATH, *Journal of Theological Studies*

As revisionist history it makes exciting reading, and it is hoped that it will spark off a lively debate on this subject.

GERALD BRAY, *Churchman*

Dr Clifford's analysis of [the] debates is lucid, stimulating and of a delectable brevity never matched in the seventeenth and eighteenth centuries. ... If revisionism means reclassification, here we have it, and no scholar of the period should miss the sport.

W. R. WARD, *Journal of Ecclesiastical History*

A learned and provocative book.

E. D. DUFFY, *Times Higher Education Supplement*

Dr Clifford finds that in important respects Baxter's mediating theology and Wesley's Arminianism were more akin to Calvin's thought than was the Calvinism of Owen and others. In some circles this is fighting talk! But those who wish to dissent from Dr Clifford's conclusions will do well to read the texts as closely as he has done.

ALAN P. F. SELL, *Huguenot Society Proceedings*

There is much that is compelling in Clifford's argument and it may be added that he expounds some difficult and complex themes with an enviable clarity and sympathy.

HENRY D. RACK, *Proceedings of the Wesley Historical Society*

Occasionally we come across a new book that is informative, stimulating, challenging and a delight to read. Such a volume I found in Dr Alan C. Clifford's *Atonement and Justification*. ... Dr Clifford writes from the perspective of being a moderate Calvinist, and among the very many good things in this book is its fairness and irenic spirit. Dr Clifford writes from wide and careful reading, sound biblical and theological scholarship, and with a desire to pursue truth with openness and candour. ... [His] book is a welcome and positive contribution to the questions raised. ... Dr Clifford subjects the views of Calvin, Owen, Baxter and Wesley to close scrutiny and constructive criticism. While too many writers of lesser ability are content with second-hand evidence, Dr Clifford has worked long and hard on these writings. He finds strengths and weaknesses in all these positions and says so. If a die-hard Calvinist or Arminian is looking for a book merely to confirm his own opinions, he will find Dr Clifford's work disturbing. ... One does not have to be a prophet to predict that in certain quarters Dr Clifford will not get an accolade for his conclusions!

H. MCGONIGLE, *The Flame*

CALVINUS:
Authentic Calvinism, A Clarification

94 pp. Charenton Reformed Publishing, Norwich, 1996. £5.95
ISBN 0-9526716-0-3

This book reflects the author's conclusions about Calvinism through his doctoral studies. He explores the hotly-debated issue of whether Calvin taught limited atonement. In the light of this, he examines the validity of interpretations of Calvinism made by subsequent theologians, particularly that of the French pastor Moïse Amyraut (1596-1664). ... After the introduction comes the focal point of the book: a selection of 90 extracts from the writings of John Calvin, directly expounding his views on the extent of the atonement. It is wonderful to have set before you a collection of quotations from Calvin's writings on this subject, which allow the reformer to speak for himself. This whole section is written without comment, leaving the reader to decide where Calvin really stood. ... Whatever one's opinions about 'authentic Calvinism', one would have to admit that Dr Clifford writes authoritatively and convincingly on a subject with which he is thoroughly acquainted and has extensively researched. ... [The] content is thought-provoking and stimulating, and challenging reading, especially for all who claim to be 'authentic' Calvinists!

KATHY CHILDRESS, *Evangelicals Now*

According to God's revealed will or intention the death of Christ is universal in its scope, but conditional upon the human response; according to his secret will or decree it is restricted in its scope but absolute and unconditional. Thus Calvin affirms *both* a conditional salvation made available to all *and* an efficacious, unconditional salvation given to the elect alone. It is this antinomy the author claims, rightly in my view, that makes sense of the diverse statements that Calvin makes on the subject. ... The debate about Calvin's teaching on the intent of the atonement looks set to run and run. Those who in future turn their minds to it will not be able to ignore this volume and will especially be grateful for the opportunity to review the wide range of Calvin material which is gathered together in the core of the book.

TONY LANE, *Evangelical Quarterly*

The great value of the book is the way in which the overall argument is related to Calvin's writings. ... Some authors give only sections of what Calvin wrote, some are historically selective, others give only one emphasis and leave the drift of the whole for the reader to search out. The author has done a fine job in rectifying that problem by presenting his arguments holistically. ... It must be said, and it is inevitably so, that the arguments are often subtle, all are closely argued, and at times, some can be philosophically quite sophisticated. ... However, despite the nature of the discussion, and the enormous literature generated, this book is a model of clarity and perspicacious argumentation. It is demanding, by its nature, but careful and diligent reading will give even the near novice a fine introduction to the whole issue. It is a valuable work in the continuing debate. Whether or not it will fulfil the author's wish that these issues 'will now be settled once and for all' remains to be seen, but it will deserve a serious reply from opponents. If Dr Kendall set the cat amongst the pigeons then Dr Clifford continues to rattle the reformed cage. Let the reader read and discern.

JOHN F. DUNN, *English Churchman*

Dr Clifford's scholarship is undoubtedly detailed, but his hope of settling the controversies in this volume presumably depends on the assumption that readers will have perused his more detailed study on *Atonement and Justification*. ... Note: 1996 is the 400th anniversary of the birth of Moïse Amyraut, whose authentic Calvinist credentials Clifford is anxious to reassert in this piece.

STEPHEN WILLIAMS, Themelios

This is an unusual book but it debates an all-to-familiar field. ... Clifford's claim that Calvin makes universal-sounding statements too strong to reconcile with Owen's approach seems formidable. Equally it suggests that whilst Calvin's work predates the classical differences between parties in the Reformed tradition, the subject was not quite as alien to the great Reformer as we might think. A surprising side benefit of the study also shows that Calvin was a missionary at heart and advocated personal evangelism. ... The author supplies a spirited introduction defending Amyraut and his successors, who challenged the seventeenth-century Calvinist 'high orthodoxy' with its belief in limited atonement. It is some time since Amyraut found an advocate, but the case presented here is more than worthy of such a distinguished figure. The argument will certainly rumble on yet, but all parties will have to take account of this little but forceful book.

ROY KEARSLEY, Scottish Bulletin of Evangelical Theology